Facebook Graph API Development with Flash
Beginner's Guide

Build social Flash applications fully integrated with the
Facebook Graph API

Michael James Williams

BIRMINGHAM - MUMBAI

Facebook Graph API Development with Flash
Beginner's Guide

First published: December 2010

Production Reference: 1081210

Published by Packt Publishing Ltd.
32 Lincoln Road
Olton
Birmingham, B27 6PA, UK

ISBN 978-1-849690-74-4

www.packtpub.com

Cover Image by Asher Wishkerman (a.wishkerman@mpic.de)

Credits

Author
Michael James Williams

Reviewer
Emanuele Feronato

Acquisition Editor
David Barnes

Development Editor
Hyacintha D'Souza

Technical Editors
Paramanand Bhat

Namita Sahni

Copy Editor
Laxmi Subramanian

Indexer
Monica Ajmera Mehta

Editorial Team Leader
Aditya Belpathak

Project Team Leader
Lata Basantani

Project Coordinator
Vishal Bodwani

Proofreader
Lynda Sliwoski

Graphics
Geetanjali Sawant

Production Coordinator
Arvindkumar Gupta

Cover Work
Arvindkumar Gupta

About the Author

Michael James Williams is a technical concept writer and freelance Flash developer. He is the technical editor for the tutorial website Activetuts+, and also runs his own blog about Flash game development.

He currently lives in England, in a nice little town that has both a river and a canal, and has been using Facebook since it was just some site that his American housemate wouldn't stop talking about.

You can follow Michael on Twitter at `http://twitter.com/MichaelJW`.

His public Facebook profile is available at `http://on.fb.me/MichaelJamesWilliams`.

Activetuts+ can be found at `http://active.tutsplus.com/`.

Michael's website is `http://michaeljameswilliams.com/`.

Acknowledgement

I'd like to thank my Dad, for teaching me how to be technical; my Mum, for teaching me how to write; and my little sister, for not being too jealous that I beat her to being a published author.

I also want to thank Ryan Henson Creighton, for inadvertently introducing me to David Barnes; all the Flash developers that make up the awesome community I'm happy to be a part of, particularly Bram, Ryan, Rasmus, Jeff and Steve, and Daniel; Tom, for letting me use his tutorial as a template for my first (and still most popular!) piece of writing; Ian Yates and the rest of Envato™, for enabling me to keep working and earning a living while writing this book; Keith Peters, for providing the awesome MinimalComponents I used throughout this book; and everyone that's ever commented on anything I've written – I really appreciate that.

Finally, I must express my appreciation for and thanks to David, Vishal, Hyacintha, Paramanand, Priya, Namita, and everyone else at Packt Publishing for all their support, help, and hard work. I know I can be stubborn, but it's been a pleasure to work with you all. In particular, thank you to David, who not only approved this book in the first place, but also gave me a huge amount of guidance in all aspects of writing it. And of course, I have to thank Emanuele, not just for doing the technical review of this book, but also for his blog, which (by a funny turn of events) was one of my key inspirations to start writing about Flash in the first place.

About the Reviewer

Emanuele Feronato has been studying programming languages since the early eighties, with a particular interest in web and game development. He taught online programming for the European Social Fund and now co-owns a web development company in Italy where he also works as a lead programmer. His blog, www.emanueleferonato.com, is one of the most visited blogs about indie programming.

> I would like to thank Vishal Bodwani at Packt Publishing for the opportunity to review this book, and my little daughter Kimora for making my life happy.

www.PacktPub.com

Support files, eBooks, discount offers and more

You might want to visit www.PacktPub.com for support files and downloads related to your book.

Did you know that Packt offers eBook versions of every book published, with PDF and ePub files available? You can upgrade to the eBook version at www.PacktPub.com and as a print book customer, you are entitled to a discount on the eBook copy. Get in touch with us at service@packtpub.com for more details.

At www.PacktPub.com, you can also read a collection of free technical articles, sign up for a range of free newsletters, and receive exclusive discounts and offers on Packt books and eBooks.

http://PacktLib.PacktPub.com

Do you need instant solutions to your IT questions? PacktLib is Packt's online digital book library. Here, you can access, read, and search across Packt's entire library of books.

Why Subscribe?

- Fully searchable across every book published by Packt
- Copy and paste, print and bookmark content
- On demand and accessible via web browser

Free Access for Packt account holders

If you have an account with Packt at www.PacktPub.com, you can use this to access PacktLib today and view nine entirely free books. Simply use your login credentials for immediate access.

Table of Contents

Preface

Facebook is big, by all meanings of the word. It's used by half a billion people—and countless businesses, bands, and public figures—for socializing and self-promotion. It's also a huge development platform, with tens of thousands of applications.

It's now common to see a Facebook "Like" button on blog posts, news articles, and many other websites. In the same way, Facebook integration is becoming more and more desirable for browser-based RIAs and games, with some, like FarmVille, even being based entirely around Facebook. That's where Flash comes in.

What this book covers

Chapter 1, Introduction, gets you up to speed with Facebook and ready to learn to develop Flash applications that connect with the Facebook platform. You'll learn why it's worth putting more time into developing for Facebook than other social networks (and why it's likely to stay that way), and get yourself technically set up for coding.

Chapter 2, Welcome to the Graph, introduces you to Facebook's model for connecting all the information in its huge data stores—the **Graph API**. You'll discover how intuitive this model is, and will start to explore the publicly available data using AS3 through utility code, which you'll build from scratch.

Chapter 3, Let Me In!, breaks down Facebook's systems for security, permissions, and authentication. You'll learn how to access the private data of Facebook users (including their photos, biographical information, and lists of friends). You will also start using the official Adobe ActionScript 3 SDK for Facebook platform alongside your own utility code.

Chapter 4, Digging Deeper into the Graph, helps you understand the concepts of paging and filtering, so that you aren't restricted to using only the default dataset that Facebook presents you with. You'll find out how to obtain data from specified dates, and how to speed up your applications by retrieving information from multiple sources at once.

Chapter 5, *Search Me*, builds on the previous chapter by teaching you how to search for data based on criteria other than dates. You'll learn how to retrieve Wall Posts by specific users, pages with specific names, and places by specific geographical coordinates.

Chapter 6, *Adding to the Graph*, takes you beyond merely retrieving data and into publishing new data to Facebook. You'll find out how to create new Wall Posts (including rich posts including images and embedded hyperlinks); how to comment on other users' Wall Posts; how to create new events, notes, and albums; and how to upload photos from your hard drive.

Chapter 7, *FQL Matters*, takes a break from the Graph API to teach you how to learn a powerful search tool—**Facebook Query Language**. You'll trade the Graph API's intuitiveness and simplicity for FQL's depth and additional features, while also understanding the benefits that each approach offers over the other.

Chapter 8, *Finishing Off*, wraps up what you've learned throughout the book and gets you ready to release your application to the wild. You'll find out how to embed your application into the Facebook website itself; how to get it into the official Facebook Application Directory; and how to export it as a desktop or Android application, while still keeping its Facebook connectivity. Finally, you'll learn how to keep up-to-date with the ever-changing Facebook platform, and discover some useful resources for taking what you've learned even further.

Appendix, *Pop Quiz Answers*, contains answers to all the Pop Quizzes in the book

What you need for this book

To develop and compile the example code in this book, you will need an AS3 compiler. Sample projects are provided for use with Flash Professional (CS3 and above), Flash Builder, and the free FlashDevelop IDE (with the Flex SDK); if you use a different workflow you will be able to convert these to fit your tools.

You'll also need previous experience with AS3 class-based coding and a Facebook account. The exact requirements here, along with what to do if you don't meet them, are detailed in Chapter 1.

Who this book is for

If you are an AS3 developer who wants to create applications and games that integrate with Facebook—either on the Facebook website itself or off it, then this book is for you. Even if you have no previous experience with Facebook, databases, or server-side programming, you can follow this book.

Conventions

In this book, you will find a number of styles of text that distinguish between different kinds of information. Here are some examples of these styles, and an explanation of their meaning.

Code words in text are shown as follows: "All we have to do is pass it an argument of type `graph.GraphObject`."

A block of code is set as follows:

```
for (var key:String in decodedJSON)
{
    graphObject[key] = decodedJSON[key];
}
```

When I wish to draw your attention to a particular part of a code block, the relevant lines or items are set in bold:

```
if (decodedJSON.data)
{
  //has a "data" property so we assume it is a Graph List
  var graphList:GraphList = new GraphList();
}
```

New terms and **important words** are shown in bold. Words that you see on the screen, in menus or dialog boxes for example, appear in the text like this: "Compile and run your SWF, then expand the **Connections** box and click on **posts**".

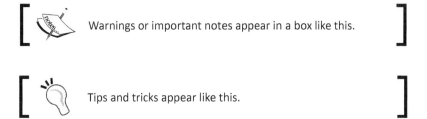

Warnings or important notes appear in a box like this.

Tips and tricks appear like this.

Reader feedback

Feedback from our readers is always welcome. Let us know what you think about this book—what you liked or may have disliked. Reader feedback is important for us to develop titles that you really get the most out of.

To send us general feedback, simply send an e-mail to feedback@packtpub.com, and mention the book title via the subject of your message.

If there is a book that you need and would like to see us publish, please send us a note in the **SUGGEST A TITLE** form on www.packtpub.com or e-mail suggest@packtpub.com.

If there is a topic that you have expertise in and you are interested in either writing or contributing to a book, see our author guide on www.packtpub.com/authors.

Customer support

Now that you are the proud owner of a Packt book, we have a number of things to help you to get the most from your purchase.

Downloading the example code for this book

You can download the example code files for all Packt books you have purchased from your account at http://www.PacktPub.com. If you purchased this book elsewhere, you can visit http://www.PacktPub.com/support and register to have the files e-mailed directly to you.

Errata

Although we have taken every care to ensure the accuracy of our content, mistakes do happen. If you find a mistake in one of our books—maybe a mistake in the text or the code—we would be grateful if you would report this to us. By doing so, you can save other readers from frustration and help us improve subsequent versions of this book. If you find any errata, please report them by visiting http://www.packtpub.com/support, selecting your book, clicking on the **errata submission form** link, and entering the details of your errata. Once your errata are verified, your submission will be accepted and the errata will be uploaded on our website, or added to any list of existing errata, under the Errata section of that title. Any existing errata can be viewed by selecting your title from http://www.packtpub.com/support.

Piracy

Piracy of copyrighted material on the Internet is an ongoing problem across all media. At Packt, we take the protection of our copyright and licenses very seriously. If you come across any illegal copies of our works, in any form, on the Internet, please provide us with the location address or website name immediately so that we can pursue a remedy.

Please contact us at copyright@packtpub.com with a link to the suspected pirated material.

We appreciate your help in protecting our authors, and our ability to bring you valuable content.

Questions

You can contact us at questions@packtpub.com if you are having a problem with any aspect of the book, and we will do our best to address it.

1
Introduction

Ready to start learning how to develop Flash Facebook applications? You will be in a few pages.

In this chapter, we will:

- Learn what the big deal is about Facebook, and why you should be interested in developing an application for it
- Get you set up with a web host, which you'll need for developing any online Facebook application
- Establish how much AS3 you need to know already, and what to do if you don't
- Take a quick look at the project that you'll be building throughout most of this book
- Find out how to deal with the debugging complications that arise when developing a "browser-only" application like this

So let's get on with it...

What's so great about Facebook?

Seems like everyone's on Facebook these days—people are on it to socialize; businesses are on it to try to attract those people's attention. But the same is true for other older social networks such as LinkedIn, Friendster, and MySpace. Facebook's reach goes far beyond these; my small town's high street car park proudly displays a "Like Us On Facebook" sign.

More and more Flash games and **Rich Internet Applications** (**RIAs**) are allowing users to log in using their Facebook account—it's a safe assumption that most users will have one. Companies are asking freelancers for deeper Facebook integration in their projects. It's practically a buzzword.

But why the big fuss?

It's popular

- ◆ Facebook benefits from the snowball effect: it's big, so it gets bigger.

- ◆ People sign up because most of their friends are already on it, which is generally not the case for, say, Twitter. Businesses sign up because they can reach so many people. It's a virtuous circle.

- ◆ There's a low barrier to entry, too; it's not just for techies, or even people who are "pretty good with computers;" even old people and luddites use Facebook. In February 2010, the technology blog **ReadWriteWeb** published an article called "Facebook Wants to Be Your One True Login," about Facebook's attempts to become the de facto login system throughout the Web. Within minutes, the comments filled up with posts from confused Facebook users:

19. This is such a mess I can't do a thing on my facebook. The changes you have made are ridiculous. I can't even login!!!!! am very upset!!!

Posted by ⬛ | February 10, 2010 10:24 AM

20. Can we log into face book? This is crazy I want to get all my info off and be done with this. I recently moved from MN to SC Myrtle Beach and facebook was a great way to keep in touch with family and friends but this is getting to be to difficult.

Posted by ⬛ | February 10, 2010 10:32 AM

21. log in please.

Posted by ⬛ | February 10, 2010 10:38 AM

22. i need the old facebook this new one is very bad bbbbbbbbbbbuuuuuuuuuuuuuuuuuuuuu!

Posted by ⬛ | February 10, 2010 10:40 AM

(Source: http://www.readwriteweb.com/archives/facebook_wants_to_be_your_one_true_login.php.)

- ❑ Evidently, the ReadWriteWeb article had temporarily become the top search result for **Facebook Login**, leading hundreds of Facebook users, equating Google or Bing with the Internet, to believe that this blog post was actually a redesigned `Facebook.com`. The comment form, fittingly, had a **Sign in with Facebook** button that could be used instead of manually typing in a name and e-mail address to sign a comment—and of course, the Facebook users misinterpreted this as the new **Log in** button.

  - ❑ And yet... all of those people manage to use Facebook, keenly enough to throw a fit when it apparently became impossible to use. It's not just a site for geeks and students; it has serious mass market appeal.

- ◆ Even "The Social Network"—a movie based on the creation of Facebook—held this level of appeal: it opened at #1 and remained there for its second weekend.

Numbers

- ◆ According to Facebook's statistics page (`http://www.facebook.com/press/info.php?statistics`), over 500 million people log in to Facebook in any given month (as of November 2010). For perspective, the population of the entire world is just under 7,000 million.

- ◆ Twitter is estimated to have 95 million monthly active users (according to the `eMarketer.com` September 2010 report), as is MySpace. **FarmVille**, the biggest game based on the Facebook platform, has over 50 million: more than half the population of either competing social network.

- ◆ FarmVille has been reported to be hugely profitable, with some outsider reports claiming that its parent company, **Zynga**, has generated twice as much profit as Facebook itself (though take this with a grain of salt). Now, of course, not every Facebook game or application can be that successful, and FarmVille does benefit from the same snowball effect as Facebook itself, making it hard to compete with—but that almost doesn't matter; these numbers validate Facebook as a platform on which a money-making business can be built.

It's everywhere

As the aforementioned ReadWriteWeb article explained, Facebook has become a standard login across many websites. Why add yet another username/password combination to your browser's list (or your memory) if you can replace them all with one Facebook login?

This isn't restricted to posting blog comments. UK TV broadcaster, Channel 4, allows viewers to access their entire TV lineup on demand, with no need to sign up for a specific Channel 4 account:

Again, Facebook benefits from that snowball effect: as more sites enable a Facebook login, it becomes more of a standard, and yet more sites decide to add a Facebook login in order to keep up with everyone else.

Besides login capabilities, many sites also allow users to share their content via Facebook. Another UK TV broadcaster, the BBC, lets users post links for their recommended TV programs straight to Facebook:

Blogs—or, indeed, many websites with articles—allow readers to **Like** a post, publishing this fact on Facebook and on the site itself:

So half a billion people use the Facebook website every month, and at the same time, Facebook spreads further and further across the Internet—and even beyond. "Facebook Messages" stores user's entire conversational histories, across e-mail, SMS, chat, and Facebook itself; "Facebook Places" lets users check into a physical location, letting friends know that they're there.

No other network has this reach.

It's interesting to develop for

With all this expansion, it's difficult for a developer to keep up with the Facebook platform. And sometimes there are bugs, and undocumented areas, and periods of downtime, all of which can make development harder still.

But the underlying system—the **Graph API**, introduced in April 2010—is fascinating. The previous API had become bloated and cumbersome over its four years; the Graph API feels well-designed with plenty of room for expansion.

This book mainly focuses on the Graph API, as it is the foundation of modern Facebook development. You'll be introduced to it properly in *Chapter 2*, *Welcome to the Graph*.

Have a go hero – get on Facebook

If you're not on Facebook already, sign up now (for free) at `http://facebook.com`. You'll need an account in order to develop applications that use it. Spend some time getting used to it:

- Set up a personal profile.
- Post messages to your friends on their **Walls**.
- See what all the FarmVille fuss is about at `http://apps.facebook.com/onthefarm`.
- Check in to a location using Facebook Places.
- Log in to some blogs using your Facebook account.
- Share some YouTube videos on your own Wall from the YouTube website.
- "Like" something.
  Go native!

Web hosts

If you've already got a publicly accessible web server or are signed up to a web host to which you can upload SWFs and HTML pages via FTP, skip to the *How much AS3 knowledge is required?* section.

What's a web host?

I'll assume that you roughly know how the Internet works: when you type a URL into a web browser on your computer and hit **Go**, it retrieves all the pages and images it needs from another computer, the **web server**, and displays them. The exact methods it uses to find the web server and the protocols for how the information gets back to your computer aren't relevant here.

You could go out and buy a computer, install some server software, and hook it up to your Internet connection, and you'd have a functional web server. But you'd have to maintain it and keep it secure, and your ISP probably wouldn't be very happy about you sending all those pages and images to other people's browsers. A better option is to pay another company to take care of all of that for you—a **web host**.

Why do you need one?

- In order to build an online SWF-based application or game that allows users to log in with their Facebook account (with the SWF being able to access their profile, list of friends, Wall, and so on), you will require control over a web page.

- Technically, you could probably come up with some hack that would allow you to get around this—perhaps by hosting everything on Google sites and MegaSWF—but in the long run it's not going to be worth it. Splash out on a web host for the sake of learning; you will definitely need access to one if you do professional Facebook application development in the future.

How do you choose one?

- There are a huge number of web hosts to choose from, and an even bigger number of configurable options between them. How much disk space do you need? How much bandwidth per month? How much processing power? Some hosts will give you a server all to yourself, while others will put your files on the same computer as other customers. And of course, you have to wonder how good the customer service is and how reliable the company is at keeping their servers online. Throw in a few terms such as "cloud hosting" and it's enough to make your head spin.

- All you need is a host that allows you to upload HTML files and SWFs; this book also assumes that you'll be able to use **FTP** to transfer files from your computer to the host, though this isn't strictly necessary.

- Want to just get started without wasting time comparing hosts? Go with Media Temple. The code in this book was all tested using a Media Temple Grid Service account, available at `http://mediatemple.net/webhosting/gs/`. It provides much more than what you'll need for completing the projects in this book, granted, and at $20/month. It's not the cheapest option available, but the extra service and features will definitely come in handy as you build your own Facebook applications and games.

Useful software

You'll need an HTML editor for editing web pages. **FlashDevelop** and **Flash Builder** both do good jobs at this; otherwise, try:

- **Notepad++** for Windows (free): `http://notepad-plus-plus.org/`
- **TextMate** for Mac: `http://macromates.com/`
- **Komodo Edit** for Mac and Windows (free): `http://www.activestate.com/komodo-edit`

And in order to transfer your files from your computer to your web host, you'll probably need an FTP client. Check out **FileZilla** (it's free and available for both Windows and Mac) at `http://filezilla-project.org/`. Documentation for this is available at `http://wiki.filezilla-project.org/Documentation`, and your web host will almost certainly provide instructions on connecting to it via FTP (Media Temple's instructions can be found at `http://kb.mediatemple.net/questions/131/Using+FTP+and+SFTP`)

What about domain names?

Web hosts will generally assign you a very generic address, such as `http://michaeljw.awesomewebhost2000.com/` or `http://sites.awesomewebhost2000.com/michaeljw`. If you want to have a more condensed personal address such as `http://michaeljw.com/`, you'll need to pay for it. This is called a **domain name**—in this specific example, `michaeljw.com` is the domain name.

Media Temple allows you to buy a domain name for $5/year at the point where you sign up to their web hosting package. If you go with another host, you may need to buy a domain name elsewhere; for this, you can use `http://www.moniker.com/`.

You don't need to own a domain name to use this book, though. The generic addresses that your web host assigns you will be fine. Throughout the book, it'll be assumed that your website address (either generic or domain name) is `http://host.com/`.

Have a go hero – get a web host, upload to it, test

Pick a web host, get your credit card out, and sign up for one of their packages.

1. Create a new directory called `/test/` in the public path of your web host.
2. Create a new plain text file on your hard drive called `index.html`. (It's a good idea to create a new folder on your computer to store all your work, too.) Open this file in your HTML editor.

3. Copy the HTML below into the file:

```
<html>
  <head>
  <title>Test</title>
  </head>
  <body>
    <h2>Hello!</h2>
  </body>
</html>
```

4. Hopefully, you know enough HTML to understand that this just writes **Hello!** in big letters.

5. Transfer `index.html` to the `/text/` directory on your host. Again, you'll probably need to use an FTP client for this.

6. Open a web browser and type `http://host.com/test/index.html` into the URL bar. Of course, you should replace `http://host.com/` with the path to your public directory, as given to you by your web host. You should see Hello! appear in a glorious default font:

7. If not, check the documentation and support for your host.

How much AS3 knowledge is required?

◆ You'll need to know some AS3 before you start using this book. Sure, it's a "Beginner's Guide", but beginner refers to your knowledge of Facebook development, not Flash development!

◆ All of the code in this book is written using classes inside AS files; there's no timeline code at all. You don't have to be an OOP guru to follow it, but you must be familiar with class-based coding. If you aren't, check out these two resources:

❑ **How To Use A Document Class In Flash**—A short tutorial to get you up to speed with using document classes in Flash CS3 and above: `http://active.tutsplus.com/tutorials/actionscript/quick-tip-how-to-use-a-document-class-in-flash/`.

❑ **AS3 101**—A series of tutorials to walk you through the basics of AS3 development. In particular, read from Part 8 onwards, as these deal with OOP in AS3: `http://active.tutsplus.com/series/as3-101/`.

◆ You should also know how to create and compile a SWF project, and be familiar enough with HTML to be able to embed a SWF in it. We'll use **SWFObject** for this purpose (this is the default embed method used by Flash CS5); if you're not sure what this means, familiarize yourself here: `http://code.google.com/p/swfobject/`.

◆ All important AS3 classes and keywords used in this book will be briefly explained as they become relevant, so don't worry if you haven't memorized the **LiveDocs** yet. Speaking of LiveDocs, remember that you can always use them to look up unfamiliar code: `http://help.adobe.com/en_US/FlashPlatform/reference/actionscript/3/index.html`.

The source code

At the start of *Chapter 2*, *Welcome to the Graph*, you'll be given a Flash project that's just an empty user interface—it'll be up to you to build the backend using the lessons you learn from Chapters 2 through 6.

This project is called **Visualizer**, and contains the class structure and all the UI for an application that can be used to represent all of the information stored on Facebook. You'll go far beyond simply allowing people to log in to the application and grabbing their username; there is so much more that can be achieved with AS3 and the Graph API, and you'll learn about all of it.

Although the project is complex, the classes have been arranged in such a way that you need to modify only a small number of them, and these have little or no code in them to begin with. This means that you don't have to dive into mountains of code that you didn't write! You can focus entirely on learning about the Facebook side of Flash development.

Each of the Chapters from 2 to 6 has two associated ZIP files: one for the start of the project at the start of the chapter, and one for the end. This means you could skip through those chapters in any order, but you'll find it must easier to learn if you go through them in sequence. All project files are available in forms that are compatible with Flash CS3 and above, Flash Builder, and FlashDevelop—and if you use a different Flash editor, you should find it easy to convert the project.

When you first compile the project, it'll look like this:

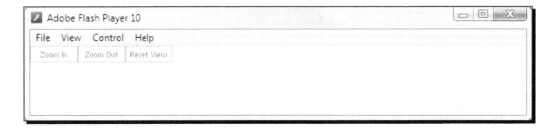

Nothing much to see. But before long, you'll have added features so that it can be used to explore Facebook, rendering different Pages and Photos:

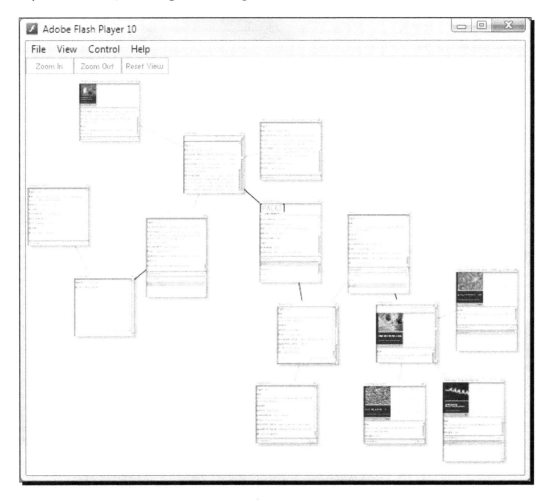

By the end of *Chapter 6*, you'll be happily adding code to search for users by name, exploring their personal profiles, and posting images and links to their Wall:

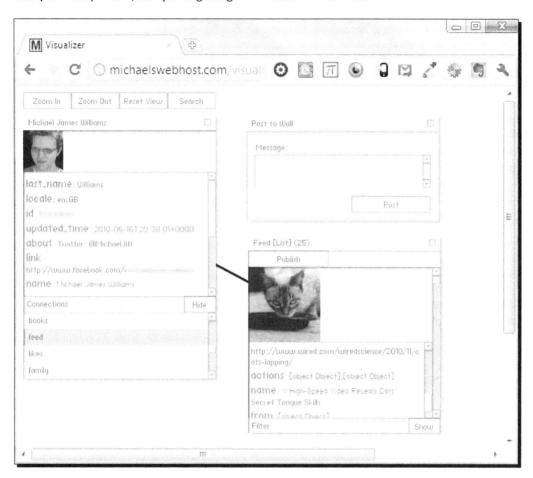

...plus plenty more besides!

Powered by...

In September 2010, Adobe released an official Adobe ActionScript 3 SDK for the Facebook Platform Graph API, which will remain fully supported by Adobe and Facebook. Read more about it at `http://www.adobe.com/devnet/facebook.html`. This book will teach you how to use this SDK, as it is a standard technology.

However, the main aim of this book is to teach you the underlying concepts of Facebook Flash development; once you understand these, the actual code and the SDK used don't matter. For this reason, this book will also teach you how to program every sort of Facebook interaction you might need from scratch. The code will be all yours, and you'll understand every line, with no abstraction in the way.

Besides the Adobe AS3 SDK for Facebook Platform, two other code libraries are used heavily:

- **MinimalComps**: Keith Peters' excellent, lightweight user interface components, available at `http://www.minimalcomps.com/` under an MIT license.
- **as3corelib**: A collection of classes and utilities for working with AS3, including classes for JSON serialization, available at `https://github.com/mikechambers/as3corelib` under a BSD license.

Debugging

From Chapter 3 onwards your SWF will need to be run from your server, through a web browser, in order to work. (Find out why in that chapter.) This makes debugging tricky—there's no **Output** panel in the browser, so `trace` statements aren't automatically visible.

The Visualizer contains a dialog feature which you can use to work around this. It can be created from any class that is in the display list. To do so, first import the `DialogEvent` class:

```
import events.DialogEvent;
```

Then, dispatch a `DialogEvent` of type `DIALOG` with an argument containing the text you wish to see output:

```
dispatchEvent(new DialogEvent(DialogEvent.DIALOG, "Example"));
```

It will look like this:

Of course, that's useful only for the Visualizer project. What can you do when you build your own?

There are a few tools that will help:

- **De MonsterDebugger**: Excellent tool for general AS3 debugging: `http://demonsterdebugger.com/`.

- **Flash Tracer for Firebug**: This Firefox tool lets you see `trace` statements from any SWF, as long as you have the debug version of Flash Player installed in your browser: `http://blog.sephiroth.it/firefox-extensions/flash-tracer-for-firebug/`.

- **Vizzy Flash Tracer**: Similar to Flash Tracer for Firebug, but also works for Internet Explorer and Chrome: `http://code.google.com/p/flash-tracer/`.

- **SOS max**: Creates a socket server on your computer to which an AS3 project can send data; this data will then be logged and can then be viewed: `http://www.sos.powerflasher.com/`.

In Chapter 3, you'll learn how to run a JavaScript function in your web page from the AS3 in your SWF. One JavaScript function, `alert()`, creates a little window containing any `String` passed to it, like so:

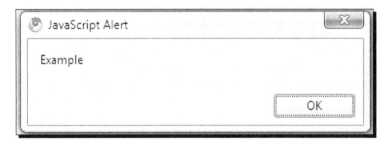

This is a quick and simple way to display one-off messages without using `trace`.

Watch out for caching

When you run a SWF using Flash Player on your desktop, it loads and runs the SWF. Well, of course, why wouldn't it?

When you run a SWF in a browser, this isn't always the case, though. Sometimes, browsers **cache** SWFs, meaning that they save a copy locally and then load that copy—rather than the online version—the next time you request it. In normal browsing, this is a great idea—it saves bandwidth and reduces loading times. You can lose huge amounts of time trying to figure out why your new code isn't working, only to finally realize that the new code isn't being run at all because you were seeing only a cached copy of your SWF.

Different browsers require different solutions. It's usually possible to disable caching for one browsing session, and it's always possible to delete some or all of the cache.

In Google Chrome, you can do this by clicking on **[Spanner] | Tools | Clear Browsing Data...**, selecting **Empty the cache**, and choosing an appropriate time period:

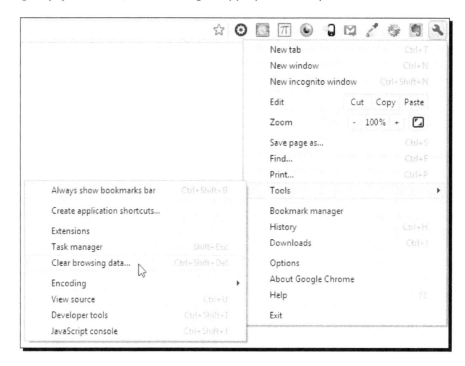

You should easily be able to find the equivalent option for your browser by searching Google for **«browser name» delete cache**.

A final note...

Facebook's developers are always tweaking the platform. This can make it exciting to develop on because new features are being added all the time, but it can also make it very frustrating to develop on because old features can be removed, or their implementations changed; anything could be altered at any time.

The new Platform API (the Graph API) is a strong foundation, and looks likely to be around for a while—remember, the previous Platform API lasted four years. But it's modular, and individual pieces might change, or even be removed.

It's possible then that parts of this book may be out-of-date by the time you read it, and some of the instructions might not give the same results with the current version of Facebook platform as they did when this book was written. If you're concerned about this, you can find out how to keep up-to-date with any platform changes in the last section of *Chapter 8, Keeping Up With The Zuckerbergs*.

But for now, dive into *Chapter 2, Welcome to the Graph* and start developing!

2
Welcome to the Graph

Facebook has a huge store of information, on people, companies, events, photo albums, and more. It also knows how all of these are linked: which person owns each album; which people appear in each photo; which company is organizing each event.

For four years, this was accessed using a huge, sprawling API, which got more complex as new abilities were bolted on to it. In April 2010, Facebook launched the **Graph API**, greatly simplifying how developers can retrieve all of this data.

In this chapter we shall:

- Explore the Facebook Graph
- Learn what the Graph API is, and how it structures all the data on Facebook
- Access public Graph data using AS3 and the Graph API

So let's get on with it.

Accessing the Graph API through a Browser

We'll dive right in by taking a look at how the Graph API represents the information from a public **Page**.

When I talk about a Page with a capital P, I don't just mean any web page within the Facebook site; I'm referring to a specific type of page, also known as a public profile. Every Facebook user has their own personal profile; you can see yours by logging in to Facebook and clicking on the "Profile" link in the navigation bar at the top of the site. Public profiles look similar, but are designed to be used by businesses, bands, products, organizations, and public figures, as a way of having a presence on Facebook.

This means that many people have both a personal profile and a public profile. For example, Mark Zuckerberg, the CEO of Facebook, has a personal profile at http://www.facebook.com/zuck and a public profile (a Page) at http://www.facebook.com/markzuckerberg. This way, he can use his personal profile to keep in touch with his friends and family, while using his public profile to connect with his fans and supporters.

There is a second type of Page: a **Community Page**. Again, these look very similar to personal profiles; the difference is that these are based on topics, experience, and causes, rather than entities. Also, they automatically retrieve information about the topic from Wikipedia, where relevant, and contain a live feed of wall posts talking about the topic.

All this can feel a little confusing – don't worry about it! Once you start using it, it all makes sense.

Time for action – loading a Page

Browse to http://www.facebook.com/PacktPub to load Packt Publishing's Facebook Page. You'll see a list of recent wall posts, an **Info** tab, some photo albums (mostly containing book covers), a profile picture, and a list of fans and links.

Packt Publishing

Wall   Info   Photos   Discussions

Basic Info

Founded: 2004

Detailed info

Website: http://www.PacktPub.com

Company Overview: Packt is a modern, IT focused book publisher, specializing in producing cutting-edge books for communities of developers, administrators, and newbies alike.

Packt published its first book, Mastering phpMyAdmin for MySQL Management in April 2004.

Facebook Page: http://www.facebook.com/PacktPub

That's how website users view the information. How will our code "see" it? Take a look at how the Graph API represents Packt Publishing's Page by pointing your web browser at `https://graph.facebook.com/PacktPub`. This is called a **Graph URL** – note that it's the same URL as the Page itself, but with a secure `https` connection, and using the `graph` sub domain, rather than `www`.

What you'll see is as follows:

```
{
   "id": "204603129458",
   "name": "Packt Publishing",
   "picture": "http://profile.ak.fbcdn.net/hprofile-ak-snc4/
     hs302.ash1/23274_204603129458_7460_s.jpg",
   "link": "http://www.facebook.com/PacktPub",
   "category": "Products_other",
   "username": "PacktPub",
   "company_overview": "Packt is a modern, IT focused book publisher,
     specializing in producing cutting-edge books for communities of
     developers, administrators, and newbies alike.\n\nPackt
     published its first book, Mastering phpMyAdmin for MySQL
     Management in April 2004.",
   "fan_count": 412
}
```

What just happened?

You just fetched the Graph API's representation of the Packt Publishing Page in your browser.

The Graph API is designed to be easy to pick up – practically self-documenting – and you can see that it's a success in that respect. It's pretty clear that the previous data is a list of fields and their values.

The one field that's perhaps not clear is `id`; this number is what Facebook uses internally to refer to the Page. This means Pages can have two IDs: the numeric one assigned automatically by Facebook, and an alphanumeric one chosen by the Page's owner. The two IDs are equivalent: if you browse to `https://graph.facebook.com/204603129458`, you'll see exactly the same data as if you browse to `https://graph.facebook.com/PacktPub`.

Have a go hero – exploring other objects

Of course, the Packt Publishing Page is not the only Page you can explore with the Graph API in your browser. Find some other Pages through the Facebook website in your browser, then, using the `https://graph.facebook.com/id` format, take a look at their Graph API representations. Do they have more information, or less?

Next, move on to other types of Facebook objects: personal profiles, events, groups. For personal profiles, the `id` may be alphanumeric (if the person has signed up for a custom Facebook Username at `http://www.facebook.com/username/`), but in general the `id` will be numeric, and auto-assigned by Facebook when the user signed up.

For certain types of objects (like photo albums), the value of `id` will not be obvious from the URL within the Facebook website; we'll look at how to find these later in the chapter.

In some cases, you'll get an error message, like:

```
{
    "error": {
        "type": "OAuthAccessTokenException",
        "message": "An access token is required to request
          this resource."
    }
}
```

Again, we'll look at what this means and how to get around it later in the book.

Accessing the Graph API through AS3

Now that you've got an idea of how easy it is to access and read Facebook data in a browser, we'll see how to fetch it in AS3.

Time for action – retrieving a Page's information in AS3

Set up the project from the Chapter 2 start files, as explained in Chapter 1. Check that the project compiles with no errors (there may be a few warnings, depending on your IDE). You should see a 640 x 480 px SWF, all white, with just three buttons in the top-left corner: **Zoom In**, **Zoom Out**, and **Reset View**:

This project is the basis for a Rich Internet Application (RIA) that will be able to explore all of the information on Facebook using the Graph API. All the code for the UI is in place, just waiting for some Graph data to render. Our job is to write code to retrieve the data and pass it on to the renderers.

I'm not going to break down the entire project and explain what every class does, as the focus of this book is on using Facebook with Flash, not on building RIAs. What you need to know at the moment is a single instance of the `controllers.CustomGraphContainerController` class is created when the project is initialized, and it is responsible for directing the flow of data to and from Facebook. It inherits some useful methods for this purpose from the `controllers.GCController` class; we'll make use of these later on.

Open the `CustomGraphContainerController` class in your IDE. It can be found in `\src\controllers\CustomGraphContainerController.as`, and should look like the listing below:

```
package controllers
{
  import ui.GraphControlContainer;

  public class CustomGraphContainerController extends GCController
  {

    public function CustomGraphContainerController
      (a_graphControlContainer:GraphControlContainer)
    {
      super(a_graphControlContainer);
    }

  }

}
```

The first thing we'll do is grab the Graph API's representation of Packt Publishing's Page via a Graph URL, like we did using the web browser. For this we can use a `URLLoader`.

The `URLLoader` and `URLRequest` classes are used together to download data from a URL. The data can be text, binary data, or URL-encoded variables.

The download is triggered by passing a `URLRequest` object, whose `url` property contains the requested URL, to the `load()` method of a `URLLoader`.

Once the required data has finished downloading, the `URLLoader` dispatches a `COMPLETE` event. The data can then be retrieved from its `data` property.

Modify `CustomGraphContainerController.as` like so (the highlighted lines are new):

```
package controllers
{
  import flash.events.Event;
  import flash.net.URLLoader;
  import flash.net.URLRequest;
  import ui.GraphControlContainer;

  public class CustomGraphContainerController extends GCController
  {

    public function CustomGraphContainerController
      (a_graphControlContainer:GraphControlContainer)
    {
      super(a_graphControlContainer);

      var loader:URLLoader = new URLLoader();
      var request:URLRequest = new URLRequest();
      //Specify which Graph URL to load
      request.url = "https://graph.facebook.com/PacktPub";
      loader.addEventListener(Event.COMPLETE,
        onGraphDataLoadComplete);
      //Start the actual loading process
      loader.load(request);
    }

    private function onGraphDataLoadComplete(a_event:Event):void
    {
      var loader:URLLoader = a_event.target as URLLoader;
      //obtain whatever data was loaded, and trace it
      var graphData:String = loader.data;
      trace(graphData);
    }

  }

}
```

All we're doing here is downloading whatever information is at `https://graph.facebook.com/PackPub` and tracing it to the output window.

Test your project, and take a look at your output window. You should see the following data:

```
{"id":"204603129458","name":"Packt Publishing","picture":"http:\/\/
profile.ak.fbcdn.net\/hprofile-ak-snc4\/hs302.
ash1\/23274_204603129458_7460_s.jpg","link":"http:\/\/www.facebook.
com\/PacktPub","category":"Products_other","username":"PacktPub",
"company_overview":"Packt is a modern, IT focused book publisher,
specializing in producing cutting-edge books for communities of
developers, administrators, and newbies alike.\n\nPackt published
its first book, Mastering phpMyAdmin for MySQL Management in April
2004.","fan_count":412}
```

If you get an error, check that your code matches the previously mentioned code. If you see nothing in your output window, make sure that you are connected to the Internet. If you still don't see anything, it's possible that your security settings prevent you from accessing the Internet via Flash, so check those.

What just happened?

The line breaks and tabulation between values have been lost, and some characters have been escaped, making it hard to read... but you can see that this is the same data as we obtained when browsing to `https://graph.facebook.com/PacktPub`. No surprise here; that's all the `URLLoader` does.

The data's not very useful to us in that form. In order to do something with it, we need to convert it to an object that we can interact with natively in AS3.

The format which Graph API uses is called **JSON** (**JavaScript Object Notation**; pronounced "Jason").

JSON is a human-readable, text-based data format standard. It allows you to represent objects as key-value pairs, like so:

```
{
  "key1": "value1",
  "key2": "value2",
  "key3": "value3"
}
```

The values can be strings (enclosed in quote marks), or numbers, Boolean values, or `null` (not enclosed in quote marks).

JSON objects can also contain arrays, using square brackets:

```
{
  "key1": "value1",
  "array":
  [
    "First item in array",
    "Second item in array",
    "Third item in array"
  ]
}
```

They can even contain other JSON objects, by nesting curly braces:

```
{
  "key1": "value1",
  "subObject":
  {
    "subKey1": "subValue1",
    "subKey2": "subValue2",
  }
}
```

These sub-objects can contain other objects and arrays, and arrays can contain other objects or arrays, too.

Note that this is very similar to the AS3 syntax for declaring an object:

```
var as3Object:Object = {
  key1:"value1",
  key2:"value2",
  subObject:{
    subKey1:"subValue1"
  },
  myArray:[1, 2, 3]
}
```

For more information, check out http://www.json.org.

Unlike with XML, AS3 has no native features for handling JSON objects – but there is an officially supported library that does.

Time for action – deserializing a JSON object

Adobe's **as3corelib** library contains a set of utility classes for serializing and deserializing JSON. It's available at `http://github.com/mikechambers/as3corelib`, but you don't need to download it, as it is already included in the `\src\` directory of the project. (It consists of every class in `com.adobe.*`)

1. In `CustomGraphContainerController.as`, import the JSON class:

   ```
   import com.adobe.serialization.json.JSON;
   ```

2. Modify the `onGraphDataLoadComplete()` function so that it deserializes the JSON string to an object, instead of simply tracing the string:

   ```
   private function onGraphDataLoadComplete(a_event:Event):void
   {
     var loader:URLLoader = a_event.target as URLLoader;
     //obtain whatever data was loaded, and trace it
     var graphData:String = loader.data;
     var decodedJSON:Object = JSON.decode(graphData);
   }
   ```

3. Trace the `name` property of this new object, to check that it worked:

   ```
   private function onGraphDataLoadComplete(a_event:Event):void
   {
     var loader:URLLoader = a_event.target as URLLoader;
     //obtain whatever data was loaded, and trace it
     var graphData:String = loader.data;
     var deserialisedJSON:Object = JSON.decode(graphData);
     trace("name:", decodedJSON.name);
   }
   ```

4. Compile and run the SWF. Resulting output:

   ```
   name: Packt Publishing
   ```

What just happened?

We passed this string to the `JSON.decode()` method:

```
{
    "id": "204603129458",
    "name": "Packt Publishing",
    "picture": "http://profile.ak.fbcdn.net/hprofile-ak-snc4/
      hs302.ash1/23274_204603129458_7460_s.jpg",
    "link": "http://www.facebook.com/PacktPub",
```

```
    "category": "Products_other",
    "username": "PacktPub",
    "company_overview": "Packt is a modern, IT focused book
      publisher, specializing in producing cutting-edge books for
      communities of developers, administrators, and newbies
      alike.\n\nPackt published its first book, Mastering
      phpMyAdmin for MySQL Management in April 2004.",
    "fan_count": 412
}
```

and it turned the string into a native AS3 object, as if we had typed this:

```
var graphObject:Object = {};
graphObject.id = "204603129458";
graphObject.name = "Packt Publishing";
graphObject.picture = "http://profile.ak.fbcdn.net/hprofile-ak-
snc4/hs302.ash1/23274_204603129458_7460_s.jpg";
graphObject.link = "http://www.facebook.com/PacktPub";
graphObject.category = "Products_other";
graphObject.username = "PacktPub";
graphObject.company_overview = "Packt is a modern, IT focused
book publisher, specializing in producing cutting-edge books for
communities of developers, administrators, and newbies alike.\n\
nPackt published its first book, Mastering phpMyAdmin for MySQL
Management in April 2004."
graphObject.fan_count = 412;
```

(Note that unlike the raw string we had earlier, the slashes in the URLs have not been escaped.)

This means we can easily access any of the information Facebook has about this Page, or even iterate through every piece of data.

Time for action – visualizing the info

Enough traces! It's time we displayed something in our actual SWF.

CustomGraphContainerController inherits a method called renderGraphObject() which will take care of this for us. All we have to do is pass it an argument of type graph. GraphObject.

GraphObject.as is a simple class; feel free to open it and take a look:

```
package graph
{
  import graph.controls.GraphObjectRenderer;
  public dynamic class GraphObject extends BaseGraphItem
```

```
{
  public var rendererObject:GraphObjectRenderer;
  public var graphObjectListRenderers:Array = [];

  public function GraphObject()
  {

  }

}

}
```

Honestly, there's no need to worry about any of the code there. All you need to know is that it's `dynamic`, which means that we can assign new properties to it during runtime, without having to specify their names beforehand. So we can do this:

```
var graphObject:GraphObject = new GraphObject();
graphObject.favoriteColor = "red";
```

When a `GraphObject` is passed to the `CustomGraphContainerController.renderGraphObject()` method, every single property of the `GraphObject` will be rendered in a fancy list, automatically. Every single property apart from the two that are defined in the class already, that is!

So what we have to do, inside `CustomGraphContainerController.onGraphDataLoadComplete()`, is:

1. Create a new instance of `GraphObject`.

2. Copy all the properties of `decodedJSON` to this new `GraphObject`.

3. Pass the `GraphObject` to `renderGraphObject()`.

4. The code for doing that is as follows:

```
private function onGraphDataLoadComplete(a_event:Event):void
{
  var loader:URLLoader = a_event.target as URLLoader;
  //obtain whatever data was loaded, and trace it
  var graphData:String = loader.data;
  var decodedJSON:Object = JSON.decode(graphData);

  var graphObject:GraphObject = new GraphObject();
  //copy all the properties from decodedJSON to graphObject
  for (var key:String in decodedJSON)
```

```
    {
      graphObject[key] = decodedJSON[key];
    }
    this.renderGraphObject(graphObject);
  }
```

5. Compile and test. The SWF is shown in the next screenshot:

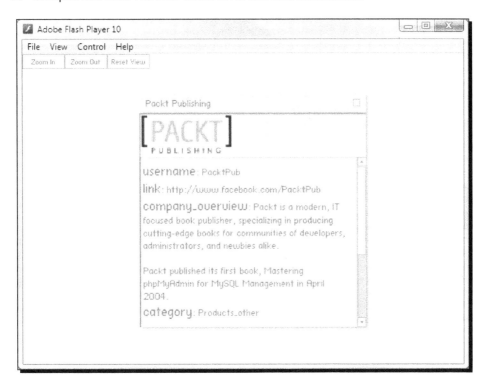

You can click the **Zoom In** button a few times to make the Renderer larger and clearer, as in the screenshot above. Your Renderer might display the fields in a different order than depicted; Facebook returns the fields in an arbitrary order.

What just happened?

The window that appeared on stage is what I call a Renderer – specifically, a **Graph Object Renderer**. It can be dragged around by the title bar, the contents can be scrolled, and you can close it by clicking the button in the top-right corner.

So, you've successfully fetched data from Facebook's Graph API and displayed it in a SWF. Your SWF is flexible; change `request.url` to point to the Graph URL of a different Facebook object and you'll see it displayed in the **Renderer**.

Most of the data from the `GraphObject` is displayed in a text area inside the window, in a simple "`key: value`" format. The Page's `name` field is displayed in the window's title bar, and if the Page has a `picture` field (we can see from the JSON that `PacktPub` does), the image is downloaded and displayed inside the renderer using a `Loader`.

Like `URLLoader`, the `flash.display.Loader` class downloads the object that a given `URLRequest` points to, dispatching a `COMPLETE` event when ready. Unlike `URLLoader`, `Loader` is used to download images and SWFs, and the event is actually dispatched by one of its sub-objects, `contentLoaderInfo`. Also, `Loader` extends `DisplayObject`, and takes the appearance of the image when it has finished downloading.

Flash's security model prevents an image's data being accessed by SWFs residing on a different domain than the image itself, unless there is a cross-domain policy file on the domain of the image that allows it. Fortunately, Facebook's cross-domain policy file is lenient, allowing such access by every domain.

So, really, this is just a graphical way of representing a Page object from the Graph API.

Understanding connections

"That's all well and good," you may be thinking, "but it doesn't show all the data associated with the Page, does it? Where are the wall posts and photos?"

Time for action – finding connections in a browser

Facebook treats wall posts, photos, videos, and even statuses as separate objects within the Graph API, rather than jamming them all into a single Page object. For instance, here's an object representing a single Post by Packt Publishing:

```
{
    "id": "204603129458_127056137323572",
    "from": {
        "name": "Packt Publishing",
        "category": "Products_other",
        "id": "204603129458"
    },
    "message": "The Amazon SimpleDB Developer Guide has been published!
        Get your copy now! http://bit.ly/b1FQUG",
    "picture": "http://external.ak.fbcdn.net/
        safe_image.php?d=c4a7887cb52dd8f93e439aaec13c034b&w=130&h=130&url
        =https%3A%2F%2Fwww.packtpub.com%2Fsites%2Fdefault%2Ffiles%2Fimage
        cache%2Fproductview%2F7344EN_MockupCover%2520Template.jpg",
    "link": "http://bit.ly/b1FQUG",
```

```
        "name": "Amazon SimpleDB Developer Guide | Packt Publishing
            Technical & IT Book Store",
        "caption": "bit.ly",
        "description": "Gain in-depth understanding of Amazon SimpleDB
            with PHP, Java, and Python examples, and run optimized
            database-backed applications on Amazon\\'s Web Services cloud",
        "icon": "http://static.ak.fbcdn.net/rsrc.php/zB010/hash/
            9yvl71tw.gif",
        "type": "link",
        "created_time": "2010-06-04T12:39:44+0000",
        "updated_time": "2010-06-04T12:39:44+0000",
        "likes": 1
    }
```

That object has expired now, and is no longer available through the Graph API, but as you could have guessed, it was available at `https://graph.facebook.com/204603129458` `_127056137323572`. It's in the same format as the Page object – albeit with a few different fields – so our Graph Object Renderer could render it just fine.

Of course, this is useless unless we know the ID of each of the Posts associated with Packt Publishing, and there's no indication of where we might find them. Or is there?

I said earlier that the Graph API was designed to be self-documenting. We can request extra, "meta" information about any Graph Object by adding a `metadata=1` flag to the end of any Graph URL. Take a look at: `https://graph.facebook.com/PacktPub?metadata=1` in your browser. A new property, `type`, appears in the JSON:

```
    "type": "page"
```

That's useful; as I said, Posts and Pages (and in fact all Graph Objects) take the same format, so this gives us a way of telling them apart.

More immediately interesting, though, is the new `metadata` object. This contains one object, `connections`, and one array, `fields`. Let's look at `fields` first:

```
    "fields": [
      {
        "name": "id",
        "description": "The page's ID"
      },
      {
        "name": "name",
        "description": "The page's name"
      },
      {
        "name": "picture",
        "description": "The pages profile picture"
```

```
      },
      {
       "name": "category",
       "description": "The page's category"
      },
      {
       "name": "fan_count",
       "description": "\\* The number of fans the page has"
      }
     ]
```

This is a list explaining what each of the fields in the main body of the Graph Object represents. At time of writing, this is still a fairly new feature, so it's possible that the list will be more complete by the time you load it.

The `connections` object is as follows:

```
     "connections": {
      "feed": "https://graph.facebook.com/packtpub/feed",
      "posts": "https://graph.facebook.com/packtpub/posts",
      "tagged": "https://graph.facebook.com/packtpub/tagged",
      "statuses": "https://graph.facebook.com/packtpub/statuses",
      "links": "https://graph.facebook.com/packtpub/links",
      "notes": "https://graph.facebook.com/packtpub/notes",
      "photos": "https://graph.facebook.com/packtpub/photos",
      "albums": "https://graph.facebook.com/packtpub/albums",
      "events": "https://graph.facebook.com/packtpub/events",
      "videos": "https://graph.facebook.com/packtpub/videos"
     }
```

Browse to one of the URLs from the previous list: `http://graph.facebook.com/ packtpub/posts`. It returns a JSON containing an array called `data` and an object called `paging`. The `data` array contains several Post objects; we'll look at `paging` later in the book.

What just happened?

The `metadata=1` parameter tells the Graph API to display all of the metadata about the current object, which, in this case, includes the type of object it is, an array of descriptions of the object's properties, and all of the URLs that contain lists of objects connected to this Page.

This layout is where the Graph API gets its name. In everyday usage, "graph" means the type of chart shown in the next diagram:

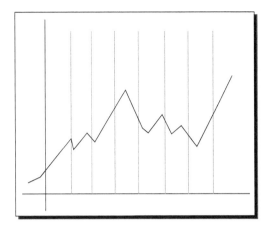

But in mathematics, "graph" refers to any set of nodes connected by edges, like the example in the next diagram:

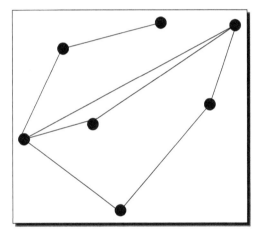

The Graph API represents Facebook's data as shown in the next diagram :

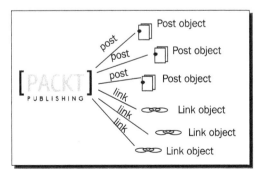

In the previous diagram, each object is a node, and the lines represent different types of connection.

Fetching `http://graph.facebook.com/packtpub/posts` gets you all the nodes joined to `PacktPub` by a "post" connection – that is, all Post objects that have been posted on Packt's wall:

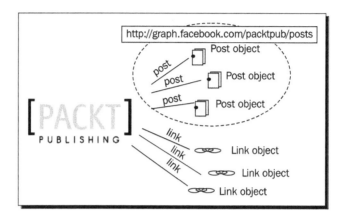

Have a go hero – exploring connections

Now that you know about the `metadata` parameter, explore the different types of connections in your browser, and see what new kinds of objects you can find.

Rendering Lists

What happens if you try to load `https://graph.facebook.com/packtpub/posts` using the same code we used to load the Packt Publishing Page object?

We get this in the output panel:

Graph Object was null!

Not a success. The way the Graph API structures the JSON here is totally different to how it structures the JSON for a Page, Post, or any other Graph Object. The same is true of the JSON for the other connection URLs. We call this structure a **Graph List**.

Time for action – rendering Lists of Posts

Since a Graph List's `data` property is an array of Graph Objects, we could just loop through the array and create a new Graph Object Renderer for each element. Feel free to have a go at this, if you like, but I've got another solution.

I've created a second renderer: this time, a **Graph List Renderer**. I've also created a class `graph.GraphList`. And `CustomGraphContainerController` inherits a method called `renderGraphList()`. Perhaps unsurprisingly, this takes an object of type `graph.GraphList` as a parameter, and creates a new Graph List Renderer to display its contents. So, we need to take a Graph List that we receive from the Graph API, and turn it into an instance of the `GraphList` class. The `GraphList` class is a little more sophisticated than the `GraphObject` class; it has a method called `addToList()`, to which we can pass any `GraphObject` instance to be added to the list.

We'll still loop through the `data` array, then, but instead of rendering each `GraphObject` on its own, we'll add each one to a `GraphList` and render that.

Modify the URL that `CustomGraphContainerController` requests, so that it loads the list of posts:

```
public function CustomGraphContainerController
  (a_graphControlContainer:GraphControlContainer)
{
  super(a_graphControlContainer);

  var loader:URLLoader = new URLLoader();
  var request:URLRequest = new URLRequest();
  //Specify which Graph URL to load
  request.url = "https://graph.facebook.com/PacktPub/posts";
  loader.addEventListener(Event.COMPLETE, onGraphDataLoadComplete);
  //Start the actual loading process
  loader.load(request);
}
```

Now, once this is loaded, we need to check whether the item returned is a Graph Object or a Graph List. We can do this by looking for a property called `data`; if one exists, we'll assume it's a List.

```
private function onGraphDataLoadComplete(a_event:Event):void
{
  var loader:URLLoader = a_event.target as URLLoader;
  //obtain whatever data was loaded, and trace it
  var graphData:String = loader.data;
  var decodedJSON:Object = JSON.decode(graphData);

  if (decodedJSON.data)
  {
    //has a "data" property so we assume it is a Graph List

  }
```

```
    else
    {
      //no "data" so we assume it is a Graph Object
      var graphObject:GraphObject = new GraphObject();
      //copy all the properties from decodedJSON to graphObject
      for (var key:String in decodedJSON)
      {
        graphObject[key] = decodedJSON[key];
      }
      this.renderGraphObject(graphObject);
    }
}
```

Inside this `if` block, we first create a new `GraphList` instance:

```
if (decodedJSON.data)
{
  //has a "data" property so we assume it is a Graph List
  var graphList:GraphList = new GraphList();
}
```

(You will need to `import graph.GraphList`.)

Next, remember than `decodedJSON.data` is an array of objects; we loop through this array, and create a `GraphObject` from each element.

```
if (decodedJSON.data)
{
  //has a "data" property so we assume it is a Graph List
  var graphList:GraphList = new GraphList();
  var childGraphObject:GraphObject;
  for each (var childObject:Object in decodedJSON.data)
  {
    childGraphObject = new GraphObject();
    for (var childKey:String in childObject)
    {
      childGraphObject[childKey] = childObject[childKey];
    }
  }
}
```

This is basically the same thing we did with the `decodedJSON` when loading a single Graph Object.

What about the other property inside the Graph List, the `paging` object? We should add that too:

```
if (decodedJSON.data)
{
  //has a "data" property so we assume it is a Graph List
  var graphList:GraphList = new GraphList();
  var childGraphObject:GraphObject;
  for each (var childObject:Object in decodedJSON.data)
  {
    childGraphObject = new GraphObject();
    for (var childKey:String in childObject)
    {
      childGraphObject[childKey] = childObject[childKey];
    }
    graphList.addToList(childGraphObject);
  }
  graphList.paging = decodedJSON.paging;
}
```

Finally, we pass the `GraphList` instance to `renderGraphList()`:

```
if (decodedJSON.data)
{
  //has a "data" property so we assume it is a Graph List
  var graphList:GraphList = new GraphList();
  var childGraphObject:GraphObject;
  for each (var childObject:Object in decodedJSON.data)
  {
    childGraphObject = new GraphObject();
    for (var childKey:String in childObject)
    {
      childGraphObject[childKey] = childObject[childKey];
    }
    graphList.addToList(childGraphObject);
  }
  graphList.paging = decodedJSON.paging;
  this.renderGraphList(graphList);
}
```

Compile the SWF and test it. The following screenshot shows the result:

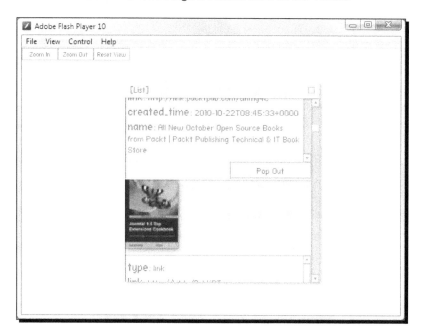

It's a scrollable window containing all the Graph Objects from the list.

What happens when you click the **Pop Out** button underneath a Graph Object?

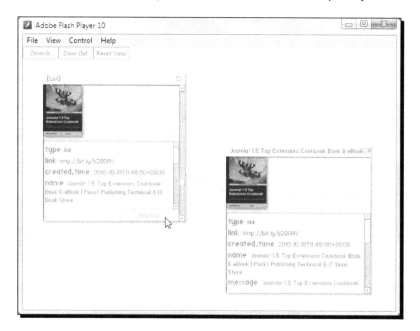

What just happened?

The Graph Object pops out into its own Graph Object Renderer, with a gray line connecting it to the list to which it belongs. This lets you look at several children of a list at the same time:

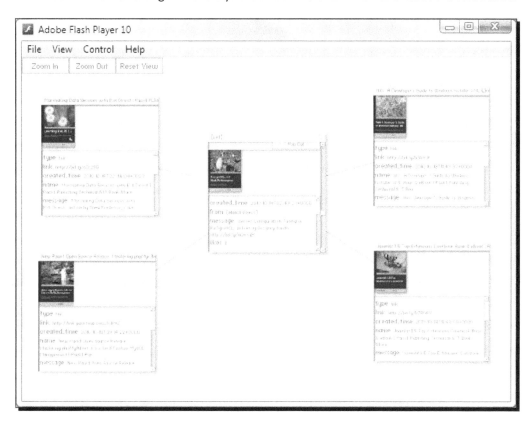

(You can drag the individual renderers to reposition them, or drag the background to move everything at once.)

This makes it clear that a Graph List is just a collection of Graph Objects.

Rendering connections

We've shown the link from a Graph List to its Graph Objects; the next step is to show the connections from a Graph Object to its Graph Lists.

Time for action – displaying a Graph Object's connections

The Graph Object Renderer has the ability to show a list of all the object's connections, if that list is included as part of the Graph Object.

All we have to do is tell the Graph API to give us that list when we request a Graph Object; since our code for creating an instance of `GraphObject` from a JSON copies all the properties of that JSON to the `GraphObject`, this metadata will be included too. So, actually, all we need to do is add the `metadata=1` flag to the end of the Graph URL that we request, and it'll do the rest for us.

We could do this by changing our request code as shown in the following excerpt:

```
public function CustomGraphContainerController
  (a_graphControlContainer:GraphControlContainer)
{
  super(a_graphControlContainer);

  var loader:URLLoader = new URLLoader();
  var request:URLRequest = new URLRequest();
  //Specify which Graph URL to load
  request.url = "https://graph.facebook.com/PacktPub?metadata=1";
  loader.addEventListener(Event.COMPLETE, onGraphDataLoadComplete);
  //Start the actual loading process
  loader.load(request);
}
```

There's a slightly more elegant way to do this, however, using a class called `URLVariables`. In `CustomGraphContainerController.as`, add a line to import this class:

```
import flash.net.URLVariables;
```

Now, modify the constructor as shown in the following lines of code:

```
public function CustomGraphContainerController
  (a_graphControlContainer:GraphControlContainer)
{
  super(a_graphControlContainer);

  var loader:URLLoader = new URLLoader();
  var request:URLRequest = new URLRequest();
  var variables:URLVariables = new URLVariables();
  //Specify which Graph URL to load
  request.url = "https://graph.facebook.com/PacktPub";
  variables.metadata = 1;
  request.data = variables;
  loader.addEventListener(Event.COMPLETE, onGraphDataLoadComplete);
  //Start the actual loading process
  loader.load(request);
}
```

As you can probably guess, setting `variables.metadata = 1` is exactly the same as sticking `?metadata=1` on the end of the URL. Doing it this way takes a few more lines, but it makes it much easier to set different parameters, and keeps the parameters separate from the URL.

Anyway, compile the SWF and you should see the following screenshot:

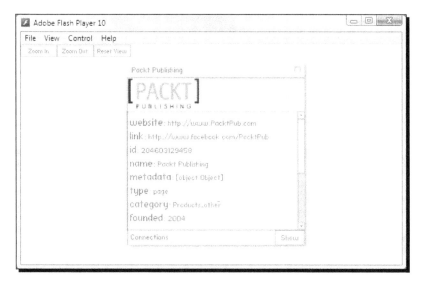

Notice the new **Connections** bar at the bottom of the Renderer? Click on the **Show** button:

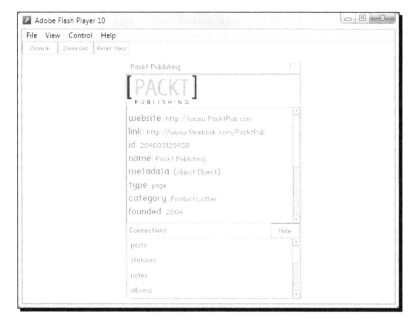

What just happened?

We can now see all of the connections of a Graph Object right there in its renderer. Of course, that's not very interesting unless we can see what's at the other end of each connection!

Introducing the Requestor

Ideally, whenever the user clicks a connection from the scrolling list, a new Graph List Renderer of that connection will be created and displayed.

To do this, we'd need to add a `MouseEvent.CLICK` listener to the list, and use it to trigger a new `URLLoader` request for the clicked connection.

Fortunately, all the UI code has already been provided elsewhere in the project; we just need to tap into that. To do this, we'll need to make use of what I call a **Requestor**.

Time for action – creating an HTTP Requestor

The idea is, we move all of the code regarding the `URLLoader` from `CustomGraphContainerController` to a separate class, called `HTTPRequestor`. We will then replace the `CustomGraphContainerController` constructor with this:

```
public function CustomGraphContainerController(a_graphControlContainer
:GraphControlContainer)
{
  super(a_graphControlContainer);

  _requestor = new HTTPRequestor();
  _requestor.request(new GraphRequest("PacktPub"));
}
```

Why bother? Well, apart from being neater, there are two main advantages:

1. It's much simpler to request several Graph Objects or Graph Lists; no need to deal with multiple instances of `URLLoader`.

2. In the next chapter, we'll see how to use the official Adobe AS3 Facebook SDK to retrieve information from the Graph API. If all the code for a request is encapsulated in one class, then we only need to change one line to switch from using HTTP to using Adobe's SDK:

```
public function CustomGraphContainerController(a_graphControlConta
iner:GraphControlContainer)
{
  super(a_graphControlContainer);

  _requestor = new SDKRequestor();
  _requestor.request(new GraphRequest("PacktPub"));
}
```

GraphRequest is a simple class; its constructor allows you to use two parameters to specify what you'd like to retrieve from the Graph API:

♦ objectID, the name of any Graph Object.

♦ connectionID, the name of any connection of that Graph Object.

So, to request the Packt Publishing Page, you would use this GraphRequest:

newGraphRequest("PacktPub");

and to request the list of Posts from the Packt Publishing Page, you'd use this:

newGraphRequest("PacktPub", "posts");

The class is already written; it's in \src\com\graph\apis\http\HTTPRequestor. as. Take a look! There are a few changes from the code we wrote in CustomGraphContainerController.as, but these all have comments to explain them:

```
package graph.apis.http
{
  import events.DialogEvent;
  import events.RequestEvent;
  import flash.events.Event;
  import flash.events.EventDispatcher;
  import flash.events.HTTPStatusEvent;
  import flash.events.IEventDispatcher;
  import flash.events.IOErrorEvent;
  import flash.net.URLLoader;
  import flash.net.URLRequest;
  import flash.net.URLVariables;
  import flash.utils.Dictionary;
  import graph.apis.base.IRequestor;
  import graph.BaseGraphItem;
  import graph.GraphList;
  import graph.GraphObject;
  import graph.GraphRequest;
  import com.adobe.serialization.json.JSON;

  //the class needs to dispatch events (see later in code for why)
  public class HTTPRequestor extends EventDispatcher implements
    IRequestor
  {
    //this is used to figure out which GraphRequest created each
    //loader
    private var _requests:Dictionary = new Dictionary();

    public function HTTPRequestor(target:IEventDispatcher = null)
    {
```

```
      //this is needed because the class extends EventDispatcher
      super(target);


   }


   public function request(a_request:GraphRequest):void
   {
     var loader:URLLoader = new URLLoader();
     var urlRequest:URLRequest = new URLRequest();
     var variables:URLVariables = new URLVariables();


     //We construct a URL from the parameters of the GraphRequest
     urlRequest.url = "https://graph.facebook.com/" + a_request.
objectID;
     if (a_request.connectionID)
     {
       urlRequest.url += "/" + a_request.connectionID;
     }


     variables.metadata = 1;
     urlRequest.data = variables;


     //this is used to figure out which GraphRequest created the
loader later
     _requests[loader] = a_request;


     loader.addEventListener(Event.COMPLETE,
onGraphDataLoadComplete);
     loader.load(urlRequest);
   }


   private function onGraphDataLoadComplete(a_event:Event):void
   {
     var loader:URLLoader = a_event.target as URLLoader;
     var graphData:String = loader.data;
     var decodedJSON:Object = JSON.decode(graphData);


     //we find the original GraphRequest used to start the loader
     var originalRequest:GraphRequest = _requests[loader] as
GraphRequest;


     if (decodedJSON.data)
     {
       var graphList:GraphList = new GraphList();
```

```
    var childGraphObject:GraphObject;
    for each (var childObject:Object in decodedJSON.data)
    {
      childGraphObject = new GraphObject();
      for (var childKey:String in childObject)
      {
        childGraphObject[childKey] = childObject[childKey];
      }
      graphList.addToList(childGraphObject);
    }
    graphList.paging = decodedJSON.paging;

    //we use the properties of the original GraphRequest to add
    //some extra data to the GraphList itself
    graphList.ownerID = originalRequest.objectID;
    graphList.connectionType = originalRequest.connectionID;

    //since this class does not have a renderGraphList() method,
    //we dispatch an event, which CustomGraphContainerController
    //will listen for, and call its own renderGraphList() method
    dispatchEvent(new RequestEvent(RequestEvent.REQUEST_COMPLETED,
      graphList));
  }
  else
  {
    var graphObject:GraphObject = new GraphObject();
    for (var key:String in decodedJSON)
    {
      graphObject[key] = decodedJSON[key];
    }

    //since this class does not have a renderGraphList() method,
    //we dispatch an event, which CustomGraphContainerController
    //will listen for, and call its own renderGraphList() method
    dispatchEvent(new RequestEvent(RequestEvent.REQUEST_COMPLETED,
      graphObject));
  }
  }
  }

  }
```

There's no need to change any of this, or even to understand any of it apart from the HTTP request code that we wrote earlier. Just remember, its purpose is to encapsulate your requests to the Graph API.

Now, go back to `CustomGraphContainerController.as` and remove all the request-related code:

```
package controllers
{
  import ui.GraphControlContainer;

  public class CustomGraphContainerController extends GCController
  {

    public function CustomGraphContainerController
      (a_graphControlContainer:GraphControlContainer)
    {
      super(a_graphControlContainer);

    }

  }

}
```

`CustomGraphContainerController` inherits a protected variable called `_requestor` of type `IRequestor`, as well as a method for adding the required event listeners to it, so all we need to do is this:

```
package controllers
{
  import graph.apis.http.HTTPRequestor;
  import graph.GraphRequest;
  import ui.GraphControlContainer;

  public class CustomGraphContainerController extends GCController
  {

    public function CustomGraphContainerController
      (a_graphControlContainer:GraphControlContainer)
    {
      super(a_graphControlContainer);
      _requestor = new HTTPRequestor();
      addEventListenersToRequestor();
      _requestor.request(new GraphRequest("PacktPub"));
    }

  }

}
```

Compile and run your SWF, then expand the **Connections** box and click on "**posts**":

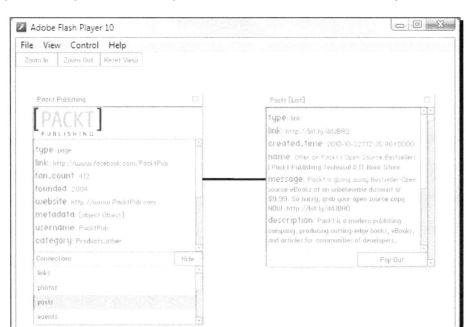

Great! The Graph List Renderer appears, with a black line to the Page to indicate that there is a connection between them. What about the other connections? Try clicking on **statuses**.

Error #2044: Unhandled ioError:.text=Error #2032: Stream Error. URL: https://graph.facebook.com/204603129458/statuses?metadata=1

Oops.

What just happened?

If you load the troublesome URL in your browser (`https://graph.facebook.com/packtpub/statuses`), you'll see the following message:

```
{
    "error": {
        "type": "OAuthAccessTokenException",
        "message": "An access token is required to request this
            resource."
    }
}
```

This error is due to not being logged in to Facebook through your SWF. We'll look at how to solve this in the next chapter.

For now, you can get around the error by adding an IO_ERROR event listener to the URLLoader. In HTTPRequestor.as, modify request():

```
public function request(a_request:GraphRequest):void
{
  varloader:URLLoader = new URLLoader();
  varurlRequest:URLRequest = new URLRequest();
  varvariables:URLVariables = new URLVariables();

  //We construct a URL from the parameters of the
  //GraphRequest
  urlRequest.url = "https://graph.facebook.com/" +
      a_request.objectID;
  if (a_request.connectionID)
  {
    urlRequest.url += "/" + a_request.connectionID;
  }

  variables.metadata = 1;
  urlRequest.data = variables;

  //this is used to figure out which GraphRequest
  //created the loader later
  _requests[loader] = a_request;

  loader.addEventListener(Event.COMPLETE,
    onGraphDataLoadComplete);
  loader.addEventListener(IOErrorEvent.IO_ERROR,
    onIOError);
  loader.load(urlRequest);
}
```

You will need to import flash.events.IOErrorEvent. Now, in the same class, create a simple event handler function to trace the error:

```
private function onIOError(a_event:IOErrorEvent):void
{
  trace(a_event.text);
}
```

This way, you can see the error in your output window, but it won't crash the SWF. Note: a try-catch block will not work for this kind of error.

Understanding Connections of Connections

Take a look at the Graph List Renderer created by clicking on the "**album**" connection:

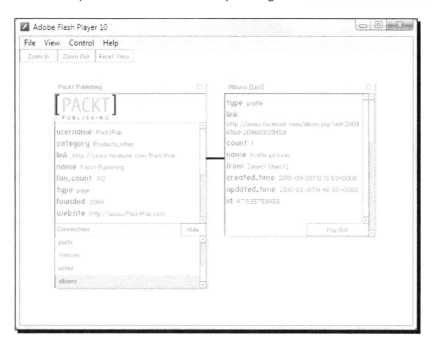

Notice anything missing?

There are no pictures! We can see lots of photos when loading the Packt Publishing Page inside the actual Facebook website, but here there are no photo URLs at all. Check it out by loading the Graph List in the browser; even with ?metadata=1, there's no indication of where the photos might be:

```
{
    "data": [
        {
            "id": "471535759458",
            "from": {
                "name": "Packt Publishing",
                "category": "Products_other",
                "id": "204603129458"
            },
            "name": "Profile pictures",
            "link": "http://www.facebook.com/
              album.php?aid=280961&id=204603129458",
            "count": 1,
            "type": "profile",
            "created_time": "2010-09-30T10:13:53+0000",
```

```
                "updated_time": "2010-03-18T14:46:50+0000"
            },
            {
                "id": "307932939458",
                "from": {
                    "name": "Packt Publishing",
                    "category": "Products_other",
                    "id": "204603129458"
                },
                "name": "Books",
                "description": "Packt Books",
                "link": "http://www.facebook.com/
                    album.php?aid=180619&id=204603129458",
                "count": 32,
                "type": "normal",
                "created_time": "2010-02-04T12:32:17+0000",
                "updated_time": "2010-03-18T16:08:42+0000"
            }
        ],
        "paging": {
            "previous": "https://graph.facebook.com/204603129458/
            albums?metadata=1&limit=25&since=2010-09-30T10%3A13%3A53%2B0000",
                "next": "https://graph.facebook.com/204603129458/
    albums?metadata=1&limit=25&until=2010-02-04T12%3A32%3A16%2B0000"
        }
    }
```

Time for action – loading photos from an album

However, as we've established, each object inside `data` is a Graph Object in its own right. Let's take a look at the Packt Books album, with id `307932939458`, by browsing to `https://graph.facebook.com/307932939458?metadata=1`:

```
{
    "id": "307932939458",
    "from": {
        "name": "Packt Publishing",
        "category": "Products_other",
        "id": "204603129458"
    },
    "name": "Books",
    "description": "Packt Books",
    "link": "http://www.facebook.com/
        album.php?aid=180619&id=204603129458",
    "count": 32,
    "type": "album",
    "created_time": "2010-02-04T12:32:17+0000",
    "updated_time": "2010-03-18T16:08:42+0000",
    "metadata": {
```

```
        "connections": {
            "photos": "https://graph.facebook.com/307932939458/photos",
            "likes": "https://graph.facebook.com/307932939458/likes",
            "comments": "https://graph.facebook.com/307932939458/
                comments"
        },
    }
}
```

This time, the metadata gives us the information we need. The photos are linked to the Album Graph Object through a connection called "photos".

Run your SWF and load the **albums** connection again. In the Renderer, scroll to the Graph Object whose name is Books, and click on **Pop Out**. Then, expand the Connections box of the **Books Renderer**, and click on **photos**.

What just happened?

When we were only considering the "posts" connection, our graph was very simple; there was a single connection between the Page and everything related to it:

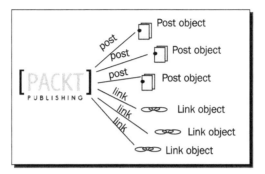

Now that we've introduced albums, it's more complicated:

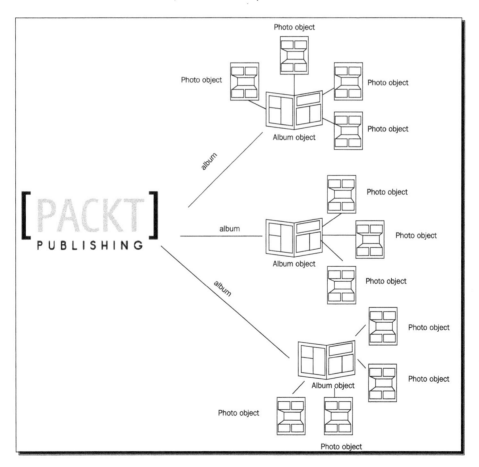

We now have to traverse two levels of connection to get from the Page to the objects we're looking for.

The connections don't stop there, though. Both Albums and Photos can be connected to Comments, too:

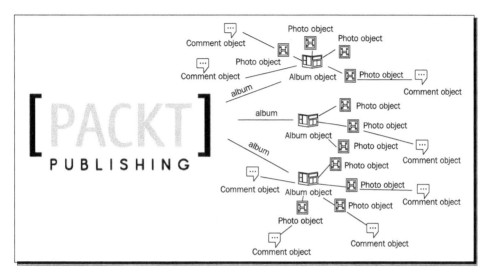

Plus, every comment has a property called `from` that connects it to the user that posted it. A user can also be "tagged" as appearing in a photo, which connects the photo and the user, as well:

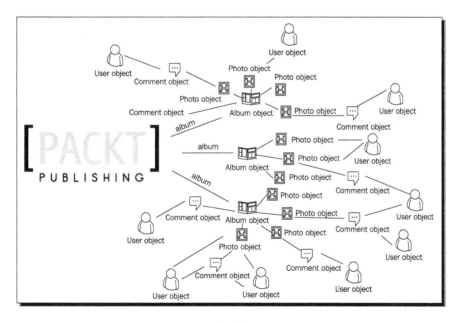

The diagram is looking more and more complex (and the similarities to the mathematical graph drawn earlier are now clear). Of course, now that people are involved, the number of connections gets ridiculous. Users can be connected to any other object, either by being friends with another User, by being tagged in a Photo, Video, or Note, by posting a Comment, Link or other item, or by clicking **Like** on any other element in Facebook.

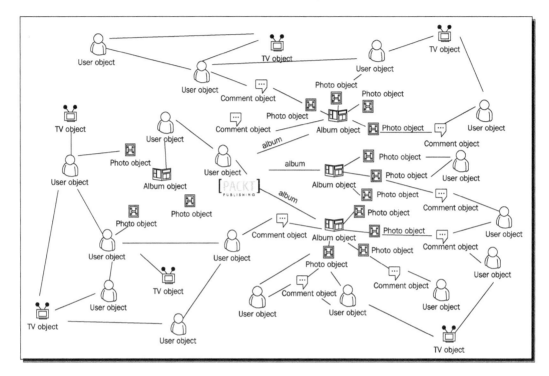

If you start with one Page and keep going through all the objects connected to it, and then all the objects connected to those, and so on, you can cover huge numbers of nodes without having to start again with a new Page.

The power of the graph lies in its flexibility. Every type of Graph Object has the same basic structure as every other type of Graph Object – with the exception of Graph Lists (which contain arrays of Graph Objects). That's why our Graph Object Renderer can easily display any kind of Graph Object.

Also, have you noticed that it's not just comments that have a `from` property? Albums do, too, and so do individual photos, and pretty much every type of object that isn't a Page or a User. This means you can start with any object, find its creator, and traverse outwards across the graph from there.

The Graph model has implications for privacy. Suppose that, if we were granted access to information about a Page, we were also allowed to access information about any object connected to that Page. Well, then we could go from the Page to:

- An Album posted by the Page, to
- A Photo in that Album, to
- A User tagged in that Photo, to
- That User's list of wall posts, to
- A Comment made on a post by a friend of the first User, to
- The User that posted the Comment, to
- A TV Show that this User Likes, to
- A Link posted on the Page for that TV Show, to
- The User who posted that link

and so on. It's no surprise, then, that Facebook uses a more detailed set of rules to determine both what a user can access, and what an app can access on behalf of a user. We'll look at these rules in the next chapter.

Putting it all together

Finally, let's see how far we can traverse through the graph, starting from the Packt Publishing Page.

Time for action – traversing the Graph

Set the Visualizer to start by requesting the PacktPub Page. Now, compile and run your SWF, and use the **Connections** box and the **Pop Out** buttons to explore the Graph, and see how far you can get. Don't forget you can drag Renderers around, and zoom out to fit even more in the Flash Player window! And remember, black lines signify connections, while gray lines signify that the object belongs to a List.

The following screenshot shows what it could look like after only a few clicks:

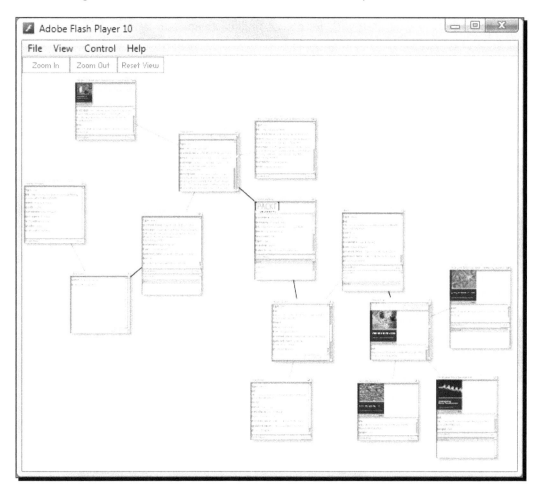

You can already see the resemblance to the sprawling diagrams of the Graph seen previously in the chapter.

What just happened?

You've written the code to power an RIA that allows you to explore the entire public Graph, starting from any point. In other words, you've made a Facebook crawler, in Flash.

Have a go hero – exploring other areas

You don't have to start exploring from the PacktPub Page. Try changing that initial `GraphRequest` instance to request the Facebook Page, `Facebook`, or *Mark Zuckerberg's* public profile, `markzuckerberg`, or the Page of any other brand, company, or famous person.

Also, realize that you're not limited to a single `GraphRequest`; you can create as many as you like. Try starting with a few at once, and see if you come across any overlaps!

Keep an eye on your output window for traces telling you that a Graph Object or List could not be retrieved. Is it always for the same reason?

Pop Quiz

1. What does the `?metadata=1` parameter do when used in a Graph API URL?

    a. It makes the metadata visible

    b. It makes the metadata invisible

2. How many levels through the Graph can you traverse, starting with any Page?

    a. One

    b. Two

    c. Ten

    d. Unlimited

3. True or false: If the JSON returned from a Graph URL contains an object called data, we can always assume it's a Graph List.

    a. True

    b. False

4. True or false: If the JSON returned from a Graph URL doesn't contain an object called data, we can always assume it's a Graph Object.

    a. True

    b. False

Summary

We learned a lot in this chapter about the Graph API: not just what it is, but also how to access it in AS3.

Key things to learn:

♦ The Graph API is so-called because it represents all of Facebook's data connected in an enormous graph of objects and connections.

♦ The Graph API has two types of elements: Graph Objects and Graph Lists.

♦ Graph Objects may have two IDs: a numeric one specified by Facebook, and possibly an alphanumeric one, specified by the Graph Object's owner.

♦ Graph Objects have connections; connections lead to Graph Lists; Graph Lists contain Graph Objects.

♦ The format of a Graph URL for retrieving a Graph Object is `https://graph. facebook.com/graph_object_id`.

♦ The format of a Graph URL for retrieving a Graph List is `https://graph. facebook.com/graph_object_id/connection_id`.

♦ Graph URLs return data in JSON format. This is a text-based format which uses key-value pairs to represent objects containing properties, arrays, and other objects.

♦ Sometimes, Graph URLs return error messages; these are also given in JSON format.

♦ We can use the `?metadata=1` parameter in a Graph URL to make it return extra information about the element, like the list of connections leading from a Graph Object.

♦ Metadata is not returned for Graph Objects that are part of a Graph List.

♦ The JSON representation of a Graph Object can be deserialized to an AS3 object we can use in code using the **as3corelib** library.

We also discussed how the Graph API is so flexible, because it uses the same basic structure for every type of object in Facebook's database.

But what about those objects that give us an authorization error when we try to get information on them? That's what we'll cover in the next chapter.

3
Let Me In!

When exploring the Graph in the previous chapter, we came across a few points where our access was blocked. Our Facebook apps need to be able to deal with this gracefully, by either avoiding such points or asking for access.

In this chapter we'll learn about:

◆ **Security**: How Facebook blocks people and apps from seeing things they shouldn't

◆ **Permissions**: How users decide what information other people and apps are allowed to see, and how your application can request to see more

◆ **Authentication**: How your application can prove that it's trusted to see all that information

So let's get on with it...

What can you see?

Let's find out what we can see on other people's Facebook accounts under different circumstances.

Time for action – snooping through other people's accounts

Log in to Facebook in your browser and go to your personal profile page. Note down the URL; it'll be something like `http://www.facebook.com/yournamehere` (or `http://www.facebook.com/profile.php?id=12345678` if you haven't signed up for a Facebook User Name at `http://www.facebook.com/username/`). Since it's your profile, you'll be able to see everything: Wall Posts, photos, links, interests, bio, and so on.

Now check out a friend's profile (and again note down the URL). You'll be able to see most of the same information as you can on your own profile—perhaps even all of it.

Are you in a network? If so, take a look at the profile of someone who is in the same network, but who isn't marked as a friend of yours. You'll be able to see some information about them, but not everything they've published; perhaps you won't be able to see their wall or their photos.

Networks are based on where you work or study; being in a network is like tagging yourself to say "I work here", and lets you find other people in your network more easily. **(Facebook used to have regional networks, too, but these were phased out in 2009.)**

Joining a network often requires having an e-mail address that's only available to employees at your workplace or students at your school or university, to stop random people pretending to belong when they don't.

For information on networks and how to join them, browse to `http://www.facebook.com/networks/networks.php`.

Finally, take a look at the profile of someone you have no connection to at all. Obviously this is tricky! Try looking at friends of friends of friends, or searching for random names. Again, you'll be restricted in what information you can see.

Okay, now, log out of Facebook (or switch to private browsing mode), and visit all the same profile pages again.

Private browsing mode allows you to open a new browser window or tab that doesn't log you in to sites automatically (and doesn't cache any information or save pages to your history). It's useful for situations like this where you want to check how the behavior of a website changes based on whether you're logged in.

Different browsers use different names for this mode:

- Google Chrome: Incognito
- Mozilla Firefox: Private browsing
- Internet Explorer: InPrivate
- Safari: Private browsing
- Opera: Private window / private tab

Check your browser's help to find out how to enable it.

What's different?

What just happened?

As you can see, Facebook's security restricts access to what information you can see about a person. It's not a simple binary setting – "you can either see *this* information or *that* information" – rather, it's based on:

◆ How you are connected to the other person

◆ Whether or not you are logged in to Facebook

What's particularly interesting is that you can often see more information about a person just by logging in to Facebook – even if you've never met them, and have no friends or networks in common. For some people, you may not even be able to view their profile page if you're not logged in; Facebook might deny that it even exists.

Every Facebook user has a list of **permissions**, which specifies the information about them that other users can see, based on their connections to the other user. If you don't have permission to view certain data, Facebook's security simply doesn't show it to you.

Permissions can be complicated to figure out. Here's a diagram of what one user's permissions might look like:

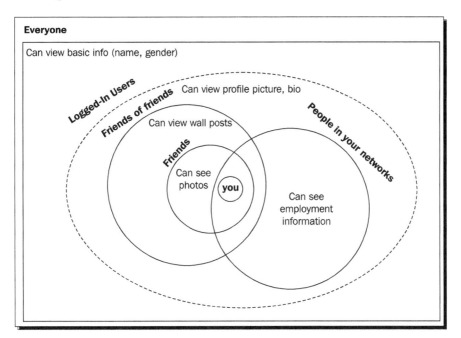

In this diagram, the label outside each set explains which group of people it belongs to, and the writing inside the sets details which permissions those people have. The permissions overlap, so a person that's a friend of a friend and in this user's network would be able to see their basic information, their profile picture, their bio, their wall posts, and their employment information, but not their photographs.

The diagram could be even more complicated; you can add sets for arbitrary groups (which users set up manually) or even for specific people.

Let's take a look at your settings to see what permissions you're giving other people.

Have a go hero – viewing your privacy settings

While logged in to Facebook, click on **Account | Privacy Settings** in the top-right-hand corner.

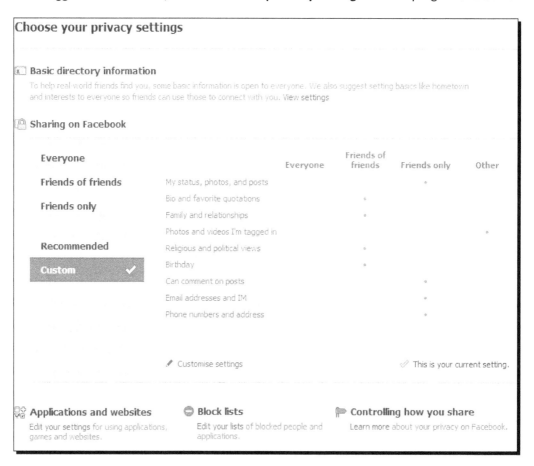

This page is split into two main sections: **Basic directory information** and **Sharing on Facebook**. Take some time to dig in to these and see what information can be viewed by whom. You might be surprised at how much information about you is available to anyone who cares to look.

While customizing your settings in either of those pages, you can click on **Preview my Profile** to see how your profile will look when viewed by any person you specify.

A few pieces of information are always viewable by anyone who's logged in: your name, your gender, your profile picture, and your list of networks. Access to everything else can be modified.

What's that got to do with the Graph API?

That's all good to know, but does it affect our application?

Try accessing the profiles of all the people you just looked at through their Graph URLs. Remember, if their Facebook URL is `http://www.facebook.com/username`, their Graph URL will be `https://graph.facebook.com/username`; if their Facebook URL is `http://www.facebook.com/profile.php?id=12345678`, their Graph URL will be `https://graph.facebook.com/12345678`.

You'll notice that the only information you can see is:

◆ Name (and separate fields for first name, last name, and so on)

◆ Profile picture (through `https://graph.facebook.com/id/picture`)

◆ Gender

All this information is publicly available. This is true even if you can see extra information on their profile page when logged out.

The Graph API can't detect whether we're logged in to Facebook in another browser window, so everything we see here is through the eyes of a logged-out user.

For instance, here's what my page looks like as shown in the following lines of code:

```
{
    "id": "«redacted»",
    "name": "Michael James Williams",
    "first_name": "Michael",
    "middle_name": "James",
    "last_name": "Williams",
    "gender": "male",
    "locale": "en_GB"
}
```

And although you can see a list of connections URLs by adding `metadata=1` to the URL, trying to access any of them leads to this error:

```
{
    "error": {
        "type": "OAuthAccessTokenException",
        "message": "An access token is required to request this
            resource."
    }
}
```

But what is an access token?

Access tokens are proof of authorization

Imagine a secure building. To get in through the front door, you need to provide the doorman with your passport, your driver's license, and your social security number – just to prove who you are. Once he's satisfied, he gives you a temporary pass, with your name on it, to clip to your jacket.

Inside the building, everybody trusts the pass. You don't need to risk showing them your important personal documents; those only get seen by the doorman.

An **access token** is like that pass. Facebook gives a logged-in user a string of characters, which says, "I am this person, and I have logged in," and this string can be passed as a parameter to a Graph URL to gain access to information that the user is permitted to see.

Except, that's not the whole story.

User/Application authorization

There are actually *two* authorizations required: the user's and the application's. It works like this:

Joe User tries to do something in Bill's Cool Application that requires the application to access some of Joe's restricted information. The application can't access it, so the two of them approach Facebook via the Graph API.

The application says, "Hey Facebook, I'm Bill's Cool Application, and I want to access Joe User's data."

Facebook replies, "First I need to see your ID, to prove that you really are Bill's Cool Application."

The application says, "Sure thing; here are my credentials."

Facebook checks them out, and says, "These look okay to me. Wait a minute, how do I know that this is the real Joe User, and not some guy in a wig?"

Joe logs in to Facebook with his e-mail address and password, obscuring them so that Bill's Cool Application never sees them. The application politely looks away.

Facebook says, "Hey Joe, good to see you. Are you happy for Bill's Cool Application to access this data it's asking for?"

Joe checks what the application is trying to get, and says, "Yeah, sure, that's fine with me."

Facebook says, "Great. Okay, Bill's Cool Application, here's an access token. If you want to access any of Joe's data, just show me that token when you ask for the info and I'll give it to you."

The application says, "Cool! So, I can just use this token whenever I want?"

Facebook says, "Well, no. It will expire within a few hours. After that, you'll have to ask for another one, and you'll need Joe to be logged in to do that. Same deal if Joe logs out; you'll need to get another token, which means getting him to log in again."

The application says, "That seems a little inconvenient. You mean I have to get Joe to say it's okay for me to access his data every couple of hours?"

Facebook replies, "Oh, no, no, no. Now that Joe's said it's okay for you to see his information, I'll remember that, and won't bother asking again. And I don't need to see his e-mail and password if he's already logged in."

Joe and the application thank Facebook and go off to do whatever it was they wanted to do in the first place.

Of course, the information isn't passed through the form of a conversation; that would be silly. The application credentials are passed to Facebook through a Graph URL, while the user give their credentials through a standard Facebook login web page. Facebook does not return the access token in a JSON, but through a parameter to the application's URL – this is why your application needs a web host.

First, you're probably wondering where we get application credentials from. We can't just make them up; we need to register our application with Facebook first. Let's do that now.

Time for action – registering an application with Facebook

Sign up to become a Facebook Developer at `http://www.facebook.com/developers/`. Don't worry; it's free, and instant.

You may be asked to verify your Facebook account by entering a valid mobile phone number or adding a credit card. You won't be charged (apart from the cost of a standard text message, if you pick that method); this is to ensure that every application is connected to a real person.

On the Developer page, click **Set Up New Application** in the top-right:

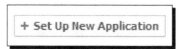

You'll be asked to enter the name of your application. It's a good idea to use your name or your company's name as part of the application's name, as this makes it more likely to be unique. (You can change the name of the application later if you like; this isn't set in stone.) You'll also be asked to agree to the **Facebook Terms and Conditions** – make sure you read them first.

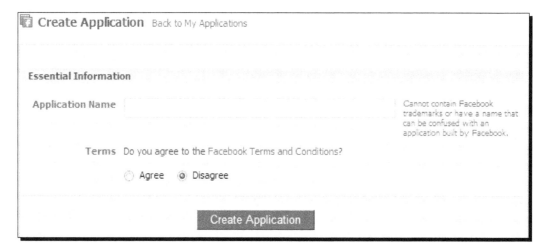

Click on **Create Application**. A huge number of new options appear! Some, like the description and logo fields, only affect the way the application looks, but many of them affect how the application behaves. For now, we don't need to worry about any of that.

What just happened?

You just created your first Facebook Application. Until we configure some more options, this is little more than a set of authentication credentials that can be used to identify your application:

- ◆ **Application ID**: Like a username for your application
- ◆ **Application secret**: Like a password, used to prove that requests come from the actual application – don't share it!
- ◆ **API key**: Used to access the Graph API

You can find these in your application's summary page; browse to `http://www.facebook.com/developers`, find your application in the list on the right-hand side (underneath the **Set Up New Application** button), and click its name.

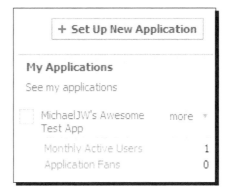

The three fields mentioned previously are easy to spot:

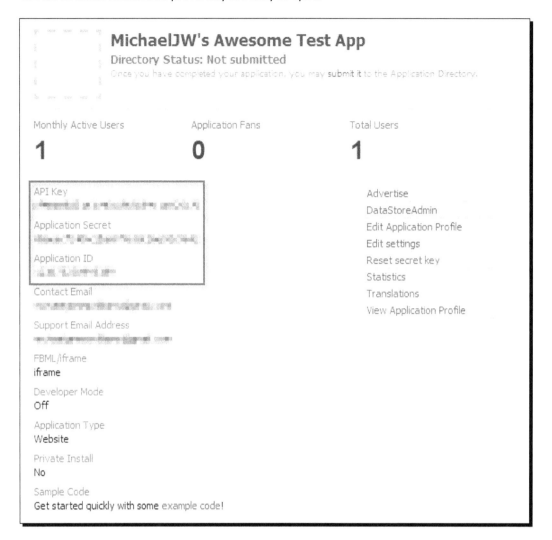

These don't change (though you can reset your secret key at any time, if you accidentally let someone else see it), so take a note of them. We'll be using them a lot throughout the book.

Application ID + logged-in user = access token

We've now got everything we need to request an access token from Facebook. So let's do it.

Time for action – requesting an access token with the browser

Open your browser and head to `https://graph.facebook.com/oauth/ authorize?client_id=«insert_application_id»` (replace «insert_ application_id» with your application's Application ID).

You'll get the following error:

```
{
    "error": {
        "type": "OAuthException",
        "message": "Missing redirect_uri parameter."
    }
}
```

Facebook won't just output the access token; it wants to redirect the browser to another web page, and pass the access token to that page. At the moment, this isn't very useful. Our Flash application is running as a standalone SWF and is not embedded in a page — so we'll use a quick workaround.

Registering a redirect URI with our application

Go to your application's **Settings** (go to `http://www.facebook.com/developers`, then click the name of your application, then click on **Edit Settings**). Click on the **Web Site** tab in the navigation bar on the left.

You'll see the panel as shown in the next screenshot:

The **Site URL** box defines the URL that Facebook redirects to after authorizing the user and the application. It's also the URL to which the access token will be passed.

Until we create our own page, let's set this to the Google home page. I'm sure they won't mind. Enter `http://google.com/` in the box, and click on **Save Changes**.

If you try browsing to `https://graph.facebook.com/oauth/authorize?client_id=«your_application_id»` again, you'll get the same error message. Even though we've specified the redirect destination page inside our application's settings, we still have to pass it to the `authorize` URL.

There is a security risk involved in passing credentials as parameters typed into a URL; they're not secure, and could be read by anyone. This poses a problem: Facebook would like to see our **Application Secret**, to prove that we really are logging in via the application whose ID we've provided, but we can't risk passing the Secret via the URL.

To get around this, we can tell Facebook that we're using a web browser on the user's side to authenticate, and Facebook will let us through without requiring our **Application Secret**. This involves passing another parameter: `type=user_agent` (**user agent** is the general term for applications like web browsers that run on the user's computer).

So, browse to the URL: `https://graph.facebook.com/oauth/authorize?client_id=«your_application_id»&redirect_uri=http://google.com&type=user_agent`.

 Note that there is an ampersand (`&`) separating the value of each parameter and the name of the next, and that the second parameter is called `redirect_uri`, not `redirect_url`. (That's not a typo; a URL is a specific type of URI.)

You should be faced with a Facebook login web page:

Enter your details and click on **Log in**. You'll be asked to give the application permission to access your basic information:

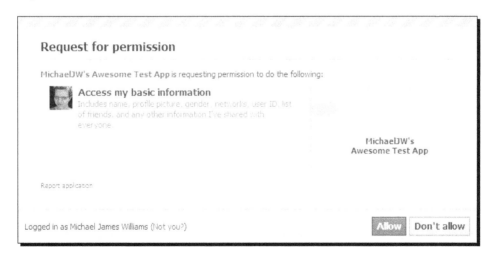

Click on **Allow**. You'll be redirected to Google—but take a closer look at the URL:

```
http://google.com/#access_token=123675230995389%7C2.hX2Png6g2LUuczfd4
tLPbQ__.3600.1276960311-169573433058884%7C8BAAidDtlt8fulZHA3bC3YxcCwM
```

At last! We have our access token. You can see it as the value of the `access_token` parameter in the URL we were redirected to. In this case, it's: `123675230995389%7C2.hX2 Png6g2LUuczfd4tLPbQ__.3600.1276960311-169573433058884%7C8BAAidDtlt8fu lZHA3bC3YxcCwM`.

(Yours will be different, because the token is based on the User ID, the Application ID, and the time of authorization, but it will look similar.)

Using the Access Token

Let's try it out. Try loading your own profile through the Graph API, as we did earlier:

```
https://graph.facebook.com/«your_username»
```

If you recall, I got this:

```
{
    "id": "«redacted»",
    "name": "Michael James Williams",
    "first_name": "Michael",
    "middle_name": "James",
    "last_name": "Williams",
    "gender": "male",
    "locale": "en_GB"
}
```

Now try again, but this time add an `access_token` parameter to the URL:

```
https://graph.facebook.com/«your_username»?access_
token=123675230995389%7C2.hX2Png6g2LUuczfd4tLPbQ__.3600.1276960311-
169573433058884%7C8BAAidDtlt8fulZHA3bC3YxcCwM.
```

This time, you'll get more data as shown in the following snippet:

```
{
    "id": "«redacted»",
    "name": "Michael James Williams",
    "first_name": "Michael",
    "middle_name": "James",
    "last_name": "Williams",
    "link": "«redacted»",
```

```
            "about": "Twitter: @MichaelJW",
            "gender": "male",
            "timezone": 1,
            "locale": "en_GB",
            "verified": true,
            "updated_time": "2010-06-16T20:38:01+0000"
    }
```

Okay, it's not a lot, but it proves that we've been successfully authorized, and can see more information than before we had an access token.

Try accessing your list of friends without an access token:

```
https://graph.facebook.com/«your_username»/friends
```

```
    {
        "error": {
            "type": "OAuthAccessTokenException",
            "message": "An access token is required to request this
                resource."
        }
    }
```

Absolutely nothing. Now, with an access token (replace «your_access_token» with the actual access token):

```
https://graph.facebook.com/«your_username»/friends?access_
token=«your_access_token»
```

```
    {
        "data": [
            {
                "name": "JohnFaikname",
                "id": "«redacted»"
            },
            {
                "name": "Sarah Toetalee-Maidup",
                "id": "«redacted»"
            },
            {
                "name": "Bob Frendomyne",
                "id": "«redacted»"
            },
        ]
    }
```

You can then take any of these IDs, use it to construct a Graph URL (like `https://graph.facebook.com/«your_friends_id»?access_token=«your_access_token»`) and see their basic information. However, you can't see much more information about them than you could without an access token – you can't even access their lists of friends:

```
https://graph.facebook.com/«your_friends_id»/friends?access_
token=«your_access_token»
```

```
{
    "error": {
        "type": "Exception",
        "message": "(#604) Can't lookup all friends of
            your_friends_id; can only lookup for the logged in user
            (your_id) or for pairs of users"
    }
}
```

You'll find that the same is true for all other users besides yourself. We will see later how to ask the user to allow the application to access more information.

Still, this is enough information to use in the Graph Visualizer; later in this chapter, we'll make our application map out list information about the current user and that user's friends.

Me, me, me

Since the access token is specific to the user that created, we can use a shortcut to get information about the currently logged-in user – "me".

Browse to:

```
https://graph.facebook.com/me?access_token=«your_access_token»
```

You'll see the same information as if you'd typed your user ID or username instead of me.

In the same way, you can grab a list of the current user's friends by visiting the following URL:

```
https://graph.facebook.com/me/friends?access_token=«your_access_
token»
```

What just happened?

Compare what you just did with the process explained in the *User/Application Authorization* section.

1. You gave Facebook your application's credentials, by passing your Application ID in a Graph URL.

2. You proved to Facebook who you were, as a Facebook user, by logging in to your account directly through a `Facebook.com` login web page.

3. Facebook asked you if you were happy to let the application access your information, and you granted it permission.

4. Facebook passed an access token back to the page that the application specified earlier (in this case, it was the Google home page).

This workflow isn't unique to Facebook. It's actually part of the **OAuth 2.0 protocol**, known as the **User Agent Flow**. This means that once you get the hang of the workflow needed to allow an application to authenticate with Facebook, you'll be able to apply that knowledge to write an application that can authenticate with any other system that uses OAuth 2.0.

 The official documentation for the OAuth 2.0 protocol is here: `http://tools.ietf.org/html/draft-ietf-oauth-v2-05#section-3.5`.

Keeping secrets

It seems odd that we don't need to pass the **Application Secret** in the Graph URL to authenticate. The reasoning is that, if we did pass the secret in that way, then the user or another program running on the user's computer could grab it, and use it to masquerade as our application – and remember, the secret is analogous to a password. So, the user agent flow lets us authenticate the application without using its secret, for unsecure situations such as this.

It's still possible for the user or a desktop application to get hold of the access token and use it to pretend to be the user, logged into our application. But there's no point in the user doing this (as any information he could access using this, he could already access via the Facebook web site anyway), and as for desktop applications, well, that's just part of the everyday risk of running a computer, along with viruses and spyware.

What did Facebook give us?

Check out the URL that Facebook redirected us to after authentication:

```
http://google.com/#access_token=123675230995389%7C2.hX2Png6g2LUuczfd4
tLPbQ__.3600.1276960311-169573433058884%7C8BAAidDtlt8fulZHA3bC3YxcCwM
.&expires_in=6561
```

There are two parameters: `access_token` and `expires_in`.

The second parameter tells us the number of seconds until the access token expires. It seems like a random number, but there is a pattern: if we request a token at 14:32:07, it will expire at 16:00:00; one requested at 9:15:34 will expire at 11:00:00. Add two hours to the token's generation time, knock off the minutes and seconds, and you'll find the expiration time.

At first glance, the access token appears to be a mess of characters. Actually, it contains some useful information.

First, you should know that %7C is code for a "pipe" character, |, which allows it to be passed in a URL. So replace both the %7Cs with pipes:

```
123675230995389|2.hX2Png6g2LUuczfd4tLPbQ__.3600.1276960311-
169573433058884|8BAAidDtlt8fulZHA3bC3YxcCwM.
```

There are three useful pieces of information in here:

1. The Application ID: the number before the first pipe –123675230995389 in this case.

2. The ID of the current user: before the last pipe, after the dash – 169573433058884 in this case.

3. The expiry time: before the user ID – 1276960311 in this case. This is given in Unix time.

The Unix time system describes points in time as the number of seconds since January 1st, 1970, at midnight UTC, ignoring leap seconds. It provides a simple way to encode any point in time (since 1970) as a single integer.

The website UnixTime.info contains a simple converter for switching between Unix timestamps and conventional date formats.

In AS3, the Date class can be used to convert between the two time formats. Pass the Date() constructor a value epochTime*1000 as its first parameter to initiate the Date with that time. The time property of a Date object will return a date in Unix format, albeit multiplied by 1000 as Flash uses milliseconds as its base time unit.

This means that, given any access token, you can find out which user requested it, when it's going to expire, and which application it's for – try browsing to https://graph.facebook.com/your_application_id.

Authenticating with AS3

You understand what we're doing and you've seen it in action. Now it's time to add authentication to our application.

We'll start by creating an access token outside the application and using it inside.

Time for action – Using an access token in our Graph visualizer

Open the AS3 Visualizer project we started working on in the previous chapter. At the moment, it's set to load the URL `https://graph.facebook.com/PacktPub`. Let's make it load a user profile instead.

Modify `CustomGraphContainerController.as` to change which object is requested:

```
package controllers
{
  import graph.apis.http.HTTPRequestor;
  import graph.GraphRequest;
  import ui.GraphControlContainer;

  public class CustomGraphContainerController extends GCController
  {

    public function CustomGraphContainerController
      (a_graphControlContainer:GraphControlContainer)
    {
      super(a_graphControlContainer);
      _requestor = new HTTPRequestor();
      addEventListenersToRequestor();
      _requestor.request(new GraphRequest("your_user_id"));
    }

  }

}
```

Replace `your_user_id` with your own User ID, naturally.

This will give you the same basic info as shown in the next screenshot:

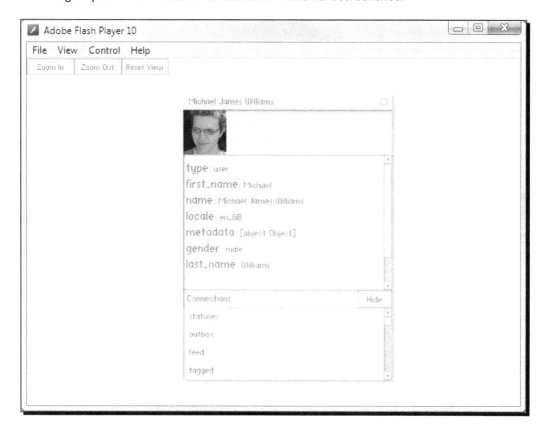

 Wondering where the Visualizer loads the profile picture from? It's not a property of the Graph Object, after all.

Earlier in the chapter, I mentioned that we could access anyone's profile picture as part of their basic information, even without an access token. A 50 x 50 pixel version is always available at `https://graph.facebook.com/«your_user_id»/picture`.

Try clicking on the friends link in the list. You'll get an empty Renderer.

We need to add the access token. The simplest way to do this is to pass it as part of the URLVariables object when the HTTPRequestor loads a Graph URL. So, open HTTPRequestor.as and add the access token as a property of the URLVariables object:

```
public function request(a_request:GraphRequest):void
{
  var loader:URLLoader = new URLLoader();
  var urlRequest:URLRequest = new URLRequest();
```

```
var variables:URLVariables = new URLVariables();

//We construct a URL from the parameters of the GraphRequest
urlRequest.url = "https://graph.facebook.com/" + a_request.objectID;
if (a_request.connectionID)
{
  urlRequest.url += "/" + a_request.connectionID;
}

variables.metadata = 1;
variables.access_token = "123675230995389%7C2.hX2Png6g2LUuczfd4tLP
bQ__.3600.1276960311-169573433058884%7C8BAAidDtlt8fulZHA3bC3YxcCwM."
urlRequest.data = variables;

//this is used to figure out which GraphRequest created the loader
later
  _requests[loader] = a_request;

loader.addEventListener(Event.COMPLETE, onGraphDataLoadComplete);
loader.addEventListener(IOErrorEvent.IO_ERROR, onIOError);
loader.load(urlRequest);
}
```

Test the application; if it doesn't load any Renderers, your access token might have expired. In this case, the Graph API will return this (when loaded in a browser):

```
{
  "error": {
    "type": "OAuthException",
    "message": "Error processing access token."
  }
}
```

and an I/O Error will be passed to your application. We can react to these errors by means of an IOErrorEvent listener, added to the URLRequest object; instructions for this are in the *What Just happened?* section of Chapter 2, *Time for Action: Creating an HTTP Requestor*.

So, if you do get an I/O Error, then generate a new access token in your browser, like we've been doing. Load https://graph.facebook.com/oauth/authorize?client_id=«your_application_id»&redirect_uri=http://google.com&type=user_agent in your browser, extract the access token from the parameters of the URL that gets loaded, and paste it into your code.

This time, when you test the application, you should see the next screenshot:

Great! We can see new fields in the list, like **verified** and **about**.

Try clicking the **friends** connection in the list again:

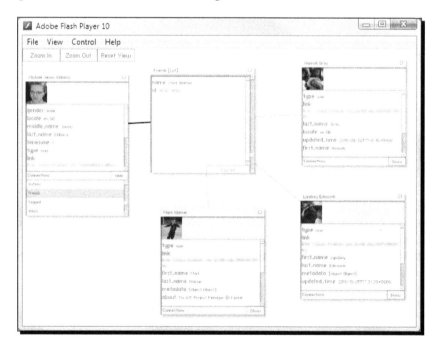

It works just as we'd expect. (Remember, `HTTPRequestor` is passing the access token as a parameter to all Graph URLs requested.)

Take a look at what's loaded when we request the user profile:

```
https://graph.facebook.com/your_user_id?access_token=«your_access_
token»&metadata=1
```

```
{
    "id": "169573433058884",
    "name": "Michael James Williams",
    "first_name": "Michael",
    "middle_name": "James",
    "last_name": "Williams",
    "link": "http://www.facebook.com/«redacted»",
    "about": "Twitter: @MichaelJW",
    "gender": "male",
    "timezone": 1,
    "locale": "en_GB",
    "verified": true,
    "updated_time": "2010-06-16T20:38:01+0000",
    "metadata": {
        "connections": {
            "home": "https://graph.facebook.com/«redacted»/
              home?access_token=«your_access_token»",
            "feed": "https://graph.facebook.com/«redacted»/
              feed?access_token=«your_access_token»",
            "friends": "https://graph.facebook.com/«redacted»/
              friends?access_token=«your_access_token»",
                «...some datacut out here, for length...»
        }
    },
    "type": "user"
}
```

Notice that the Graph URLs in the `connections` list already have the `access_token` parameter filled in. The Visualizer's code doesn't use these Graph URLs – it constructs them using the form `https://graph.facebook.com/«id_of_object»/«name_of_connection»` – but this knowledge may come in useful for your own projects.

As you can see from the Visualizer, the `friends` connection Graph List only includes very basic information: the users' IDs and names. However, much more information is loaded in the full Graph Objects of your friends – though the exact amount depends on your friends' privacy settings.

To see how much information your friends can access about you through applications, log in to the Facebook website, click on **Account | Privacy Settings**, select **Edit your settings for using applications, games and websites**, and view the settings for **Information accessible through your friends**:

Info accessible through your friends

Use the settings below to control which of your information is available to applications, games and websites when your friends use them. The more info you share, the more social the experience.

☐ Bio	☐ My videos
☐ Birthday	☐ My links
☐ Family and relationships	☐ My notes
☐ Interested in and looking for	☐ Photos and videos I'm tagged in
☐ Religious and political views	☐ Hometown
☑ My website	☐ Current location
☑ If I'm online	☐ Education and work
☐ My status updates	☐ Activities, interests, things I like
☐ My photos	☑ Places I check in to

Your name, profile picture, gender, networks and user ID (along with any other information you've set to everyone) is available to friends' applications unless you turn off platform applications and websites.

[Save Changes] [Cancel]

That's cheating!

Okay, fine, generating an access token in the browser and then pasting it directly into the source code is not a great way of handling authentication. We need to obtain an access token in our application itself.

Time for action – authenticating through the application

When authenticating in the browser, we visit `https://graph.facebook.com/oauth/authorize?client_id=«your_application_id»&redirect_uri=http://google.com&type=user_agent`, so let's start by loading that URL in our code.

Start by creating a new function, `attemptToAuthenticate()`, in `HTTPRequestor.as`:

```
public function attemptToAuthenticate():void
{
  var loader:URLLoader = new URLLoader();
  var urlRequest:URLRequest = new URLRequest();
```

```
    var variables:URLVariables = new URLVariables();

    urlRequest.url = "https://graph.facebook.com/oauth/authorize";
    variables.client_id = "«your_application_id»";
    variables.type = "user_agent";
    variables.redirect_uri = "http://google.com";
    urlRequest.data = variables;

    loader.addEventListener(Event.COMPLETE, onAuthenticationComplete);
    loader.addEventListener(IOErrorEvent.IO_ERROR, onIOError);
    loader.load(urlRequest);
}
```

Make sure that you replace «your_application_id» with your actual application ID.

We're using the same IO_ERROR handler function as when we load a Graph object, but we need a new function, onAuthenticationComplete(), for when the loading has finished; add it to HTTPRequestor.as:

```
private function onAuthenticationComplete(a_event:Event):void
{
    trace("Authentication complete");
    var loader:URLLoader = URLLoader(a_event.target);
    trace(loader.data);
}
```

Nothing complicated there; it will trace whatever gets sent back.

In CustomGraphContainerController.as, let's change the constructor function so that it kicks this authentication off instead of loading a user profile:

```
public function CustomGraphContainerController(a_graphControlContainer
:GraphControlContainer)
{
    super(a_graphControlContainer);
    _requestor = new HTTPRequestor();
    addEventListenersToRequestor();
    _requestor.attemptToAuthenticate();
    //_requestor.request(new GraphRequest("«your_user_id»"));
}
```

Before this can work, we need to add the function to the IRequestor interface. Modify \src\graph\apis\base\IRequestor.as to:

```
package graph.apis.base
{
    import flash.events.IEventDispatcher;
```

```
import graph.GraphRequest;

public interface IRequestor extends IEventDispatcher
{
  function request(a_request:GraphRequest):void;
  function attemptToAuthenticate():void;
}

}
```

Test it. What gets traced? A lot of HTML, which (when pasted into a blank .html file and opened in a browser) looks like this:

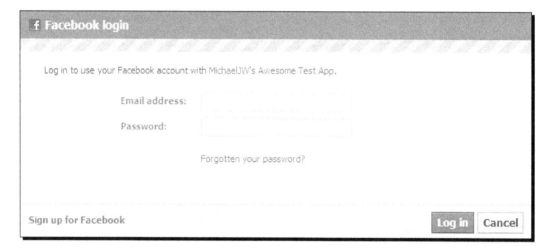

 If you get an error, or no data returned at all, load the URL in your browser to see what error message is returned. Make sure that all the properties of your `URLVariables` object are set correctly.

What just happened?

Oh, right, we need to log in first. But here's a problem: since we're loading the URL inside Flash Player, rather than in a browser, we don't have access to the browser cookies, so Facebook can't remember who we are and directs us to the login page. Of course, since we're not in a browser, we can't actually see the page!

We could write code to create a Flash login form, and post the user's e-mail address and password to the real Facebook login form, but why would the user trust our application not to hijack their data?

A different approach

There are a few ways around this, depending on whether we're using AIR or Flash Player. In this chapter, we'll use the simplest method: embedding the SWF in a web page and using JavaScript to open the login page and pass the access token back to Flash Player.

Time for action – authenticating via JavaScript

Here's what is going to happen:

1. We'll embed our application's SWF in a web page, and load the page in a browser.

2. The application will call a JavaScript function inside the web page, telling it to load the "authorize" URL in a new browser window.

3. The new window may ask us to log in; once we're authenticated, it'll redirect to the Redirect URI page, just as when we used it earlier.

4. This time, however, we'll have changed the Redirect URI page to one that we control (rather than using the Google home page). It will obtain the access token and pass it back to a JavaScript function in the page containing our application's SWF.

5. That JavaScript function will pass the access token to an AS3 function in our application, which will then be able to use it everywhere.

For this to work, the web page that Facebook redirects us to (in *Step 4*, containing the SWF) needs to be online. That means we need to have a web host. See Chapter 1 for details on setting one up.

Publish your project for the web, so that you end up with a web page containing the Visualizer SWF – again, the method for doing this is outlined in Chapter 1 – and upload it to your host. Let's suppose that the web page is called `index.html`, and that you uploaded all the files to `http://host.com/visualizer/`.

Load `http://host.com/visualizer/index.html` in your browser. You'll see, well, nothing much, because the application is still set to try to authenticate rather than loading any data, and it's failing at that. But if you look in the top-left-hand side corner, you should see the familiar UI controls: **Zoom In**, **Zoom Out**, and **Reset View**. (If you see "Movie Not Loaded", check that your HTML page is set to load the correct SWF, and that you uploaded all of the files to the web host, rather than just `index.html`.)

To open a new window containing the Facebook login page, we need to run this JavaScript code from inside `index.html`:

```
window.open('https://graph.facebook.com/oauth/authorize?client_
id=«your_application_id»&redirect_uri=http://google.com&type=user_
agent', '«window_name»', 'height=370,width=670');
```

You can probably guess what the code does, as JavaScript syntax is very similar to ActionScript; it loads a pop-up window, with the height, width, and URL specified. The «window_name» parameter is a value we can use to refer to the window later.

We could put this code inside the HTML of the page. However, rather than risk messing up the SWF embedding code (and to make our SWF a little more flexible), we'll use **ExternalInterface** to inject it into the page from our SWF instead.

 The `flash.external.ExternalInterface` class allows ActionScript code within an SWF to communicate with JavaScript code within an HTML page containing that SWF. This means that the SWF can call JavaScript methods, and vice-versa.

Open `HTTPRequestor.as` and import the `ExternalInterface` class:

```
import flash.external.ExternalInterface;
```

Now, remove all the code we put in `attemptToAuthenticate()` earlier, and replace it with an `ExternalInterface` call:

```
public function attemptToAuthenticate():void
{
  ExternalInterface.call("window.open",

    "https://graph.facebook.com/oauth/authorize?client_id=«your_
      application_id»&type=user_agent&redirect_uri=http://google.com"

    "facebookLoginWindow",

    "height=370, width=600");

}
```

This will call the JavaScript function from above, passing it the three arguments needed. Note that I've given the pop-up window a name of `facebookLoginWindow` in case we need to refer to it in code later.

Compile your SWF (avoid testing it in the standalone Flash Player, as it won't be able to access `ExternalInterface` outside of a browser) and upload it to your web host, overwriting the previous one. Then, refresh `index.html` in your browser.

The pop-up window will probably be blocked. To prevent you from being able to load a million pop-up windows automatically, pop ups opened by a call to `window.open()` are blocked by the browser, unless the call comes from within the handler of a `MOUSE_CLICK` event.

Feel free to add a "log in" button to the application and move the contents of the `attemptToAuthenticate()` function to the buttons click handler function; I'm just going to click on **Allow pop ups** in my browser.

Once the pop up is working, you'll either see the Facebook login page or the Google home page, depending on whether you're currently logged in to Facebook. To make sure you can see the login page, log out of Facebook, or load `index.html` in Private browsing mode. Eventually, you'll see the next screenshot:

Creating a callback web page

Once you log in, you'll be redirected to Google. However, we need the page that the user is redirected to – the **callback** webpage – to be one that we control, so that we can put some JavaScript inside it to grab the access token and pass it back to our application.

Create a new HTML page, `callback.html`, and enter the following code:

```
<html>
<head>
  <script type="text/javascript">
  <!--
    window.opener.setAccessToken(window.location.hash);
  //-->
```

```
    </script>
  </head>
  <body>
  <h2>Close this window</h2>
  <p>The access token has been passed back to index.html.</p>
  </body>
  </html>
```

You may later want this window to close automatically once it's done its job. This is simple to do: just add another line to the JavaScript as shown in the following code:

```
    <script type="text/javascript">
    <!--
      window.opener.setAccessToken(window.location.hash);
      self.close();
    //-->
    </script>
```

I've highlighted the most important line; this finds the window that opened the pop up, and calls a JavaScript function named setAccessToken() inside that window's page, passing it the "**hash**" of the pop up's URL (everything after the # character). Remember, the pop up's URL will be :

http://www.google.com/#access_token=123675230995389%7C2._X2CYJw2h7tOH
9T9i7tkCg__.3600.1277610200-169573433058884%7Cy3fkK9oobNvC6DSSFChUVFe
JrM0., so the hash will contain the access token.

We need to write that setAccessToken() function – but first, let's make this the official callback webpage. Upload callback.html to the same directory as index.html on your web host, then go to the Facebook Developers page and edit your application's settings.

In the **Web Site** tab, enter the base domain name of your host into the **Site URL** box. For instance, if your callback.html page is at http://host.com/visualizer/callback.html, enter http://host.com/.

Now, in HTTPRequestor.as, in your attemptToAuthenticate() function, change the redirect_uri parameter of the URL to point to callback.html:

```
  public function attemptToAuthenticate():void
  {
    ExternalInterface.call("window.open",
      "https://graph.facebook.com/oauth/authorize?
        client_id=165373950152944&type=user_agent&redirect_uri=
        http://host.com/visualizer/callback.html"
      "facebookLoginWindow",
      "height=370, width=600");
  }
```

Recompile your application, and upload it to your web host, overwriting the old version. Refresh `index.html` in your browser. You should see the pop up appear, and (once you've logged in) it will load `callback.html`:

It's telling a lie at the moment, though. The access token hasn't been passed back, because there's no `setAccessToken()` function to pass it back to!

Receiving the access token

Using `ExternalInterface`, we can allow JavaScript inside `index.html` to call an ActionScript function inside our SWF.

1. Let's create an ActionScript function that will take the hash value and extract the access token from it.

2. Add this new function to `HTTPRequestor.as`:

```
private function setAccessToken(a_hashValue:String):void
{
  var hashParams:Array = a_hashValue.substr(1).split("&");
  var hashKeyAndValue:Array;

  for (var i:int = 0; i < hashParams.length; i++)
  {
    hashKeyAndValue = (hashParams[i] as String).split("=");
    if (hashKeyAndValue[0] == "access_token")
    {
      this.accessToken = hashKeyAndValue[1];
      break;
    }
  }
  this.request(new GraphRequest("me"));
}
```

3. First, this function takes the hash value (whose format we already know) from the callback URL and removes the first character (the # symbol).

4. Next, it splits the hash by the ampersands (in case there are any; in the past, Facebook has supplied an `expires_in` parameter as part of the hash) to separate the parameters as `"key=value"` strings.

5. Then, it splits each of those by the equals signs to separate the keys from the values.

6. Once it finds a key called `access_token`, it takes the corresponding value as the token.

Finally, it attempts to load the logged-in user's Profile page. That code refers to `this.accessToken`, but we haven't declared such a variable yet. Let's make it public, so that we can retrieve it from outside the class if we need it elsewhere. Add the following line to `HTTPRequestor.as`:

```
public var accessToken:String = "";
```

If an access token has been set, we'll naturally want to use it for all Graph requests, so modify `HTTPRequestor.request()` as follows:

```
public function request(a_request:GraphRequest):void
{
  var loader:URLLoader = new URLLoader();
  var urlRequest:URLRequest = new URLRequest();
  var variables:URLVariables = new URLVariables();

  //We construct a URL from the parameters of the GraphRequest
  urlRequest.url = "https://graph.facebook.com/" + a_request.objectID;
  if (a_request.connectionID)
  {
    urlRequest.url += "/" + a_request.connectionID;
  }

  variables.metadata = 1;
  if (accessToken != "")
  {
    variables.access_token = accessToken;
  }
  urlRequest.data = variables;

  //this is used to figure out which GraphRequest created the loader
  //later
  _requests[loader] = a_request;

  loader.addEventListener(Event.COMPLETE, onGraphDataLoadComplete);
  loader.addEventListener(IOErrorEvent.IO_ERROR, onIOError);
  loader.load(urlRequest);
}
```

Before we can test this, we need to expose the `setAccessToken()` function to the JavaScript in `index.html`. We can do this with `ExternalInterface`; add a new line to the `HTTPRequestor()` constructor function:

```
public function HTTPRequestor(target:IEventDispatcher = null)
{
  //this is needed because the class extends EventDispatcher
  super(target);
  ExternalInterface.addCallback("setAccessToken", setAccessToken);
}
```

This will allow any JavaScript in `index.html` to call «`visualizer`».`setAccessToken()`, where «`visualizer`» is JavaScript's object name for our SWF (as defined by SWFObject).

However, `callback.html` is going to attempt to call a function named `setAccessToken()` inside `index.html` – not inside the SWF!

That's not a problem, though; we'll just create such a JavaScript function in `index.html` and make it call `setAccessToken()` in our SWF. As before, we'll generate our JavaScript inside our ActionScript, and use `ExternalInterface` to put it in the web page.

This is the JavaScript we need the page to call:

```
window.setAccessToken = function(hashValue){
  var visualizer = document.getElementById('«id_of_embedded_swf»');
  visualizer.setAccessToken(hashValue);
}
```

Pretty simple. It creates a new JavaScript function called `setAccessToken()` inside that window, which finds the SWF inside the page and calls the SWF's `setAccessToken()` function, passing it whatever value the JavaScript function was passed.

You might be wondering what the ID of our embedded SWF is; don't worry, it's quite obvious from the source code of `index.html`. Open that HTML file in a text editor and look for the following lines in the code:

```
var attributes = {
  id:"Visualizer"
};
```

In this case, the SWF's ID is "`Visualizer`". So, replace «`id_of_embedded_swf`» with this value.

Now, add the following code to your `HTTPRequestor()` constructor function:

```
public function HTTPRequestor(target:IEventDispatcher = null)
{
  //this is needed because the class extends EventDispatcher
  super(target);
  ExternalInterface.addCallback("setAccessToken", setAccessToken);

  ExternalInterface.call("function() {"
    + "window.setAccessToken = function(hashValue){"
    +   "var visualizer = document.getElementById('Visualizer');"
    +   "visualizer.setAccessToken(hashValue);"
    + "}"
    + "}");
}
```

The highlighted code creates and calls an anonymous function which contains the actual function we want to call. It's a bit messy, but it works.

Recompile your SWF and upload it to your host. Refresh `index.html`. The pop up will appear, may prompt you to log in, and will redirect to the **Close this window** page. Shortly after that we will see the following screenshot:

Success!

What just happened?

You just added true Facebook authentication to your Flash application.

The user logs in on Facebook itself, rather than through your application, minimizing the security risk. Facebook passes the access token back to a callback page that you wrote, which in turn passes it back through another web page to your SWF, which is now able to use it when requesting Graph API data.

What about users who haven't used the application before?

We haven't fully tested the authentication yet, since we had already granted the application permission to access our data earlier on, when we were experimenting with the browser.

Fortunately it's very easy to undo all that and pretend we've never seen the application before. Log in to Facebook and click on **Account | Application Settings**. Find your application in the list, and click on the **X** button as shown in the next screenshot:

Facebook will ask you to confirm this decision. (The application will remain on your Developers Page, even though it will be removed from your Applications Page.)

Refresh `index.html`. This time, the pop up will ask for permission to access your information:

Click on **Allow**, and the pop up is redirected to `callback.html`, which passes the access token to the visualizer, just as before.

Have a go hero – dealing with the undecided

What if your user clicks on the **Don't allow** dialog box?

At the moment, the application doesn't do anything without an access token; it just sits patiently and waits. If, when the pop up window appears, the user doesn't click on **Allow** – or if the user doesn't see the pop up , perhaps because it's blocked – the application won't fail gracefully. It will just sit there and wait.

Add some features to your application to make it deal with this kind of situation. Maybe it could pop up a message after a few seconds, saying "You need to log in to Facebook and approve this application in order to use it." Or perhaps you could load a different Graph object to start with, and only request a login when the user tries to access something they need an access token for.

Now that your application's online, you can let other people see it by directing them to `index.html`. Get some friends to test it out.

Extended permissions

We don't have access to everything yet, though. In your browser, try loading
`https://graph.facebook.com/me/inbox` (with an access token passed as a
parameter). You'll get the following message:

```
{
    "error": {
        "type": "Exception",
        "message": "(#612) mailbox requires the read_mailbox extended
            permission."
    }
}
```

Much like how you, as a user, can restrict other users from seeing certain parts of your
Facebook profile, you can also restrict certain apps from accessing certain information via
the Graph API.

In this case, we're trying to access my inbox, as an application, and are being told we don't
have permission. But how do we get permission?

Time for action – obtaining extended permissions

It's actually really easy to request permission to do something beyond the basic: when calling
the `authorize` URL, pass it an extra parameter named `scope`.

Set the value of the `scope` parameter to the name of the extended permission you want to
request. For example, to request access to the user's inbox, use this URL:

```
https://graph.facebook.com/oauth/authorize?client_id=«your_
application_id»&type=user_agent&redirect_uri=«your_callback_
url»&scope=read_mailbox
```

Try this in the browser, and you'll get this dialog:

What just happened?

Once the user clicks on **Allow**, Facebook will remember that decision, and your application won't have to ask for this permission again – just like when the user authorized the application to see their basic information for the first time.

You can request more than one extended permission at a time; just separate them with commas:

```
https://graph.facebook.com/oauth/authorize?client_id=«your_
application_id»&type=user_agent&redirect_uri=«your_callback_
url»&scope=read_mailbox,user_photos,user_interests
```

Extended permissions aren't just about you, though. Allowing the `user_interests` extended permission will allow the application to access the user's list of interests (which are, of course, represented as a list of Graph objects) – but there's also a `friends_interests` extended permission, which allows the application to access the lists of interests of all the user's friends.

Actually, most of the extended permissions have a user-only version and a friends version; check out the official documentation for a list of all of them: `http://developers.facebook.com/docs/authentication/permissions`.

Time for action – requesting extended permissions

To make your application always request the `user_interests` extended permission, we merely have to modify `HTTPRequestor.attemptToAuthenticate()` to:

`public function attemptToAuthenticate():void` as shown in the following code:

```
{
  ExternalInterface.call("window.open",
    "https://graph.facebook.com/oauth/authorize?
      client_id=«your_application_id»&type=user_agent&
      redirect_uri=«your_callback_url»"
    + "&scope=user_interests",
    "facebookLoginWindow",
    "height=370, width=600");
}
```

That'll work fine; it'll give you the pop-up window asking you if it's okay for the application to access your profile information.

If that's all you need – and all you'll ever need – then you could leave it at that. But what if you want to make this a little more flexible?

First, let's allow the `attemptToAuthenticate()` function to take an arbitrary number of extended permissions as arguments, and append them to the `scope` parameter as a comma-separated list:

```
public function attemptToAuthenticate(...permissions):void
{
  var scope:String = "";
  if (permissions.length > 0)
  {
    scope = "&scope=" + permissions.join(",");
  }
  ExternalInterface.call("window.open",
    "https://graph.facebook.com/oauth/authorize?client_
id=165373950152944&type=user_agent&redirect_uri=http://gamedev.
michaeljameswilliams.com/scrap/visualizer/callback.html"
    + scope,
    "facebookLoginWindow",
    "height=370, width=600");
}
```

Using `permissions` as the sole argument for the function means that we can pass it as many arguments as we like, and they'll form an array called `permissions`. (This is called the **... (rest) parameter**, in case you want to look it up.)

We can then use the `Array.join()` method to combine all the strings in this array into a single string, in the form of a comma-separated list.

We have to change the signature of the method in `IRequestor.as` to match the changes we've made to the function:

```
package graph.apis.base
{
  import flash.events.IEventDispatcher;
  import graph.GraphRequest;

  public interface IRequestor extends IEventDispatcher
  {
    function request(a_request:GraphRequest):void;
    function attemptToAuthenticate(...permissions):void;
  }

}
```

Now we just need to pass the extended permissions that we desire to this method. In `CustomGraphContainerController.as,` modify the constructor function:

```
public function CustomGraphContainerController(a_graphControlContainer
:GraphControlContainer)
{
  super(a_graphControlContainer);
  _requestor = new HTTPRequestor();
  addEventListenersToRequestor();
  _requestor.attemptToAuthenticate("friends_interests",
    "read_mailbox");
}
```

Compile the SWF and upload it to your host. When you test it in your browser, it will ask you to grant both permissions:

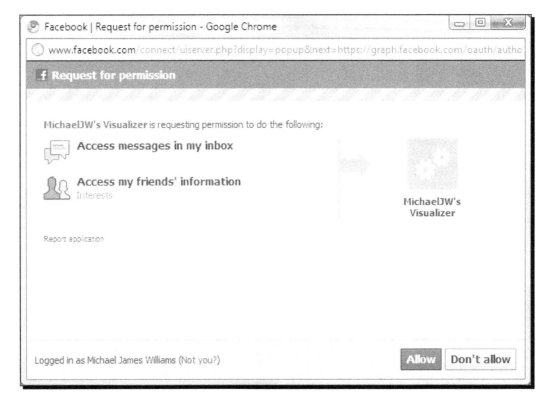

The Visualizer project includes a class, `ExtendedPermissions.as,` designed to make this a little easier. It contains a `public static const` for every one of the extended permissions, each with a short description of what it does in a comment.

This means that, if you're using a code editor that supports auto completion, you can speed up your code to request extended permissions. First, import the class in `CustomGraphContainerController.as`:

```
import graph.apis.base.ExtendedPermissions;
```

Then, type `ExtendedPermissions`, followed by a dot, and the list will appear:

```
    super(a_graphControlContainer);
    _requestor = new HTTPRequestor();
    addEventListenersToRequestor();
    _requestor.attemptToAuthenticate(ExtendedPermissions.READ_);
```

public static const READ_STREAM : String = "read_stream" ... Provides read access to all the posts in the user's News Feed. Also allows application to perform searches against the user's News Feed.	▣ READ_FRIENDLISTS ▣ READ_INSIGHTS ▣ READ_MAILBOX ▣ READ_REQUESTS ▣ READ_STREAM

You could then rewrite the previous code as:

```
public function CustomGraphContainerController(a_graphControlContainer
:GraphControlContainer)
{
  super(a_graphControlContainer);
  _requestor = new HTTPRequestor();
  addEventListenersToRequestor();
  _requestor.attemptToAuthenticate
    (ExtendedPermissions.FRIENDS_INTERESTS,
      ExtendedPermissions.READ_MAILBOX);
}
```

Have a go hero – using a permanent access token

One particularly useful extended permission to ask for is `offline_access`. If the user grants this to your application, then their access token will never expire – meaning they don't have to go through the whole routine of logging in to Facebook every time they use your application.

Make your application request this permission, and then save the access token so that it can be retrieved later on, even after the user has closed and re-opened your application. A `SharedObject` is ideal for this – see the Adobe documentation on `flash.net.SharedObject`.

I want it all, and I want it now

It's tempting to copy and paste a comma-separated list of all the possible extended permissions into the scope parameter, and ask for all of them the very first time the user tries your application. After all, then you know there's no limit to what your application can do, right?

Trouble is, the user knows this as well. Asking them to allow your application to access their inbox, friend lists, wall posts, photos, and everything else they've ever put on Facebook, as soon as they "meet" your application, will scare off all but the most security-lax users.

Make sure the user can do plenty with the application without signing over their entire digital life. Your application can ask for extra permissions at any time, even if the user has already authenticated and granted some other permissions; you don't have to decide which ones it's going to need in advance and ask for them all at once. Let them use it first, and build up a sense of trust (or at least a sense of wanting to use the features that require extended permissions).

Have a go hero – dealing with extended permissions

Following on from the last Have A Go Hero, make sure your application can deal with not having the required permissions gracefully. If the user tries to access a connection that they won't allow the associated extended permission for, let them know what the problem is.

If you're up for a challenge, try reading the error message to see which extended permission is required, and then request it automatically!

 Unfortunately it's not possible to use the Graph API to request a list of the extended permissions currently granted to the user, but in Chapter 7 we will look at how to do this via another means.

Using the Adobe ActionScript 3 SDK for Facebook platform

So far, we've been creating our own methods for accessing the graph. Now let's take a look at how to use Adobe's official AS3 Facebook SDK.

Time for action –implementing the SDK

The SDK source files have already been downloaded and copied into the Visualizer project directory; find them in `\src\com\facebook\`. (For information on downloading the latest version of the SDK and including it in your own project, refer to Chapter 1.)

We're going to build another Requestor, but this time it'll be powered by the SDK, rather than by our own `URLRequest`. Start by creating a new folder in `\src\apis\` called `\sdk\`. Then, create a new file inside this folder called `SDKRequestor.as`. Make it extend `EventDispatcher` and implement `IRequestor`, just like `HTTPRequestor`.

Here's the basic code for that class:

```
package graph.apis.sdk
{
  import flash.events.EventDispatcher;
  import flash.events.IEventDispatcher;
  import graph.apis.base.IRequestor;
  import graph.GraphRequest;

  public class SDKRequestor extends EventDispatcher
    implements IRequestor
  {

    public function SDKRequestor(target:IEventDispatcher = null)
    {
      super(target);

    }

    public function request(a_request:GraphRequest):void
    {

    }

    public function attemptToAuthenticate(...permissions):void
    {

    }

  }

}
```

Next, import the `Facebook` class. This is the API for web-based applications:

```
import com.facebook.graph.Facebook;
```

We need to initialize this class before we can do anything with it. To do so, we must pass it our application's ID and a callback function. Do this in the `SDKRequestor()` constructor:

```
public function SDKRequestor(target:IEventDispatcher = null)
{
  super(target);

  Facebook.init("«your_application_id»", initComplete);
}
```

Next we must create this `initComplete()` function, which will be called once the initialization process finishes. Add this to `SDKRequestor.as` as shown in the following code:

```
private function initComplete(success:Object, fail:Object):void
{

}
```

The function needs those two parameters – `success` and `fail` – or the code won't compile. If there were no problems with the initialization, then `success` will be an object of type `com.Facebook.graph.data.FacebookSession`; otherwise, `success` will be `null`, and `fail` will contain details. Let's deal with this using the following code:

```
private function initComplete(success:Object, fail:Object):void
{
  if (success is FacebookSession)
  {
    //was a success.
  }
  else
  {
    //was a failure. See contents of 'fail' object.
  }
}
```

You must import the `FacebookSession` too as shown in the following code:

```
import com.facebook.graph.data.FacebookSession;
```

Let's make it dispatch a COMPLETE event when it's ready, so that we know it's safe to call other methods:

```
private function initComplete(success:Object, fail:Object):void
{
  if (success is FacebookSession)
  {
    dispatchEvent(new Event(Event.COMPLETE))
  }
  else
  {
    //was a failure. See contents of 'fail' object.
  }
}
```

You must import flash.events.Event for this to work.

Once the API is initialized, we can authenticate the user using the Facebook.login() method. The call to this should go in attemptToAuthenticate():

```
public function attemptToAuthenticate(...permissions):void
{
  Facebook.login(loginComplete);

}
```

This will cause a pop-up window to appear, asking the user to log in and allow our application to access the user's profile. If no pop-up appears, check that cookies are enabled; it won't work otherwise.

The loginComplete parameter passed to Facebook.login() is another callback function, of the same form as initComplete(), which is called once the user has authenticated. Add this to SDKRequestor.as:

```
private function loginComplete(success:Object, fail:Object):void
{
  if (success is FacebookSession)
  {
    //was a success.
  }
  else
  {
    //was a failure. See contents of 'fail' object.
  }
}
```

Assuming all went well, the `success` object will contain several properties, including the access token (`accessToken`) and the user's ID (`uid`).

When our `HTTPRequestor` successfully authenticates, it requests the user's profile as a Graph Object by means of a `GraphRequest`. Let's do the same here:

```
private function loginComplete(success:Object, fail:Object):void
{
  if (success is FacebookSession)
  {
    this.request(new GraphRequest("me"));
  }
  else
  {
    //was a failure. See contents of 'fail' object.
  }
}
```

Ah, but the `request()` function is empty at the moment. How can we use the SDK to request something from the Graph?

We use the `Facebook.api()` method. This has two mandatory arguments:

◆ A string containing the name of the Graph Object or connection to request.

◆ A callback function (you guessed it!).

The format of the string is "`/object`" or "`/object/connection`" – it's the part that is tacked on to the end of `https://graph.facebook.com/` in any Graph URL, minus any URL parameters. This makes it easy to fill in the `request()` function:

```
public function request(a_request:GraphRequest):void
{
  var graphItem:String = "/" + a_request.objectID;
  if (a_request.connectionID)
  {
    graphItem+= "/" + a_request.connectionID;
  }
  Facebook.api(graphItem, requestComplete);
}
```

We've almost finished building our basic `SDKRequestor`; we just need to create a `requestComplete()` function that converts whatever it receives into a `GraphObject`.

The required form of the `requestComplete()` callback is almost the same as the others, as shown in the next lines of code:

```
private function requestComplete(result:Object, fail:Object):void
{
  if (result != null)
  {
    //was a success.
  }
  else
  {
    //was a failure. See contents of 'fail' object.
  }
}
```

Add that to `SDKRequestor.as`. Notice that this time, instead of a `success` parameter we have a `result` parameter (not that this really matters, but it's a more accurate name), and it is just an `Object`, rather than an instance of `FacebookSession`.

In fact, `result` is in exactly the same form as the `decodedJSON` object that we created ourselves in `HTTPRequestor.onGraphDataLoadComplete()`. This means we can copy and paste the code we wrote earlier to deal with it – so do so:

```
private function requestComplete(result:Object, fail:Object):void
{
  if (result != null)
  {
    var decodedJSON:Object = result;
    if (decodedJSON.data)
    {
      var graphList:GraphList = new GraphList();
      var childGraphObject:GraphObject;
      for each (var childObject:Object in decodedJSON.data)
      {
        childGraphObject = new GraphObject();
        for (var childKey:String in childObject)
        {
          childGraphObject[childKey] = childObject[childKey];
        }
        graphList.addToList(childGraphObject);
      }
      graphList.paging = decodedJSON.paging;

      graphList.ownerID = originalRequest.objectID;
```

```
      graphList.connectionType = originalRequest.connectionID;

      dispatchEvent(new RequestEvent(RequestEvent.REQUEST_COMPLETED,
        graphList));
    }
    else
    {
      var graphObject:GraphObject = new GraphObject();
      for (var key:String in decodedJSON)
      {
        graphObject[key] = decodedJSON[key];
      }

      dispatchEvent(new RequestEvent(RequestEvent.REQUEST_COMPLETED,
        graphObject));
    }
  }
  else
  {
    //was a failure. See contents of 'fail' object.
  }
}
```

You'll also need the following imports:

```
import graph.GraphList;
import graph.GraphObject;
import events.RequestEvent;
```

There's a big problem here, though. We refer to `originalRequest` in the code, but we have no way of obtaining the original `GraphRequest` instance!

The solution is to use a coding trick called **currying**. This allows us to pass extra values to the callback function at the time that we make the request.

 Don't worry if you don't understand how currying works. I'm not going to explain it here, as it's fairly advanced and not really relevant to Facebook – the code that uses it is specific to the Visualizer. For an excellent explanation of currying, see the article by Jackson Dunstan at: `http://jacksondunstan.com/articles/338.`

Change the `request()` function to:

```
public function request(a_request:GraphRequest):void
{
  var graphItem:String = "/" + a_request.objectID;
  if (a_request.connectionID)
  {
    graphItem += "/" + a_request.connectionID;
  }
  Facebook.api(graphItem, function(result:Object, fail:Object):void {
    requestComplete.call(this, result, fail, a_request); } );
}
```

Now, modify the signature of `requestComplete()` to accept an extra parameter:

```
private function requestComplete(result:Object, fail:Object, originalR
equest:GraphRequest):void
```

`SDKRequestor` is now ready for testing. Switch to `CustomGraphContainerController.
as`, and change it to:

```
package controllers
{
  import flash.events.Event;
  import graph.apis.base.ExtendedPermissions;
  import graph.apis.http.HTTPRequestor;
  import graph.apis.sdk.SDKRequestor;
  import graph.GraphRequest;
  import ui.GraphControlContainer;

  public class CustomGraphContainerController extends GCController
  {
    public function CustomGraphContainerController
      (a_graphControlContainer:GraphControlContainer)
    {
      super(a_graphControlContainer);
      _requestor = new SDKRequestor();
      addEventListenersToRequestor();
      //we must wait for the SDK to initialize before we can do
      //anything else with it
      _requestor.addEventListener(Event.COMPLETE, onSDKInitialize);
    }

    private function onSDKInitialize(a_event:Event):void
    {
      _requestor.attemptToAuthenticate();
    }
  }
}
```

All we have to do now is create an HTML page to contain the SWF. We cannot use the standard `index.html` page we have been using so far, as the SDK requires certain JavaScript functions in order to work.

Adobe has provided some **wrapper** HTML pages to use as containers for our SWFs. One of the pages, `sdkindex.html`, is in the `\bin\adobesdk\` folder, alongside a JavaScript file called `FBJSBridge.js`. Copy both `sdkindex.html` and `FBJSBridge.js` into your `\bin\` directory.

Open `sdkindex.html` in a text editor, and find the following line:

```
embedSWF("Visualizer.swf", "flashContent", "600", "300", "10.0");
```

Replace `Visualizer.swf` with the name of your SWF.

Finally, upload `sdkindex.html`, `FBJSBridge.js` and your SWF to your web host to the same directory as usual, and load `http://host.com/sdkindex.html` in your web browser.

What just happened?

You just added the official Adobe ActionScript 3 SDK for Facebook Platform to your application as an alternative to the classes that we built earlier in the chapter.

The SDK works in a very similar way to our classes, albeit with a lot more polish; it also uses `URLRequest` objects to retrieve data, and decodes the resulting JSON to a native AS3 object.

In order for the SDK to work, it imports two JS files containing JavaScript functions, which actually power the Facebook login and integration. Those two files are called: `FBJSBridge.js`, which is included in the project; and `all.js`, which is loaded from the Facebook server. As long as your webpage uses SWFObject and imports those JavaScript files, you should be able to use the SDK.

Have a go hero – requesting extended permissions with the SDK

The `Facebook.login()` method takes a second parameter: `options`, a native AS3 `Object`. This is used to request extended permissions; simply provide an object with a string property called `perms`, which is a comma-separated list of the permissions.

Use this to modify your `SDKRequestor.attemptToAuthenticate()` method so that it can take an arbitrary number of extended permissions as parameters and request them using the `Facebook.login()` method.

Pop Quiz

1. What does "me" do?

    a. Returns the authenticated user's ID

    b. Stands in as the authenticated user's ID when used in a Graph URL.

    c. It represents the ID of a Facebook user called Mike Eddington

2. Why didn't we obtain an access token using AS3 alone?

    a. `URLRequest` objects can't load the Facebook login page

    b. It's only possible to obtain a token using JavaScript

    c. We wanted to present the user with a genuine Facebook login page, for trust reasons

3. Why shouldn't you ask for all the extended permissions your application might possibly need at once?

    a. It's likely to scare users away

    b. Only five permissions can be granted at any one time

    c. This is a violation of the Facebook terms of service

Summary

In this chapter, the key words were security, permissions, and authentication. We learned about:

- How Facebook restricts us from accessing information we're not supposed to
- How users determine which information other users (and apps) can see
- How apps can request permission to see more information from users
- How users and apps work together to authenticate with Facebook

Key takeaways

- The Graph API will only give certain details about a person if you try to access a Graph Object without proof of authentication.
- An access token is proof of authorization, and is associated with both a user and an application.
- Users have two credentials: e-mail address and password.
- Applications have three credentials: application ID (which is like a username), application secret (which is like a password, and can be changed), and API key (which is used to access the Graph API).

- ❏ The application credentials are passed to Facebook through a Graph URL, while the user submits their credentials through a standard Facebook login web page. Facebook does not return the access token in a JSON, but through a parameter to the application's callback URL.

- ❏ The Graph URL used to authorize is `https://graph.facebook.com/oauth/authorize?client_id=«your_application_id»&redirect_uri=«site_url»&type=user_agent`. This redirects to `«callback_url»/#access_token=«access_token»`, so the callback page can use JavaScript to extract the access token, and `ExternalInterface` to pass it to the SWF.

- ❏ Access tokens are passed as parameters in Graph URLs like so: `https://graph.facebook.com/«graph_object»?access_token=«access_token»`.

- ❏ A 50 x 50 px version of a user's profile picture is always available at `https://graph.facebook.com/«user_id»/picture`.

- ❏ To access certain Graph Objects and Graph Lists, extended permissions are required. A list of all extended permissions is available here: `http://developers.facebook.com/docs/authentication/permissions`.

- ❏ To ask the user to grant the application a set of extended permissions, add them as a comma-separated list in a parameter called `scope`, passed to the Graph URL used to authorize, as shown in the following code: `https://graph.facebook.com/oauth/authorize?client_id=«your_application_id»&redirect_uri=«site_url»&type=user_agent&scope=user_interest, friends_interest,offline_access`.

Digging Deeper into the Graph

We've seen how to access both public and private Facebook data from the surface of the Graph. As long as we only need the most recent items in a list, we're fine. But what if that's not the case?

In this chapter we shall learn how to:

- Read more than just the most recent 25 posts on a page
- Filter posts by date
- Grab several different Objects at once

And we'll do all of this using the same form of URL-based queries we've been using so far.

Right, let's get on with it.

Getting more results with paging

As we discovered in *Chapter 2*, there are two types of results we can get back from a Graph URL: Graph Objects and Graph Lists. (Well, and errors, too.)

How many Graph Objects are in a Graph List, though? Let's find out.

Time for action – displaying the number of objects in a list

Open your `Visualizer` project. We're going to turn on a hidden option that makes the title of List Renderer windows contain the number of items in the Graph List.

1. First, though, let's switch back from our `SDKRequestor` to our `HTTPRequestor`.

Open `CustomGraphControllerContainer.as` and change the line that creates the new Requestor:

```
public function CustomGraphContainerController(a_graphControlConta
iner:GraphControlContainer)
{
  super(a_graphControlContainer);
  _requestor = new HTTPRequestor();
  addEventListenersToRequestor();
  //we must wait for the Requestor to initialise before we can do
anything else with it
  _requestor.addEventListener(Event.COMPLETE,
onRequestorInitialize);
}
```

We will come back to the SDK Requestor later in the chapter.

2. There's a slight problem: this class is waiting for the Requestor to dispatch a `COMPLETE` event, stating that it has finished initializing, but our `HTTPRequestor` does not do this. We could remove the event listener, but it'll be easier to modify the Requestor; open `HTTPRequestor.as`, and add a new function:

```
public function initialize():void
{
  dispatchEvent(new Event(Event.COMPLETE));
}
```

3. Modify `SDKRequestor.as`, too, moving the call to `Facebook.init()` from the constructor function to a new function, `initialize()`:

```
public function SDKRequestor(target:IEventDispatcher = null)
{
  super(target);

  //Facebook.init("165573950152944", initComplete);
}

public function initialize():void
{
  Facebook.init("165573950152944", initComplete);
}
```

4. Add the `initialize()` function to the `IRequestor.as` interface:

```
package graph.apis.base
{
  import flash.events.IEventDispatcher;
  import graph.GraphRequest;

  public interface IRequestor extends IEventDispatcher
  {
    function request(a_request:GraphRequest):void;
    function attemptToAuthenticate(...permissions):void;
    function initialize():void;
  }

}
```

5. Finally, add a call to this new `initialize()` function to
`CustomGraphContainerController.as`, in the constructor:

```
public function CustomGraphContainerController(a_graphControlConta
iner:GraphControlContainer)
{
  super(a_graphControlContainer);
  _requestor = new HTTPRequestor();
  addEventListenersToRequestor();
  //we must wait for the Requestor to initialise before we can do
anything else with it
  _requestor.addEventListener(Event.COMPLETE,
onRequestorInitialize);
  _requestor.initialize();
}
```

6. Compile and test your SWF. Remember that you can load `index.html` rather than `sdkindex.html`, since we've changed which Requestor we're using.

Open any connection and notice that the Graph List Renderer's caption displays the type of the connection and the word **[List]**. We'll now make it display the number of Graph Objects in that list.

7. Still in `CustomGraphContainerController.as`, at the start of the `constructor`, set the inherited `_showListCounts` Boolean property to `true`:

```
public function CustomGraphContainerController
  (a_graphControlContainer:GraphControlContainer)
{
  super(a_graphControlContainer);
  this._showListCounts = true;

  _requestor = new HTTPRequestor();
  addEventListenersToRequestor();
  //we must wait for the Requestor to initialise before we can do
  //anything else with it
  _requestor.addEventListener(Event.COMPLETE,
    onRequestorInitialize);

  _requestor.initialize();
}
```

This changes a setting elsewhere in the project which in turn tells new Graph List Renderers to display their total count of Graph Objects in the caption of the Renderer's window. You've no need to understand how this works; it suffices to say that it uses the `length` property of the `list`array inside the appropriate `GraphList`instance.

8. Recompile the SWF and load the same connection:

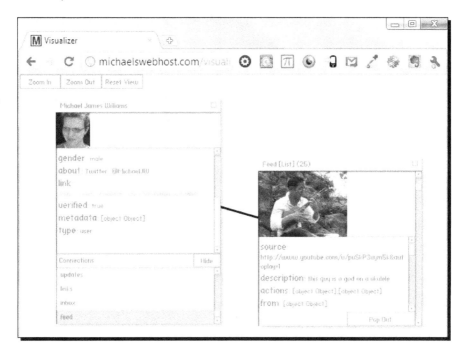

What just happened?

We can now see how many Objects are in the Graph List returned by my profile's feed connection: 25. But naturally, I've written more than 25 status updates since joining Facebook. What's going on? A little more exploration shows that 25 seems to be the default maximum number of items you'll get back when requesting a List. Sometimes you'll get less than this (even if there are more than 25 objects in the album or feed).

That might be okay for a news feed, where only the most recent entries are relevant, but it's useless for an album; naturally, you'd like to see all the photos.

How can we get Facebook to give us more Objects?

Time for action – requesting more Objects

1. We can ask for a larger number of Objects to be returned in the List by using – you guessed it – a URL parameter. To ask for 50 items to be returned instead of 25, we just add this to the URL:

```
limit=50
```

2. Let's add this as a default. Modify the `request()` function in `HTTPRequestor.as` to add this extra parameter, like so:

```
public function request(a_request:GraphRequest):void
{
  var loader:URLLoader = new URLLoader();
  var urlRequest:URLRequest = new URLRequest();
  var variables:URLVariables = new URLVariables();

  //We construct a URL from the parameters of the GraphRequest
  urlRequest.url = "https://graph.facebook.com/" +
    a_request.objectID;
  if (a_request.connectionID)
  {
    //remember, this means a connection (and thus a list)
    //was requested
    urlRequest.url += "/" + a_request.connectionID;
    variables.limit = 50;
  }

  variables.metadata = 1;
  if (accessToken != "")
  {
    variables.access_token = accessToken;
  }
  urlRequest.data = variables;

  //this is used to figure out which GraphRequest created the
  //loader later
  _requests[loader] = a_request;

  loader.addEventListener(Event.COMPLETE,
    onGraphDataLoadComplete);
  loader.addEventListener(IOErrorEvent.IO_ERROR, onIOError);
  loader.load(urlRequest);
}
```

3. Try loading the connection again:

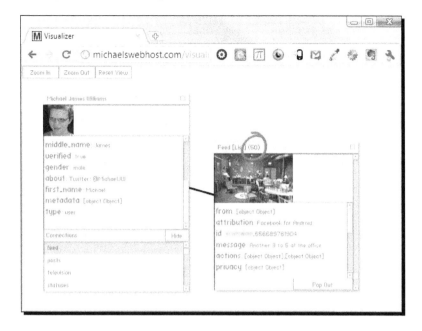

Great! It' s got the most recent **50** posts. What happens if the connection has less than 50 items? To find out, try loading Packt Publishing' s photo album called "Books", which (at time of writing) contains 32 photos:

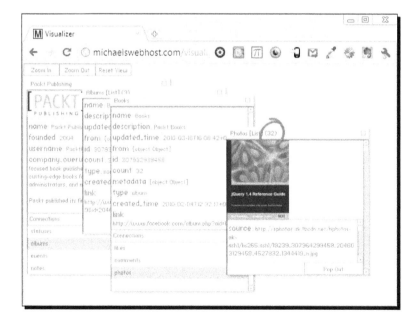

What just happened?

Here we can see that requesting more Graph Objects than there are in the connection still results in a valid Graph List; Facebook doesn't reject our request on the basis that we've asked for too many.

Still, some connections contain far more than 50 Objects – like the number of posts in my `feed`, for example. How can we deal with this?

Time for action – requesting more Objects at once

1. Let's increase the limit to 5000, just to be safe. Edit `HTTPRequestor.as`:

```
public function request(a_request:GraphRequest):void
{
  var loader:URLLoader = new URLLoader();
  var urlRequest:URLRequest = new URLRequest();
  var variables:URLVariables = new URLVariables();

  //We construct a URL from the parameters of the GraphRequest
  urlRequest.url = "https://graph.facebook.com/" +
    a_request.objectID;
  if (a_request.connectionID)
  {
    //remember, this means a connection (and thus a list)
    //was requested
    urlRequest.url += "/" + a_request.connectionID;
    variables.limit = 5000;
  }
  variables.metadata = 1;
  if (accessToken != "")
  {
    variables.access_token = accessToken;
  }
  urlRequest.data = variables;

  //this is used to figure out which GraphRequest created the
  //loader later
  _requests[loader] = a_request;

  loader.addEventListener(Event.COMPLETE,
    onGraphDataLoadComplete);
  loader.addEventListener(IOErrorEvent.IO_ERROR, onIOError);
  loader.load(urlRequest);
}
```

2. Recompile the project, re-upload the SWF to your host, and try loading your `feed`. (If you don' t have a huge feed, try loading the official Facebook Page' s feed instead; the ID of that Page is `facebook`.)

What just happened?

One of four things just happened:

1. Your SWF became very slow and eventually crashed
2. No data came through to the SWF
3. The SWF rendered a new List, but it didn't' t contain 5,000 Objects
4. The SWF rendered a new List of 5,000 Objects

It' s hard to predict which result you'll see. Previously, the Graph API couldn't handle a request for even 500 Objects at once – it would time out and return a completely blank page (not even an empty JSON or error message).

More recently the situation has improved massively; it seems that Facebook returns as many Objects as it can in one shot, up to and including the number that you specified as the `limit`. If there are any problems, they' re more likely to be caused by your code taking too long to process the data than by Facebook timing out.

This means that, in a lot of practical cases, you can request a large number of Objects in a List and get everything you need. But this is sloppy. Let's look at an alternative.

Paging

Instead of requesting, say, 250 Objects all at once, we can have the List split into several **pages**, with each Page containing a smaller number of Objects.

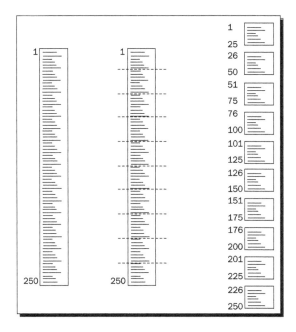

The previous diagram shows an example. The actual Graph List contains 250 pieces of information – they could be wall posts, photos, whatever. We tell the Graph to split the List into pages with 25 pieces of information each, leaving us with 10 Pages.

That's essentially what the `limit=X` parameter does; it tells the Graph to split the List into pages with (at most) X pieces of info, and return the first page to us.

 Note: be careful not to confuse a Facebook Page Object with a single "page" of data, or a web page. It's unfortunate that the three separate concepts share a name!

To get additional information, then, we just have to specify that we want a particular page. We use the `offset` parameter to do this:

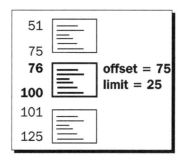

There are two things to note here:

1. We don't say, "give me the Nth page," we say, "give me the page starting with item number N."

2. Just like in an AS3 array, this is zero-based – that is, the first piece of information is numbered 0, the second is numbered 1, the 76th is numbered 75, and so on.

Time for action – obtaining data in pages

Using `limit` and `offset` together, we should be able to obtain specific pages of posts from the Facebook Page' s feed. So, if we load this URL in a browser:

```
https://graph.facebook.com/facebook/feed?offset=300&limit=25
```

We should be able to see the 301st – 325th posts in the feed. Try it out. The result at the time of writing is as follows:

```
{
    "data": [

    ]
}
```

Wait, what?

What just happened?

The Graph API puts limitations on what can be retrieved from a User's or Page's stream and status updates (which includes their `feed` connection). The official documentation says that these connections are limited to the last 30 days or 50 posts, whichever is greater.

That' s not the only problem with the `limit-offset` parameters. Try loading this URL:

`https://graph.facebook.com/facebook/feed?offset=2&limit=1`

...and you'll get the same empty JSON as before – but load this URL:

`https://graph.facebook.com/facebook/feed?offset=2&limit=4`

...and you'll receive exactly one result. However, you can set the `limit` as high as 6 without receiving any additional Objects!

It doesn't make any sense. And the more you look into this, the less logical it appears to be.

This is an ongoing issue; if you would like to keep up-to-date with any changes made in this area, subscribe to the official Facebook Bug Tracker thread for it at this link:

`http://bugs.developers.facebook.net/show_bug.cgi?id=10576`

 Of course, it's possible that by the time you read this book, these issues will have been sorted out. In that case, lucky you!

Still, we can see how `limit` and `offset` work for other connections.

Have a go hero – using limit and offset for other connections

Try loading some of your User profile's connections using `limit` and `offset`. You'll have to use an access token, naturally.

For example:

```
https://graph.facebook.com/me/likes?limit=25&offset=50&access_
token=«access_token»
```

Does it work? Can you access other people's connections in the same way? What about those of other Graph Objects, like Pages and Albums?

Time for action – adding limit and offset to GraphRequest instances

1. To make it a little easier to use `limit-offset` with our Requestors, let's add parameters for setting them to `GraphRequest.as`:

```
package graph
{
  public class GraphRequest
  {
    public var objectID:String = "";
    public var connectionID:String = "";
    public var limit:int = 25;
    public var offset:int = 0;

    public function GraphRequest(a_objectID:String = "",
      a_connectionID:String = "")
    {
      this.objectID = a_objectID;
      this.connectionID = a_connectionID;
    }

  }

}
```

2. We can make the HTTPRequestor use these by editing the `request()` function in `HTTPRequestor.as`:

```
public function request(a_request:GraphRequest):void
{
  var loader:URLLoader = new URLLoader();
  var urlRequest:URLRequest = new URLRequest();
  var variables:URLVariables = new URLVariables();
```

```
//We construct a URL from the parameters of the GraphRequest
urlRequest.url = "https://graph.facebook.com/" +
  a_request.objectID;
if (a_request.connectionID)
{
  //remember, this means a connection (and thus a list)
  //was requested
  urlRequest.url += "/" + a_request.connectionID;
  //variables.limit = 5000;
}

variables.metadata = 1;
variables.limit = a_request.limit;
variables.offset = a_request.offset;
if (accessToken != "")
{
  variables.access_token = accessToken;
}
urlRequest.data = variables;

//this is used to figure out which GraphRequest created the
//loader later
_requests[loader] = a_request;

loader.addEventListener(Event.COMPLETE,
  onGraphDataLoadComplete);
loader.addEventListener(IOErrorEvent.IO_ERROR, onIOError);
loader.load(urlRequest);
}
```

3. It's just as easy to add this feature to the SDK Requestor. Modify the call to `Facebook.api()` in the `request()` function of `SDKRequestor.as`:

```
public function request(a_request:GraphRequest):void
{
  var graphItem:String = "/" + a_request.objectID;
  if (a_request.connectionID)
  {
    graphItem += "/" + a_request.connectionID;
  }
  Facebook.api(
    graphItem,
    function(result:Object, fail:Object):void {
      requestComplete.call(this, result, fail, a_request); },
    {metadata: 1, limit:a_request.limit, offset:a_request.offset}
  );
}
```

What just happened?

We've now added `limit-offset` paging capabilities to both of our Requestors: the HTTP Requestor that we built from scratch, and the SDK Requestor that's based on the official SDK.

To test this, create a new `GraphRequest` instance in `CustomGraphContainerController.as`, used after the current Requestor has been initialized:

```
private function onRequestorInitialize(a_event:Event):void
{
  _requestor.attemptToAuthenticate(ExtendedPermissions.READ_STREAM);
  var testRequest:GraphRequest = new GraphRequest("me", "likes");
  testRequest.limit = 20;
  testRequest.offset = 50;
  _requestor.request(testRequest);
}
```

Don't forget to test it with both Requestors!

Date-Based filtering

Do you notice any potential problems with the paging system outlined above (Other than that it doesn't work as expected at the moment)?

What about for getting the list of comments on a particularly popular post?

Suppose you wish to get the 100 most recent comments on a post, and need to use paging to do so. You request comments 1-25, 26-50, and then 51-75. However, at this point, someone else posts a comment, which is added as the new #1. The old #1 becomes the new #2, the old #2 becomes the new #3, and so on, so that when you request 76-100, you've actually received comment #76 twice – it was #75 a few seconds ago!

Worse than that, you now don't have the new comment #1. So instead, you could try obtaining the pages in reverse order: 76-100, 51-75, and then 26-50. This time, if a new comment is added as #1, the old #25 becomes #26. But you now request comments 1-25; the old #25 doesn't make it into your list, so there's a gap. And that's not even mentioning what would happen if a comment were deleted.

Realistically, these aren't huge problems; they just serve to show that the limit-offset paging method is not perfect. As an alternative, we can page data based on time and date.

Time for action – requesting data based on date

What was happening around March, 2009, on the Facebook Page? If you look at the actual page (http://facebook.com/facebook), you'll have to click on **Older posts** a lot of times to get back that far.

With the Graph API it's easy. We just use the until parameter:

https://graph.facebook.com/facebook/feed?until=31march2009

A sample of the JSON returned is shown in the following code:

```
{
    "data": [
        {
            "id": "[redacted]",
            "from": {
                "name": "[redacted]",
                "id": "[redacted]"
            },
            "to": {
                "data": [
                    {
                        "name": "Facebook",
                        "category": "Technology",
                        "id": "20531316728"
                    }
                ]
            },
            "message": "[redacted]",
            "type": "status",
            "created_time": "2008-01-21T15:42:11+0000",
            "updated_time": "2009-05-31T21:26:30+0000",
            "likes": 2,
        }
    ]
}
```

What just happened?

This should have returned the 25 most recent wall posts from the end of March, 2009 (or even earlier), starting with the newest ones. Yet, clearly this is not the case – the top post was created in January, 2008 and updated at the end of May, 2009.

Also, notice that the "30 days or 50 posts" limit does not seem to apply here, as this post is much older than a year, and there have been far more than 50 posts made since.

Unfortunately, this is just what using paging with Graph URLs is like, at least for the time being. Sometimes it works as expected, but sometimes it behaves in strange and mysterious ways, as we' ve seen. Again, it' s possible that all the issues will have been sorted out by the time you read this – but just in case they haven't, take care if designing a project around Graph URL paging.

In the situations where it works, the `until` parameter can take dates in lots of different forms:

- 31march2009
- May-4th-2010
- 2010-12-25
- Yesterday
- First Monday of September 2009
- 12 days ago
- -7 weekdays

You can specify time, too:

- 31march2009 15:10
- May-4th-2010 noon
- 2010-12-25T08:00:00
- 12 days ago 8pm
- Today 7:30AM

A full list of formats is available at: `http://www.php.net/manual/en/datetime.formats.php`.

> **Remember: URLs don't like characters like** + (or even spaces, really), so be sure to encode your URL before passing it to a `URLRequest`. You can use AS3's built-in `escape()` method for this:
>
> `var urlEncodedString:String = escape(unencodedURL);`
>
> For more information, check out the LiveDocs Page on `escape()`: `http://www.adobe.com/livedocs/flash/9.0/ActionScriptLangRefV3/package.html#escape()`.

So, the until parameter lets us specify the latest day and time to filter our data by; it also has a sister parameter that lets us specify the earliest date: since. It works in exactly the same way and allows exactly the same formats of dates and times.

> To requests posts from the Facebook page from April 21st, 2010 (the day the Graph API was released), we would use this URL:
>
> https://graph.facebook.com/facebook/photos?since=21april2010T00:00:01&until=21april2010T23:59:59
>
> If there were more than 25 posts on that day, then we could even use offset and limit alongside since and until to split that list into further pages.
>
> That exact URL won't return any data (since it's more than 30 days ago), but this example shows the format that you have to use.

Okay, let's get this into our application.

Time for action – adding since and until to GraphRequest instances

The procedure for allowing us to use since-until with our GraphRequest instances is almost identical to that for allowing us to use limit-offset.

1. Add since and until string properties to GraphRequest.as as shown in the following code:

```
package graph
{
  public class GraphRequest
  {
    public var objectID:String = "";
    public var connectionID:String = "";
    public var limit:int = 25;
    public var offset:int = 0;
    public var since:String = "";
    public var until:String = "";

    public function GraphRequest(a_objectID:String = "",
      a_connectionID:String = "")
    {
      this.objectID = a_objectID;
      this.connectionID = a_connectionID;
    }

  }

}
```

2. In `HTTPRequestor.as`, set the properties of the `URLVariables` object depending on these new strings:

```
public function request(a_request:GraphRequest):void
{
  var loader:URLLoader = new URLLoader();
  var urlRequest:URLRequest = new URLRequest();
  var variables:URLVariables = new URLVariables();

  //We construct a URL from the parameters of the GraphRequest
  urlRequest.url = "https://graph.facebook.com/" +
    a_request.objectID;
  if (a_request.connectionID)
  {
    //remember, this means a connection (and thus a list)
    //was requested
    urlRequest.url += "/" + a_request.connectionID;
  }

  variables.metadata = 1;
  variables.limit = a_request.limit;
  variables.offset = a_request.offset;
  variables.since = a_request.since;
  variables.until = a_request.until;
  if (accessToken != "")
  {
    variables.access_token = accessToken;
  }
  urlRequest.data = variables;

  //this is used to figure out which GraphRequest created the
  //loader later
  _requests[loader] = a_request;

  loader.addEventListener(Event.COMPLETE,
    onGraphDataLoadComplete);
  loader.addEventListener(IOErrorEvent.IO_ERROR, onIOError);
  loader.load(urlRequest);
}
```

3. Modify the third parameter passed to the `Facebook.api()` method in the `request()` function inside `SDKRequestor.as`:

```
public function request(a_request:GraphRequest):void
{
```

```
      var graphItem:String = "/" + a_request.objectID;
      if (a_request.connectionID)
      {
        graphItem += "/" + a_request.connectionID;
      }
      Facebook.api(
        graphItem,
        function(result:Object, fail:Object):void {
          requestComplete.call(this, result, fail, a_request); },
        {metadata: 1, limit:a_request.limit, offset:a_request.offset,
          since:a_request.since, until:a_request.until}
      );
    }
```

What just happened?

You' ve added the `since-until` date-based paging capabilities to Visualizer, and to both types of Requestor.

Now you can test this by altering the properties of the `GraphRequest` instance in `CustomGraphContainerController.as`:

```
    private function onRequestorInitialize(a_event:Event):void
    {
      _requestor.attemptToAuthenticate(ExtendedPermissions.READ_STREAM);
      var testRequest:GraphRequest = new GraphRequest("me", "likes");
      testRequest.since = "September 30 2010";
      testRequest.until = "14-Oct-2010";
      _requestor.request(testRequest);
    }
```

Again, don' t forget to try it with both types of Requestor.

Time for action – filtering by date using the UI

1. Rather than hardcoding the `since` and `until` values, we could use a UI element to filter Graph Lists while the project is running.

2. The Visualizer includes another hidden option to allow this. To enable it, edit the constructor of `CustomGraphContainer.as` again:

```
    public function CustomGraphContainerController(a_graphControlConta
    iner:GraphControlContainer)
    {
      super(a_graphControlContainer);
      this._showListCounts = true;
```

```
   this._showListFilters = true;

   _requestor = new HTTPRequestor();
   addEventListenersToRequestor();
   //we must wait for the Requestor to initialise before we can do
   //anything else with it
   _requestor.addEventListener(Event.COMPLETE,
     onRequestorInitialize);

   _requestor.initialize();
}
```

3. Save, compile, and upload your project, then open any connection to create a List Renderer. (If you don' t get many results, remove the lines in `onRequestorInitialize()` that set specific `since-until` or `limit-offset` values.)

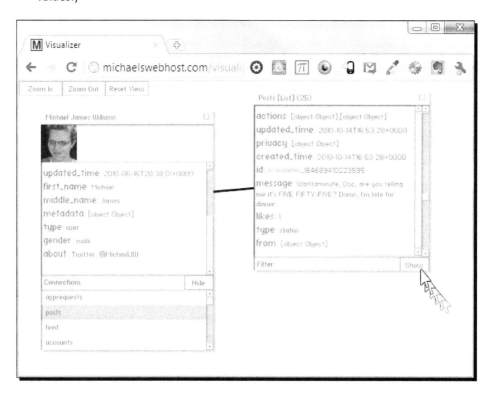

4. Click on the **Show** button on the new **Filter** bar as shown in the previous screenshot.

5. This new panel allows you to enter dates to use for `since`-`until` filtering.

6. Type any date and time into the boxes, or use the **C** buttons to bring up calendar controls which can be used instead.

7. When the user clicks the **Filter** button in this panel, it calls a protected function, `listFilterCallback()`, in the class that `CustomGraphContainerController` extends, and passes it the dates entered and the IDs of the Graph Object and connection that the List Renderer represents.

This means that `CustomGraphContainerController` inherits that function, so we can make it create a new `GraphRequest` for this Graph Object and connection, using those dates.

8. So, open `CustomGraphContainerController.as` and override the function:

```
override protected function listFilterCallback(a_objectID:String,
a_connectionType:String, a_since:String, a_until:String):void
{
   super.listFilterCallback(a_objectID, a_connectionType, a_since,
a_until);
}
```

The inherited function is just a stub – it doesn't do anything.

9. Now, create and use a new `GraphRequest` using the information passed in the parameters:

```
override protected function listFilterCallback(a_objectID:String,
a_connectionType:String, a_since:String, a_until:String):void
{
  super.listFilterCallback(a_objectID, a_connectionType, a_since,
a_until);
  var filterRequest:GraphRequest = new GraphRequest(a_objectID,
a_connectionType);
  filterRequest.since = a_since;
  filterRequest.until = a_until;
  _requestor.request(filterRequest);
}
```

10. Compile and upload the SWF, then test the changes by entering two dates in the Filter panel and clicking the **Filter** button.

What just happened?

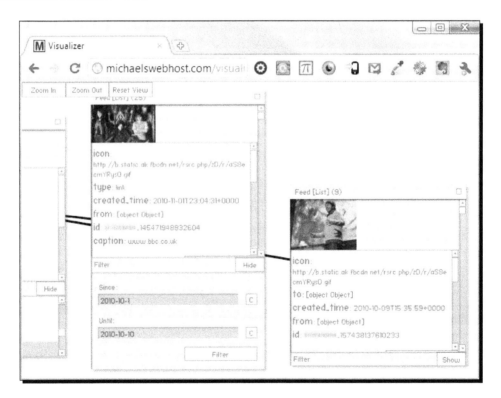

In the previous screenshot, the List Renderer on the left-hand side shows the latest 25 posts in my profile's `feed`; the **Since** and **Until** fields in the **Filter** panel have been filled in with the dates **2010-10-1** and **2010-10-10**, respectively, and the resulting List Renderer appears on the right-hand side. The right-hand side Renderer only contains nine Graph Objects, and the latest is from **2010-10-09** – just as we'd expect!

We gon' party like it's yo' birthday

Now, let's use the Filter panel for a much more interesting task: seeing who posted on your wall on your last birthday. (This will come in handy when deciding who goes on your Christmas card list this year.)

Have a go hero – loading birthday wall posts

- So who posted what on your wall on your last birthday? Unless your birthday was very recent, this would be difficult to find out through the Facebook web site. Fortunately, it's easy to find out with the Visualizer.

- Remember, posts on your wall come under the `feed` connection. Also, bear in mind that you can enter times in the values of **Since** and **Until**, as well as dates. Plus, since Facebook stores dates according to its own time zone, which is not necessarily your local one, it may disagree with you on which posts were written on the day itself.

Once you've investigated that, take a look at your friends' walls on their birthdays, or on other important dates. Remember, you'll need a certain extended permission for this – can you remember which one?

Date-based paging

Take a look at the end of a JSON returned from any List object – for example, here's Packt Publishing's "Books" photo album, with all but one item removed:

`https://graph.facebook.com/307932939458/photos`

```
{
    "data": [
        {
            "id": "307944374458",
            "from": {
                "name": "Packt Publishing",
                "category": "Products_other",
                "id": "204603129458"
            },
            "name": "Drupal 6 Themes\r\n\r\n\r\nWritten by Ric Shreves\r\n\r\n\r\
                nBuy this book now via Packt: http://www.packtpub.com/
                drupal-6-themes/book",
```

```
            "picture": "http://photos-c.ak.fbcdn.net/hphotos-ak-snc3/
    hs185.snc3/19239_307944374458_204603129458_4527791_8102041_s.jpg",
            "source": "http://sphotos.ak.fbcdn.net/hphotos-ak-snc3/hs185.
    snc3/19239_307944374458_204603129458_4527791_8102041_n.jpg",
            "height": 666,
            "width": 540,
            "link": "http://www.facebook.com/photo.php?pid=4527791&
    id=204603129458",
            "icon": "http://static.ak.fbcdn.net/rsrc.php/z2E5Y/
    hash/8as8iqdm.gif",
            "created_time": "2010-02-04T12:40:07+0000",
            "updated_time": "2010-03-18T16:08:42+0000"
        }
    ],
    "paging": {
        "previous": "https://graph.facebook.com/307932939458/
    photos?limit=25&since=2010-03-18T16%3A00%3A38%2B0000",
        "next": "https://graph.facebook.com/307932939458/
    photos?limit=25&until=2010-02-04T12%3A40%3A06%2B0000"
    }
}
```

See that node called `paging`? It obviously contains two URLs, though they seem to have some junk attached to the end of them. Actually, it's not junk; it's just URL-encoded. Here's how the `previous` URL looks when decoded:

```
https://graph.facebook.com/307932939458/photos?limit=25&since=2010-
03-18T16:00:38+0000
```

It's clearly a date with a timestamp, passed to a `since` parameter, just like we've been using.

Facebook provides these as an easier alternative to the `offset`/`limit`-based paging we explored earlier in the chapter. Paging based on time makes a lot more sense than paging based on the items position in a list (as we explored before), because the date and time that an item was created will never change, while the item's position in a list will change whenever a new item is added to that list.

It's true that items being deleted could cause problems: if we've already downloaded the item then we may not detect that it's gone, leaving us with incorrect data. Even if we do a double-check and remove it, it's going to leave a gap, meaning that the page of items that used to contain it will be shorter than the other pages. Whether these are serious problems depends on the application.

Since these paging links are bundled with the JSON, they're often easier to implement than working out our own system based on `limit` and `offset` parameters. That' s not really true in our case, because we would have to extract the `since` and `until` parameters from the `next` and `previous` URLs and then feed them to a `GraphRequest` object – it would be easier to extract the dates of the earliest and latest Graph Objects in the collection, and use those.

Still, this may come in useful for other projects you work on in the future, so it' s worth mentioning.

Requesting multiple IDs at once

Earlier in the chapter we learned how to retrieve a list of wall posts from a specific date range. How would you get the basic information about all the people that wrote these posts?

Based on what we've seen so far, the obvious answer is to loop through all of the IDs of all of the people, and request the User object for each of them.

That's fine, but it's a bit clunky, and we have no way of associating those people with each other. Wouldn't it be nicer if we could obtain them all in a single List?

Time for action – using the ids parameter in a Graph URL

Load the following URL in your browser:

```
https://graph.facebook.com/?ids=facebook,packtpub

    {
        "facebook": {
            "id": "20531316728",
            "name": "Facebook",
            "picture": "http://profile.ak.fbcdn.net/hprofile-ak-snc4/
              hs624.ash1/27535_20531316728_5553_s.jpg",
            "link": "http://www.facebook.com/facebook",
            "category": "Technology",
            "username": "facebook",
            "founded": "February 4, 2004",
            "company_overview": "«overview»",
            "mission": "Facebook's mission is to give people the power to
              share and make the world more open and connected.",
            "fan_count": 12672143
        },
        "packtpub": {
            "id": "204603129458",
            "name": "Packt Publishing",
```

```
        "picture": "http://profile.ak.fbcdn.net/hprofile-ak-snc4/
          hs302.ash1/23274_204603129458_7460_s.jpg",
        "link": "http://www.facebook.com/PacktPub",
        "category": "Products_other",
        "username": "PacktPub",
        "company_overview": "«overview»",
        "fan_count": 437
    }
}
```

What just happened?

We passed the IDs of two Pages at once to the Graph, using the `ids` parameter, and it returned a JSON containing the basic information of both of them.

So this is a List, right?

Wrong!

Well, it's not a List according to the definition we've been using so far, as there's no `data` node. I'll call it a Compound Object. Compare the above to the result you get if requesting the Facebook Page directly:

`https://graph.facebook.com/facebook`

```
{
    "id": "20531316728",
    "name": "Facebook",
    "picture": "http://profile.ak.fbcdn.net/hprofile-ak-snc4/
      hs624.ash1/27535_20531316728_5553_s.jpg",
    "link": "http://www.facebook.com/facebook",
    "category": "Technology",
    "username": "facebook",
    "founded": "February 4, 2004",
    "company_overview": "«overview»",
    "mission": "Facebook's mission is to give people the power to share
      and make the world more open and connected.",
    "fan_count": 12672338
}
```

You can see that when requesting more than one Graph object at once, the objects are jammed together as sub-nodes of a single object, each labeled with their ID.

Naturally, you don't have to use Page IDs; you can use the ID of any object in the Graph, including Albums, Photos, and Users. What's more, you can mix the types of ID you request, so you could request an Event, three Users, and a dozen Photos all at once, and they'll be returned in the same JSON.

The difference between a native Graph List and a Compound Object is very small.

The Graph List is as follows:

```
{
  "data": [
    {
      "key1": "value1",
      "key2": "value2",
      "key3": "value3"
    },
    {
      "key1": "value1",
      "key2": "value2",
      "key3": "value3"
    }
  ]
}
```

The Compound Object is as follows:

```
{
  "id1": {
    "key1": "value1",
    "key2": "value2",
    "key3": "value3"
  },
  "id1": {
    "key1": "value1",
    "key2": "value2",
    "key3": "value3"
  }
}
```

Compound objects don't have a `data` node, and the individual objects have names, but that's it – the actual data inside the nodes is the same.

Is it surprising that these two types of Graph item should be so similar? Not really. They both have a similar purpose, after all: to store more than one individual Graph Object. And there's absolutely no reason why those individual objects should have a different structure based solely on their context.

This is another great example of the "keep it simple" philosophy that underlies the Graph API. Every single item is presented in the same basic format, regardless of context or type.

Have a go hero – creating a Compound Object based on results from a List

Revisit what we looked at earlier—finding people that posted on your wall on your last birthday – but this time, request and render a Compound Object containing all of those User objects.

This is a big challenge: the best place to do this is not inside the Visualizer itself, but inside a brand new project. Can you create a project from scratch that can do this? Naturally, you can re-use any of the useful classes from Visualizer, like the Requestors and the `ExtendedPermissions` class.

Summary

Paging means splitting a long collection of data into multiple smaller components, called **Pages**. Do not confuse this type of page with a Facebook Page Object or a web page.

◆ The number of records in a page can be set using a parameter called `limit`. The default value for `limit` is 25.

◆ The `offset` parameter can be used to specify the first object in the collection that should be returned. The default value for `offset` is 0.

◆ Pages can be defined by combining `offset` and `limit` parameters – although the Graph API is a little unstable on that point at time of writing.

◆ The `since` and `until` parameters filter a Graph List to a specified range of dates and times.

◆ Dates and times can be written in a wide range of formats; see `http://www.php.net/manual/en/datetime.formats.php` for a full list.

◆ All four parameters – `limit`, `offset`, `since`, and `until`– can be used together at the same time.

◆ To specify these parameters via a Graph URL, simply pass them as URL parameters, or using an instance of the AS3 `URLVariables` class.

◆ To specify these parameters via the SDK, include them as properties of an object, passed as the third parameter to the `Facebook.api()` function.

◆ Graph Lists, returned as JSON objects, have a property called `paging`, which contains URLs for the next and previous pages of data. These URLs use `since`-`until` paging, rather than `limit`-`offset`.

◆ A **Compound Object** can be obtained using a Graph URL of this format: `https://graph.facebook.com/?ids=id1,id2,id3,...`. This contains multiple objects in a similar JSON format to a Graph List, but with no `data` node.

◆ We've learned how to dig deeper into the Graph, revealing more about Graph Objects and connections whose IDs we already know, but what about finding Graph Objects based on their contents, rather than their IDs? In the next chapter, we'll learn about searching the Graph to do just that.

Pop Quiz

1. Why does Facebook split Graph Lists into pages by default, rather than just providing all of the data at once whenever it's requested?

    a. Facebook only retains the last week's worth of information in its data banks

    b. It's a compromise between speed of access and amount of information provided

    c. Privacy concerns

2. What do the parameters `limit`, `offset`, `since`, and `until` do?

    a. Allow you to narrow down the results returned from a collection

    b. Restrict user access to a Graph Object for a certain time period

3. When paging, why is it better to use the "next" and "previous" URLs from a Graph List's JSON object, rather than constructing your own URLs using `limit` and `offset`?

    a. Date-based paging gives finer control of which posts to request

    b. Date-based paging means Graph Objects won't be missed out between pages

    c. Date-based paging means Graph Objects won't be missed out if created or removed while paging

5
Search Me

We've learned how to obtain all sorts of information about Graph Objects whose Graph URLs we already know. But what about finding those URLs in the first place?

This chapter's all about searching. We'll learn how to filter all of these by certain search terms:

- ◆ Pages, Events, and Groups
- ◆ User names
- ◆ Posts (both in the public feed and those from our friends)

So let's get on with it...

Using the website's Search box

The quote on Facebook's front page states, **Facebook helps you connect and share with the people in your life**.

To do that, Facebook needs to help you find the people in your life – without having to memorize their profile page URLs or wait for them to pop up in your news feed. That's what the Search box at the top of every page is for.

Of course, as Facebook (and its social graph) has grown to contain so many more types of objects, the Search box has needed to grow in functionality, too.

Time for action – examining quick search results

Log in to Facebook in your browser, type "test" into the **Search** bar at the top of the page, and see what appears in the drop-down list:

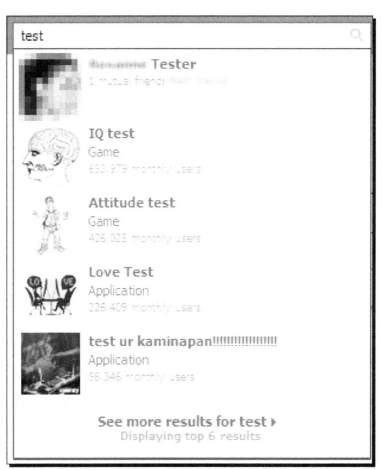

Now try a name:

What just happened?

Facebook uses a smart search for names; notice that when I typed in "bob" it found results containing "Bob," "Rob," and "Robert." Similarly, if you search for "Jim" it'll find "James."

(This can be confusing; I was scratching my head for a long time trying to find out why searching for "Liz" listed my friend Beth – whose name is not short for Elizabeth!)

This isn't a wildcard search, though. Searching for "obert" won't find you people called "Robert."

You can see from my results that the search results include Groups, Applications, and Games, mixed in with fellow users. If I'd picked a different search term, the search could have found Events and Pages.

As well as the smart name recognition search, Facebook also uses a smart sort to order the list, ranking the results to try to give you the ones you're likely to be looking for first: Pages and Groups that you 'like' are ranked higher, as are Events that you're on the guest list for, and Applications and Games that you've added. And there are a few things Facebook checks to figure out which people you might be seeking:

◆ Are you friends with the person already?

◆ Do you have a lot of friends in common?

◆ Do you both live in the same area?

◆ Are you in the same networks (college, school, workplace)?

This way, most of the time, you'll find the person or object you're looking for in the short drop-down list of results. But, if not, you'll need to go to the Full Search.

Time for action – Using the Full Search results

Type a query into the Search box, and click on the Magnifying Glass icon or the **See More Results** item at the bottom of the drop-down list to get to the Full Search page:

The full page is shown in the next screenshot:

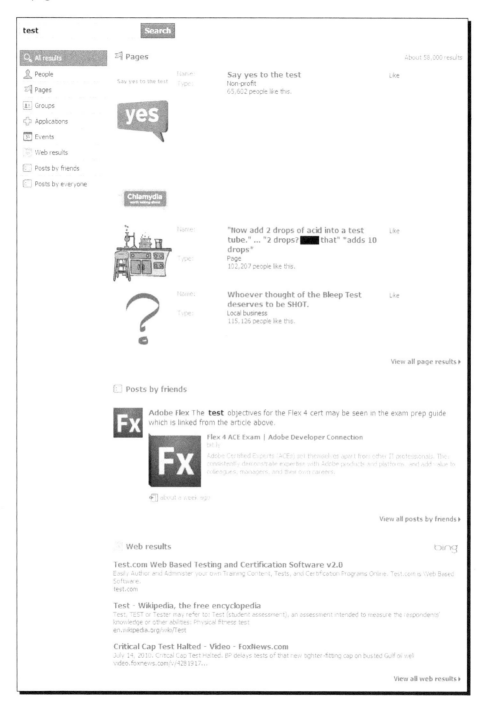

The first thing to notice is that the items in this list are different from the items in the drop-down list; the quick results aren't simply the first six items in the full list.

Second, note that these results are segmented into the different types of object: **Pages**, **People**, and so on. In the drop-down list, the different types were mixed together, and then sorted by perceived relevance.

Third, you can narrow the results down to a single type of object by using the list on the left-hand side:

(Also, note that these lists allow you to page through the results.)

Fourth, the options on the left include some types of objects that won't appear in the drop-down list:

- Web results (powered by Bing) – essentially a frontend for the search engine, inside the Facebook site

- Posts by friends – wall posts, notes, links, videos, photos, and statuses

- Posts by everyone – just wall posts, notes, links, and statuses

Finally, there are a number of sub-options you can alter for these searches: narrow posts down by locale or location; filter people by their school or workplace; look for events happening today, tomorrow, this week, or this month, and so on.

What just happened?

This is all pretty straightforward. The one point of confusion here is: why don't the top results from the Full Search match those from a Quick Search?

(I searched "Liz", and the Quick Search listed my friend Beth at the top spot and my friend Elizabeth at the second; when I do a Full Search, neither of them turn up in the **All results** tab and only Beth appears in the **People** results – Elizabeth is nowhere to be seen!)

Sure, it's not too surprising that the two pages would use different algorithms for searching, but it doesn't make a lot of sense for them to be this different. Since we're only looking at the website itself at the moment, it doesn't really matter – however, we will come across a similar issue when searching via the Graph API, which is what we're going to do next.

Searching with a Graph URL

You knew it was coming.

We'll start by searching for Graph Objects that can be seen by the public.

Time for action – searching without authorization

The basic search query Graph URL is:

```
https://graph.facebook.com/search?type=«type»&q=«query»
```

The `type` parameter lets you choose an option (as in from the left-hand side of the Full Search), and `q` (for query) specifies the search terms.

Let's try searching for the Packt Publishing page:

```
https://graph.facebook.com/search?type=page&q=PacktPub
```

```
{
    "data": [
        {
            "name": "Packt Publishing",
            "category": "Products_other",
            "id": "204603129458"
        }
    ]
}
```

We're cheating here; I've searched for the exact name of the page, which sort of defeats the point of a search. Note that PacktPub does not appear anywhere in the results, though – this implies that, sometimes, you (and your application) may not be able to tell why a certain result appears in the listings.

Let's try a similar search without cheating – we'll just look for "Packt" instead of "PacktPub":

```
https://graph.facebook.com/search?type=page&q=Packt
```

```
{
    "data": [
        {
            "name": "\u00bb Packt like sardines in a crushd tin box.",
            "category": "Public_figures_other",
            "id": "106807812689840"
        },
        {
            "name": "Packt",
            "category": "Author",
            "id": "105143859532023"
        },
        {
            "name": "Grossmama Packt Aus",
            "category": "Unknown",
            "id": "107744965912183"
        }
    ],
    "paging": {
        "next": "https://graph.facebook.com/
            search?type=page&q=Packt&limit=25&offset=25"
    }
}
```

Packt is a German word, so we get hundreds of results of German pages (many have been cut out in the listing above). Unfortunately, Packt Publishing is nowhere to be seen.

We can use spaces in the search query by replacing them with `%20`:

```
https://graph.facebook.com/search?type=page&q=Packt%20Publishing
{
    "data": [
        {
            "name": "Packt Publishing",
            "category": "Products_other",
            "id": "204603129458"
        },
        {
            "name": "Packt Publishing",
            "category": "Company",
            "id": "109477139072966"
        },
        {
            "name": "Job - System Admin(1-2 Y),Andheri E for Publishing
              House {Walk in-11am-3pm} -
              Mumbai - Packt Publishing Pvt. Ltd. -
              1-to-2 years of experience - Jobs India",
            "category": "Website",
            "id": "115106601845387"
        }
    ]
}
```

The first result is the PacktPub page we've been using (follow it through to the Graph URL that uses that ID, if you want to check).

What other types of search can we do? We can retrieve all public wall posts, links, status updates, videos, and photos using the `post` option:

```
https://graph.facebook.com/search?type=post&q=Packt
{
    "data": [
        {
            "id": "«redacted»",
            "from": {
                "name": "«redacted»",
                "id": "«redacted»"
            },
            "message": "packt seine 7 sachen .... und sieht danach
              evtl mal in Lenkersheim nach dem REchten",
            "type": "status",
            "created_time": "2010-07-31T18:16:32+0000",
```

```
        "updated_time": "2010-08-01T02:04:34+0000",
        "likes": 1
      },
      {
        "id": "204603129458_144653245560929",
        "from": {
          "name": "Packt Publishing",
          "category": "Products_other",
          "id": "204603129458"
        },
        "message": "'ColdFusion 9 Developer Tutorial' has been
          published. Get your copy now : http://bit.ly/bEqb9n",
        "link": "http://bit.ly/bEqb9n",
        "name": "ColdFusion 9 Developer Tutorial Book & eBook |
          Packt Publishing Technical & IT Book Store",
        "description": "Get up to speed in ColdFusion and learn how
          to integrate it with other Web 2.0 technologies",
        "type": "link",
        "created_time": "2010-07-31T10:04:39+0000",
        "updated_time": "2010-07-31T10:04:39+0000"
      },
      {
        "id": "139708256052538_136219896414668",
        "from": {
          "name": "The Entertainer",
          "category": "Film",
          "id": "139708256052538"
        },
        "message": "Noch 7 Tage, dann wird die gro\u00dfe
          Konzertszene in Scheifling gedreht. Wir brauchen dringend
          noch Statisten, die einfach nur als Konzertg\u00e4ste im
          Publikum sitzen! Packt also bitte eure Familie ein und
          macht einen Ausflug zum Filmdreh. Ihr werdet es auf keinen
          Fall bereuen!\n\nSamstag, 7. August\nTreffpunkt 12:30\
          nehemaliges Kino Scheifling",
        "link": "http://www.facebook.com/",
        "type": "link",
        "created_time": "2010-07-31T08:21:24+0000",
        "updated_time": "2010-07-31T08:21:24+0000"
      }
    ],
    "paging": {
      "previous": "https://graph.facebook.com/search?type=post&q=
        Packt&limit=25&since=2010-07-31T18%3A16%3A32%2B0000",
      "next": "https://graph.facebook.com/search?type=post&q=
        Packt&limit=25&until=2010-07-24T14%3A13%3A51%2B0000"
    }
  }
```

This is roughly the same as the **Posts by everyone** option in the Full Search.

All the possible values for the `type` parameter are:

◆ `page`

◆ `post`

◆ `event`

◆ `group`

◆ `checkin`

◆ `place`

◆ `user`

It's obvious what `event` and `group` do. The `checkin` option lets you search for recent checkins on Facebook Places. The `place` option lets you search by name for a place in Facebook Places, and requires two other parameters:

◆ `center` – a longitude and latitude, separated by a comma

◆ `distance` – the distance from `center`, in meters, within which to search

For example, the latitude and longitude of the White House are 38.898648 and 77.037692, respectively, so to search for libraries within 2,000 meters of the White House, you would use the following Graph URL:

◆ `https://graph.facebook.com/search?type=place&center=38.898648,77037692&distance=2000&q=library`

The `user` option just searches for any person that's signed up to Facebook. Let's try searching for someone:

`https://graph.facebook.com/search?type=user&q=Bob`

```
{
    "error": {
        "type": "OAuthAccessTokenException",
        "message": "An access token is required to request this
            resource."
    }
}
```

Hmm. We get the same message when trying to search for groups, events, and checkins.

What just happened?

Even though you can use a cut down version of Facebook's web page-based person search when not logged in (via `http://www.facebook.com/srch.php`), you can't get any search results for people, groups, or events through the Graph API unless you provide an access token.

As we've seen, search results support paging; results for Pages allow for `offset`/`limit` pagination, and results for public posts can be narrowed down to a specific date range using `until`/`since` parameters. (See Chapter 4 for more information on these types of paging.)

The search query is very simple; it doesn't allow operators like `and` and `or`, or phrase-based searching. This is not Google. Fancy queries don't work in the web page-based Search, and they won't work through a Graph URL.

In fact, the Graph URL search has fewer features than the web page-based search:

◆ There is no application value for the `type` parameter

◆ There are no additional parameters to filter results for Pages by their sub-type (place, product, service, and so on)

Let's authorize ourselves so that we can use an access token to check out the other types of search.

Time for action – searching while authorized

Grab an access token (see Chapter 3 for a reminder on how to do this) and use it to try that person search again:

```
https://graph.facebook.com/search?type=user&q=Bob&access_
token=«access_token»
```

```
{
    "data": [
        {
            "name": "Robert H.",
            "id": "«redacted»"
        },
        {
            "name": "Robert W.",
            "id": "«redacted»"
        },
        {
            "name": "Bob Bob Bob",
            "id": "«redacted»"
```

```
      },
      {
         "Name": "bob t.",
         "Id": "«redacted»"
      },
      {
         "Name": "bob p.",
         "Id": "«redacted»"
      }
   ],
   "Paging": {
      "Next": "https://graph.Facebook.Com/
   search?Type=user&q=bob&access_token=«access_token»&limit=25&offset=25"
   }
}
```

This has used both the "smart" features of the web page-based search: it found "Robert" when searching for "Bob", and ordered the results so that people I'm more likely to be looking for (friends, friends of friends, and locals) are nearer the top.

 Remember, the access token is not just tied to the application but also to the current user, which is how the search knows which results are more relevant to you. This means that your search results will be considerably different from the previous results.

With an access token we can also search for Events and Groups, and you'll find that the smart searching works with these, too.

What about Pages? Do we get different search results when authenticated?

Let's try it out by searching for "Packt" again. Recall that last time there were lots of German results and the Packt Publishing page was not in the top results. This time use the following URL:

```
https://graph.facebook.com/search?type=page&q=packt&access_
token=«access_token»
```

```
{
   "data": [
      {
         "name": "\u00bb Packt like sardines in a crushd tin box.",
         "category": "Public_figures_other",
         "id": "106807812689840"
      },
      {
```

```
         "name": "Packt Publishing",
         "category": "Products_other",
         "id": "204603129458"
      },
      {
         "name": "Packt",
         "category": "Author",
         "id": "105143859532023"
      },
      {
         "name": "Grossmama Packt Aus",
         "category": "Unknown",
         "id": "107744965912183"
      }
   ],
   "paging": {
      "next": "https://graph.facebook.com/
search?type=page&q=packt&access_token=«access_
token»&limit=25&offset=25"
   }
}
```

Great! Because I'm a fan of the Packt Publishing Page, it appears higher in my search results. This makes it easier to provide relevant search results through our apps.

> Although I've never even heard of `Packt like sardines in a crushd tin box`, Facebook puts it at the top of my search results because it has a huge number of fans.

Since the Full Search has two options for searching for posts – **Posts by friends** and **Posts by everyone** – one would imagine that, when authorized, the Post search would return only posts by friends. Unfortunately, this isn't the case.

What just happened?

With an access token we can search through much more of the Graph than we could without one. Also, because access tokens are specific to one person, the search results are tailored to be more relevant to that user; this is all done at Facebook's end, without us having to change anything in our application. Some search types require a particular extended permission to be granted before returning any results. See `http://developers.facebook.com/docs/authentication/permissions` for more info, and refer to Chapter 3 for information on granting these permissions.

Differences

However, even when authenticated, the results we get through a Graph URL search don't always match the results we see in a Full Search. This is particularly true when looking for people; by default, all apps are able to access an authenticated user's friends' names and IDs, but other information may be hidden.

For example, by entering an e-mail address as the query in a User search, we can find anyone with that exact email address – unless they've noted in their privacy settings that they don't want that information to be available to other apps. (See also the options in **Account | Privacy Settings | Applications and websites | Information accessible through your friends**, as described in Chapter 3.)

Sometimes this will cut particular results out entirely; sometimes it will make the same results appear, but in a different order. Remember this when testing: If the results you get when searching through your application are different from those you get when searching through the web site, that doesn't necessarily mean there's a bug in your application.

Restrictions

The sub-options available when searching via a Graph URL are very limited when compared to the Full Search. We can't filter Users by their location or school, Groups by their type, or Events by their date (even using `since`/`until` paging).

Nor can we restrict Posts to a specific language, which makes them far less useful than they might be (as we saw when searching for "Packt", a common German word). But we can do something similar.

There is a parameter called `locale` which accepts languages like "`en_US`" (for US English) and "`fr_FR`" (for French). This can be used in two ways.

First, we can use it to transform information that we receive. For example, here's Facebook CTO *Bret Taylor's* User object:

```
https://graph.facebook.com/btaylor

  {
    "id": "220439",
    "name": "Bret Taylor",
    "first_name": "Bret",
    "last_name": "Taylor",
    "link": "http://www.facebook.com/btaylor",
    "gender": "male",
    "locale": "en_US"
  }
```

In the next code snippet, we have the User object with the locale set to French:

```
https://graph.facebook.com/btaylor?locale=fr_FR
```

```
{
    "id": "220439",
    "name": "Bret Taylor",
    "first_name": "Bret",
    "last_name": "Taylor",
    "link": "http://www.facebook.com/btaylor",
    "gender": "homme",
    "locale": "en_US"
}
```

Not much has changed – except the value of `gender`, which has gone from `male` to `homme`. This is useful if you need to make basic information available in different languages, without hiring a translator.

Second, notice that Bret's locale is set to `en_US`. All users have a locale; it can be set in **Account | Language**, and defines which language you view the Facebook website in. We can filter Post search results to only show results from users that have a certain locale, using the following Graph URL :

```
https://graph.facebook.com/search?type=post&q=test&locale=fr_FR
```

It's not quite the same as searching for posts in a specified language – so we can't eliminate all the results that use "Packt" as part of a German sentence – but it's close. And this is the same sub-option that we can set in the **Posts** searches in the Full Search.

A full list of locales is available at `http://www.facebook.com/translations/FacebookLocales.xml`.

A sample is as follows:

```
<?xml version='1.0'?>
<locales>
  <locale>
    <englishName>Catalan</englishName>
    <codes>
      <code>
      <standard>
        <name>FB</name>
        <representation>ca_ES</representation>
      </standard>
      </code>
    </codes>
  </locale>
</locales>
```

There are some peculiar choices in there, like `English (Upside-Down)`, so take a look.

Time for action – implementing a Search window in the Visualizer

Okay, now that we know what we can do with the Graph URL search, let's use it in our application.

The Visualizer project includes a window with UI elements for searching the Graph. It's hidden, but we can enable it in the same way that we enabled the Filter panel on the List Renderers.

Load the Visualizer project and open `CustomGraphContainerController.as`. In the constructor function, set the `_canShowSearchUI` property (which is inherited from the class that CustomGraphContainerController extends) to `true`:

```
public function CustomGraphContainerController
  (a_graphControlContainer:GraphControlContainer)
{
  super(a_graphControlContainer);
  this._showListCounts = true;
  this._showListFilters = true;
  this._canShowSearchUI = true;

  _requestor = new HTTPRequestor();
  addEventListenersToRequestor();
  //we must wait for the Requestor to initialise before we can do
  //anything else with it
  _requestor.addEventListener(Event.COMPLETE, onRequestorInitialize);

  _requestor.initialize();
}
```

Compile the project, upload the SWF to your web host, and load it in your browser using the usual URL. The result is shown in the next screenshot:

As you can see, there's a new **Search** button in the top-left corner, which makes the new **Search** window appear in the main stage area. You'll recognise the first six radio buttons as corresponding to allowed values for the `type` parameter; don't worry about **My News Feed** or **Friend's Posts** for now.

When the **Search** button inside the window is clicked, it calls a function called `search()` inside the class that `CustomGraphContainerController.as` extends, passing it three values:

- ◆ Query
- ◆ Type
- ◆ User ID (which contains the value in the lower textbox – again, we'll come to this later)

This function is completely empty, so clicking that button doesn't do anything at the moment; we'll have to override `search()` and make it work!

1. In `CustomGraphContainerController.as`, add the following function:

```
override public function search(a_query:String = "", a_type:String
= "", a_userID:String = ""):void
{

}
```

2. Now to add the actual search code. Let's start with the HTTP Requestor. The process is very similar to requesting a Graph Object or Graph List directly – in fact, it's even simpler. Open `HTTPRequestor.as` and create a new function as so:

```
public function search(a_query:String = "", a_type:String =
""):void
{
  var loader:URLLoader = new URLLoader();
  var urlRequest:URLRequest = new URLRequest();
  var variables:URLVariables = new URLVariables();

  urlRequest.url = "https://graph.facebook.com/search";

  variables.metadata = 1;
  if (accessToken != "")
  {
    variables.access_token = accessToken;
  }
  variables.q = a_query;      //not variables.query!
  variables.type = a_type;
```

```
urlRequest.data = variables;

loader.addEventListener(Event.COMPLETE, onGraphSearchComplete);
loader.addEventListener(IOErrorEvent.IO_ERROR, onIOError);
loader.load(urlRequest);
}
```

See? It's like a cut-down version of `request()`. The Visualizer project doesn't require us to store information about the original `GraphRequest` object, which makes it simpler.

3. The JSON that the `URLLoader` returns is in the form of a Graph List, not a Compound Object, so we can use a List Renderer to render it. This means, in turn, that we can use a cut-down version of the `onGraphDataLoadComplete()` function to handle the search data load. Create a new function, `onGraphSearchComplete()`, as shown in the following lines of code:

```
private function onGraphSearchComplete(a_event:Event):void
{
  var loader:URLLoader = a_event.target as URLLoader;
  var graphData:String = loader.data;
  var decodedJSON:Object = JSON.decode(graphData);

  if (decodedJSON.data)
  {
    var graphList:GraphList = new GraphList();
    var childGraphObject:GraphObject;
    for each (var childObject:Object in decodedJSON.data)
    {
      childGraphObject = new GraphObject();
      for (var childKey:String in childObject)
      {
        childGraphObject[childKey] = childObject[childKey];
      }
      graphList.addToList(childGraphObject);
    }
    graphList.paging = decodedJSON.paging;

    dispatchEvent(new RequestEvent(RequestEvent.REQUEST_COMPLETED,
      graphList));
  }
}
```

The two functions we've just created are very similar to the ones we made in Chapter 2 and Chapter 3, so have a look at those if you need a reminder of how they work.

We need to make the `CustomGraphContainerController.search()` function pass its parameters to `HTTPRequestor.search()`, so load `CustomGraphContainerController.as` and modify the search() function as shown in the following code:

```
override public function search(a_query:String = "", a_type:String
= "", a_userID:String = ""):void
{
(_requestor as HTTPRequestor).search(a_query, a_type);
}
```

The `as` keyword tells Flash to treat an object as though it were an instance of a specific class; this is known as **casting**. In this code, we're forcing Flash to treat `_requestor` as an `HTTPRequestor`, since neither the `SDKRequestor` nor the `IRequestor` have a `search()` method.

Make sure that the `_requestor` object is being created as an instance of `HTTPRequestor`, rather than `SDKRequestor`, in the constructor, then compile, upload, and test your SWF. When you type in a query, select any of the first six radio buttons and click **Search**, and you should see a List Renderer appear with the results as shown in the next screenshot:

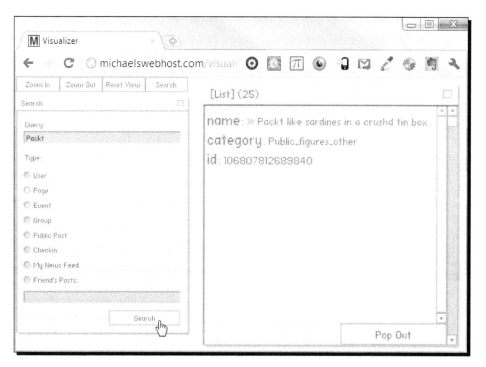

Fantastic!

What just happened?

Our Visualizer can now search for Graph objects based on a query that you enter. Since the results are returned in the form of a Graph List, our application will then grab all the info about those objects – and this means we can see their connections, too.

Time for action – searching via the SDK

It's easy to make our search work via the SDK, too. Start by opening SDKRequestor.as and adding a new function called search(), just as we did with the HTTPRequestor:

```
public function search(a_query:String = "", a_type:String = ""):void

  {

  }
```

As with a request, we pass three parameters to the Facebook.api() method:

1. /search (a string containing the key part of the Graph URL)
2. A reference to a callback function
3. An object containing the parameters (q and type – remember not to use query as the name of the parameter!)

So, add this call to your search() function as shown in the following code:

```
public function search(a_query:String = "", a_type:String = ""):void
{
  Facebook.api(
    "/search",
    searchComplete,
    { metadata: 1, q:a_query, type:a_type }
  );
}
```

 There was no need to use currying this time, as we don't need to maintain a reference to the original GraphRequest object.

That's it for the search() function. We still need to write the callback for when the data is loaded though, so create a new function, searchComplete(), as shown in the following lines of code:

```
private function searchComplete(success:Object, fail:Object):void
{

}
```

Like the other SDK callbacks, this function must accept two parameters: `result` and `fail`.

Since the search results are returned in the form of a Graph List, we can re-use most of the code from the `requestComplete()` function. Modify `searchComplete()` as shown in the following lines of code:

```
private function searchComplete(result:Object, fail:Object):void
{
  if (result != null)
  {
    var decodedJSON:Object = result;
    var graphList:GraphList = new GraphList();
    var childGraphObject:GraphObject;
    for each (var childObject:Object in decodedJSON)
    {
      childGraphObject = new GraphObject();
      for (var childKey:String in childObject)
      {
        childGraphObject[childKey] = childObject[childKey];
      }
      graphList.addToList(childGraphObject);
    }
    graphList.paging = decodedJSON.paging;

    dispatchEvent(new RequestEvent(RequestEvent.REQUEST_COMPLETED,
      graphList));
  }
  else
  {
    //was a failure. See contents of 'fail' object.
  }
}
```

Just as with the HTTP Requestor, check Chapter 2 and Chapter 3 if you want a reminder of how this all works.

Now that both Requestors have a `search()` method; we can add that method to the `IRequestor` interface. Modify `IRequestor.as` like so:

```
package graph.apis.base
{
  import flash.events.IEventDispatcher;
  import graph.GraphRequest;

  public interface IRequestor extends IEventDispatcher
  {
```

```
    function request(a_request:GraphRequest):void;
    function attemptToAuthenticate(...permissions):void;
    function initialize():void;
    function search(a_query:String = "", a_type:String = ""):void;
  }


}
```

This means we don't have to cast `_requestor` as an `HTTPRequestor` in
`CustomGraphContainerController.search()` any more, so open
`CustomGraphContainerController.as` and alter that method:

```
override public function search(a_query:String = "", a_type:String =
"", a_userID:String = ""):void
{
  _requestor.search(a_query, a_type);
}
```

All that's left before we can test it is to change the constructor so that `_requestor` is
created as an `SDKRequestor` rather than an `HTTPRequestor`. This is done as follows:

```
public function CustomGraphContainerController(a_graphControlContainer
:GraphControlContainer)
{
  super(a_graphControlContainer);
  this._showListCounts = true;
  this._showListFilters = true;
  this._canShowSearchUI = true;

  _requestor = new SDKRequestor();
  addEventListenersToRequestor();
  //we must wait for the Requestor to initialise before we can do
anything else with it
  _requestor.addEventListener(Event.COMPLETE, onRequestorInitialize);

  _requestor.initialize();
}
```

Save, compile, and upload the SWF. Load it in your browser – remember to use
`sdkindex.html`.

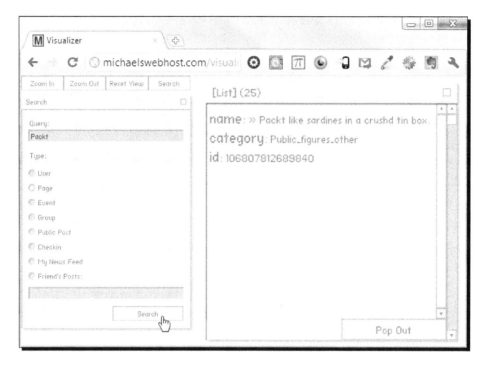

Great, it works!

What just happened?

We just added the same search functionality as before, but this time we made it work
via the SDK. Bear in mind that this means that the access token is automatically used,
if the user is authenticated.

Have a go hero – setting the locale

Now that we can search for posts, how about restricting the search to posts written by
people with a specified locale?

You could hardcode the locale to use within the `search()` method, or (if you're comfortable
with manipulating XML) you could make your project pick one of the locales at random, from
`http://www.facebook.com/translations/FacebookLocales.xml`.

Searching feeds and wall posts

The Graph URL search may be limited compared to Facebook's Full Search, but there are two types of search that can only be done via the Graph API:

◆ Searching for specific items in your news feed
◆ Searching for things that a specific friend has posted

Time for action – searching your news feed

Your news feed is the list you see when you log in to the Facebook website; all the status updates, links, videos, and photos that your friends (and other Graph website to which you are subscribed, such as pages you "like") have posted.

We've seen that we can access this feed through your profile's `home` connection:

```
https://graph.facebook.com/me/home?access_token=«access_token»
```

which returns a Graph List, as you'd expect.

We can search within this feed by specifying a value for the `q` parameter:

```
https://graph.facebook.com/me/home?q=test&access_token=«access_token»
```

```
    "data": [
      {
        "id": "151673724649_415202504649",
        "from": {
          "name": "Activetuts",
          "category": "Products_other",
          "id": "151673724649"
        },
        "message": "Test Your Observation Skills With an AS3
          Difference Game \u2013 Active Premium",
        "link": "http://feedproxy.google.com/~r/Flashtuts/~3/
          i8-bZF-Mvhc/",
        "description": "Today, we have another Active Premium
          tutorial exclusively available to Premium members. If you
          want to take your ActionScript skills to the next level,
          then we have an awesome tutorial for you, courtesy of
          Stephan Meesters",
        "type": "link",
        "created_time": "2010-07-28T11:07:12+0000",
        "updated_time": "2010-07-28T11:07:12+0000"
      }
    ],
    "paging": {
```

```
        "previous": "https://graph.facebook.com/61300894/
          home?q=test&access_token=«access_token»&limit=25&since=
          2010-07-28T11%3A07%3A12%2B0000",
        "next": "https://graph.facebook.com/61300894/home?q=test&access_
    token=«access_token»&limit=25&until=2010-07-20T15%3A01%3A01%2B0000"
    }
}
```

What just happened?

Perhaps this should be thought of more as a filter than a search. Regardless, the end result is a Graph List of posts from your news feed containing the specified query.

The search terms don't have to appear in the actual text of the post; suppose it's my friend Bill's birthday. If I load:

```
https://graph.facebook.com/me/home?q=Bill&access_token=«access_token»
```

then I will see:

◆ My own post on Bill's wall, saying "Happy Birthday, Bill!" (because the post contains the word "Bill")

◆ My friend Bob's post on Bill's wall, saying "Happy Birthday!" (because the person receiving the post is called "Bill" – which means that there are two reasons for my own post to be in these results)

◆ Bill's post saying "Thanks for the birthday wishes, everyone!" (because his name is Bill)

Unfortunately there's no way to narrow this down and specify where you want to look for matches – at least, not using a Graph Search URL.

You're probably wondering whether we can substitute another person's User ID instead of "me", and thus see what posts will be appearing in their news feed. We can't do this, for privacy reasons, but we can do something similar.

Time for action – searching a friend's Wall Posts

It's confusing that the Graph URL for your news feed (which you'll see when you log in) is:

```
https://graph.facebook.com/me/home?access_token=«access_token»
```

The link to your wall is:

```
https://graph.facebook.com/me/feed?access_token=«access_token»
```

It's just something to memorize, I'm afraid.

Now, while we can't access someone else's `home` connection, we can access their `feed` connection as long as they're a friend; in other words, we can get data from:

```
https://graph.facebook.com/«username»/feed?access_token=«access_token»
```

And we can actually run a search query on this list:

```
https://graph.facebook.com/«username»/feed?q=«query»&access_token=«access_token»
```

Try loading that URL.

What just happened?

The result is probably not what you expected.

Unlike the `feed` URL, adding a query parameter does not act like a filter here. Instead of retrieving all the posts on the user's wall that contain the search terms, this URL will retrieve everything the user has posted which contains the search terms. (And even then, you'll only be able to see things that are posted publicly or on the walls of friends.)

For example, on Bill's `feed` connection list, I can see all sorts of birthday wishes to Bill:

```
https://graph.facebook.com/BillSmith/feed?access_token=«access_token»
    {
        "data": [
            {
                "id": "«redacted»",
                "from": {
                    "name": "Joe Q Bananas ",
                    "id": "«redacted»"
                },
                "to": {
                    "data": [
                        {
                            "name": "Bill Smith",
                            "id": "«redacted»"
                        }
                    ]
                },
                "message": "Happy Birthday Bill!! Have a Good one!!",
                "type": "status",
            },
            {
                "id": "«redacted»",
```

```
            "from": {
               "name": "JohnSmith",
               "id": "«redacted»"
            },
            "to": {
               "data": [
                  {
                     "name": "Bill Smith",
                     "id": "«redacted»"
                  }
               ]
            },
            "message": "happy birthday bill",
            "type": "status",
         }
      ],
      "paging": {
         "previous": "https://graph.facebook.com/502630189/feed?&access_
token=«access_token»&limit=25&since=2010-08-01T12%3A09%3A34%2B0000",
         "next": "https://graph.facebook.com/502630189/feed?&access_
token=«access_token»&limit=25&until=2010-07-31T08%3A59%3A06%2B0000"
      }
}
```

When we search for the term `"birthday"` within the same connection, however, we see the
following output :

```
https://graph.facebook.com/BillSmith/feed access_token=«access_
token»&?q=birthday
```

```
{
   "data": [
      {
         "id": "«redacted»",
         "from": {
            "name": "Bill Smith",
            "id": "«redacted»","
         },
         "to": {
            "data": [
               {
                  "name": "JerryJohnson",
                  "id": "«redacted»","
               }
            ]
```

```
        },
        "message": "Happy birthday mate!",
        "type": "status",
    }
],
"paging": {
    "previous": "https://graph.facebook.com/502630189/
feed?q=birthday&access_token=«access_token»&limit=25&since=2010-07-
27T22%3A08%3A16%2B0000",
    "next": "https://graph.facebook.com/502630189/
feed?q=birthday&access_token=«access_token»&limit=25&until=2010-07-
23T12%3A22%3A47%2B0000"
    }
}
```

All I can see is the birthday wish that Bill posted on our mutual friend Jerry's wall. I can't even see my own birthday greeting on Bill's wall.

It's also possible to see posts that the user has made on a Page, an Event, or a Group. Overall, it's a very different set of data to the base `feed` connection.

Time for action – searching feeds through the Visualizer

Let's get these two new types of search into our application.

Presumably the purpose of the bottom three fields is a lot clearer now:

My News Feed searches /me/home, and **Friend's Posts** searches /«username»/feed, where «username» is the value typed into the textbox.

Let's first add the **My News Feed** search to both Requestors. The only change we have to make is to the URL that gets requested; instead of /search we use /me/home. The Search window returns "home" as the value of type if **My News Feed** is checked, so modify the search() method in HTTPRequestor.as as shown in the following code:

```
public function search(a_query:String = "", a_type:String = ""):void
{
  var loader:URLLoader = new URLLoader();
  var urlRequest:URLRequest = new URLRequest();
  var variables:URLVariables = new URLVariables();

  if (a_type == "home")
  {
    urlRequest.url = "https://graph.facebook.com/me/home";
  }
  else
  {
    urlRequest.url = "https://graph.facebook.com/search";
  }

  variables.metadata = 1;
  if (accessToken != "")
  {
    variables.access_token = accessToken;
  }
  variables.q = a_query;      //not variables.query!
  variables.type = a_type;
  urlRequest.data = variables;

  loader.addEventListener(Event.COMPLETE, onGraphSearchComplete);
  loader.addEventListener(IOErrorEvent.IO_ERROR, onIOError);
  loader.load(urlRequest);
}
```

Similarly, make the following changes to the search() method inside SDKRequestor.as:

```
public function search(a_query:String = "", a_type:String = ""):void
{
  var urlStub:String;
  if (a_type == "home")
  {
    urlStub = "/me/home";
  }
  else
  {
    urlStub = "/search";
```

```
    }
    Facebook.api(
      urlStub,
      searchComplete,
      { metadata: 1, q:a_query, type:a_type }
    );
}
```

We don't need to change anything else, as these searches will still return a Graph List. Test it out:

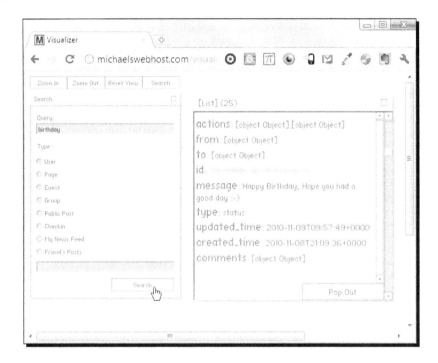

Success. Adding the **Friend's Posts** search will be a little trickier, but not much. First we have to allow the Requestors' search() functions to accept another parameter: User ID.

Open IRequestor.as and add this parameter to the function signature:

```
package graph.apis.base
{
  import flash.events.IEventDispatcher;
  import graph.GraphRequest;

  public interface IRequestor extends IEventDispatcher
  {
    function request(a_request:GraphRequest):void;
    function attemptToAuthenticate(...permissions):void;
```

```
    function initialize():void;
    function search(a_query:String = "", a_type:String = "", a_
userID:String = ""):void;
    }


}
```

Now, open `HTTPRequestor.as` and `SDKRequestor.as` and edit their implementations of `search()` to accept this parameter:

```
public function search(a_query:String = "", a_type:String = "", a_
userID:String = ""):void
```

If the **Friend's Posts** radio button is selected, then the **Search** window will return `"feed"` as the value of `a_type`. Remember, in this situation we need to query the `/«username»/feed` URL, so in `HTTPRequestor.as`, modify the `search()` function as follows:

```
public function search(a_query:String = "", a_type:String = "", a_
userID:String):void
{
  var loader:URLLoader = new URLLoader();
  var urlRequest:URLRequest = new URLRequest();
  var variables:URLVariables = new URLVariables();

  if (a_type == "home")
  {
    urlRequest.url = "https://graph.facebook.com/me/home";
  }
  else if ((a_type == "feed") && (a_userID != ""))
  {
    urlRequest.url = "https://graph.facebook.com/";
    urlRequest.url += a_userID + "/";
    urlRequest.url += "feed";
  }
  else
  {
    urlRequest.url = "https://graph.facebook.com/search";
  }

  variables.metadata = 1;
  if (accessToken != "")
  {
    variables.access_token = accessToken;
  }
  variables.q = a_query;    //not variables.query!
```

```
        variables.type = a_type;
        urlRequest.data = variables;

        loader.addEventListener(Event.COMPLETE, onGraphSearchComplete);
        loader.addEventListener(IOErrorEvent.IO_ERROR, onIOError);
        loader.load(urlRequest);
    }
```

Make a similar change in SDKRequestor.as:

```
    public function search(a_query:String = "", a_type:String = "", a_
    userID:String = ""):void
    {
      var urlStub:String;
      if (a_type == "home")
      {
        urlStub = "/me/home";
      }
      else if ((a_type == "feed") && (a_userID != ""))
      {
        urlStub = "/" + a_userID + "/feed";
      }
      else
      {
        urlStub = "/search";
      }
      Facebook.api(
        urlStub,
        searchComplete,
        { metadata: 1, q:a_query, type:a_type }
      );
    }
```

Finally, modify CustomGraphContainerController.as so that its search() method passes the User ID to the Requestor's search() method:

```
    override public function search(a_query:String = "", a_type:String =
    "", a_userID:String = ""):void
    {
      _requestor.search(a_query, a_type, a_userID);
    }
```

That's all that is needed. Test it out as shown in the next screenshot:

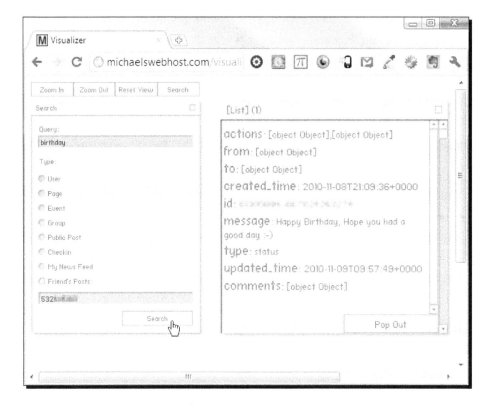

Cool.

What just happened?

You've built two types of extra search functionality into your application:

◆ Search posts in your news feed

◆ Search posts by a specific friend

Since your news feed is made up of posts by friends (and other Graph Objects that you've subscribed to), the first post is essentially the same as the **Posts by friends** options that is in the Full Search but was missing from the Search URL.

Searching posts made by a specific friend is something that cannot be done through the Facebook website. Congratulations! Your application now has more functionality than Facebook.

Did you notice that we still passed the `type` parameter to the Graph API, even when we weren't using a search that needed it? Technically we don' t need to do that, but it doesn't hurt to leave it there. Feel free to improve the code so that the type is not passed if it's "`feed`" or "`home`", though.

Summary

We've learned a lot about how to find data in the Graph. Are you surprised by how limited our search options are? After all, even the website search can be narrowed down with more options than we have available.

Don't worry – in Chapter 7 we'll see how to use a more powerful resource than Graph URLs to search and sort data from the Graph. But before that, I think it's time we stopped merely looking at Graph data, and started creating some of our own. That's what we'll cover in the next chapter.

Key takeaways:

- The basic search query Graph URL is: `https://graph.facebook.com/search?type=«type»&q=«query»`
- The `type` parameter can be any of the following:
    - `page`
    - `post` (which is the default, if `type` is unspecified)
    - `event`
    - `group`
    - `user`
    - `checkin`
    - `place`
- If type is set to `place`, then two other parameters are required:
    - `center`, a location specified by a latitude and longitude, separated by a comma
    - `distance`, the maximum distance in meters from the `center` location that the place being searched for can be
- Search data is returned in Graph List JSON format, not as a Compound Object
- Paging works; all Graph Lists of results support `offset`/`limit` paging, and `since`/`until` paging is supported when sensible (example for posts)
- You can also provide an access token in the URL, using `access_token=«access_token»` as usual

- Without an access token, certain types of search (like `user`) cannot be performed

- When using an access token, search results are tailored to the authorized user: people are ranked higher in the search if they live nearby, for example

- Some search types require a certain extended permission to be granted before returning any results – see `http://developers.facebook.com/docs/authentication/permissions` for more details

- You can set the locale of certain properties of JSON objects returned by using the locale URL parameter: `https://graph.facebook.com/«id»?locale=fr_FR`

- You can also filter Post search results to only shows those made by people that use a certain locale: `https://graph.facebook.com/search?type=post&q=«query»&locale=fr_FR`

- A full list of locales is available at `http://facebook.com/translations/FacebookLocales.xml`

- You can filter the entries from your news feed using this Graph URL: `https://graph.facebook.com/me/home?access_token=«access_token»&q=«query»`

- You can filter the Graph for everything that a given friend has posted using this Graph URL: `https://graph.facebook.com/«username»/feed?access_token=«access_token»&q=«query»`

Pop Quiz

1. What's gone wrong if the results you obtain from a Graph URL search don't match those from a website search?

    a. Incorrect parameters were passed to the Graph URL

    b. An incorrect Graph URL was used

    c. A user's privacy settings don't allow applications to access their data

    d. Potentially any of the above

2. What's odd about the results you get from `https://graph.facebook.com/«username»/feed?q=«query»` and those you get from `https://graph.facebook.com/«username»/feed`?

    a. They can be obtained even if the user's privacy settings are turned all the way up

    b. The first doesn't act as a filter for the second, unlike all the other Graph Search URLs

    c. The two URLs always return exactly the same JSON as each other

3. What difference does it make to use an access token when searching through a Graph URL?

    a. Results are personalised so that more relevant results rank higher

    b. Results are returned faster

    c. More search parameters are available

    d. More types of search (like `user`) can be used

6
Adding to the Graph

We've spent a lot of time observing the Graph, both as anonymous outsiders and as authenticated users. We understand the different types of node and the connections between them. Now it's time to create some of our own.

In this chapter, you will learn:

- How to create new Graph Objects using the Graph API
- How to delete existing objects from the Graph
- The limitations of the Graph API for adding to the Graph versus the Facebook website

Let's get started...

Hello, Facebook!

I'm not usually a fan of "Hello World" applications, but it's so relevant here that I will make an exception. We'll start by posting a message to the logged-in user's Wall.

Time for action – posting to the user's feed

We'll keep it simple to start with. Just let the user enter a line of text, and post it to their Wall.

The Visualizer project contains a UI window for doing this—it looks like the following screenshot:

To make this window appear, we must enable another hidden option in `CustomGraphContainerController.as`. Open that file and tell it that we want to use "basic" publishing capabilities by adding the line highlighted in the following code:

```
public function CustomGraphContainerController(a_graphControlContainer:
   GraphControlContainer)
{
   super(a_graphControlContainer);
   this._showListCounts = true;
   this._showListFilters = true;
   this._canShowSearchUI = true;
   this._publishingCapability = PublishingCapabilities.BASIC;

   _requestor = new SDKRequestor();
   addEventListenersToRequestor();
   //we must wait for the Requestor to initialise before we can do
   // anything else with it
   _requestor.addEventListener(Event.COMPLETE, onRequestorInitialize);

   _requestor.initialize();
}
```

You must import the `PublishingCapabilities` class for this to compile, so do so:

```
import graph.controls.publishing.PublishingCapabilities;
```

Compile and upload the application, then load it in your browser. Load your profile's `feed` connection, and notice the new **Publish** button that appears:

Clicking on this button will make the **Post to Wall** window appear.

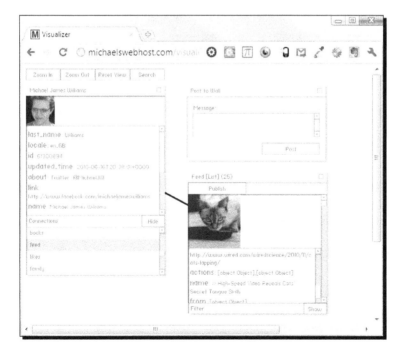

When the user types in their message and clicks on **Post**, we want the message to get posted to their Wall. At the moment, the code is set up to pass an AS3 object containing the message to a method called `publish()` in the class which `CustomGraphContainerController` extends. Just as in previous chapters, we'll override this method and write new code to handle the Facebook integration.

In `CustomGraphContainerController.as`, add this function:

```
override public function publish(a_publishObject:PublishObject):void
{
   super.publish(a_publishObject);
}
```

The `PublishObject` class contains a property called `message` that holds the message which the user typed into the **Post to Wall** window. We need to import this class:

```
import graph.apis.base.PublishObject;
```

That takes care of the UI. Next, we'll pass this object to a method inside our `Requestor` to deal with publishing the post on Facebook. Add a new function, `publish()`, to `IRequestor.as`:

```
package graph.apis.base
{
   import flash.events.IEventDispatcher;
   import graph.GraphRequest;

   public interface IRequestor extends IEventDispatcher
   {
      function request(a_request:GraphRequest):void;
      function attemptToAuthenticate(...permissions):void;
      function initialize():void;
      function search(a_query:String = "", a_type:String = "",
        a_userID:String = ""):void;
      function publish(a_publishObject:PublishObject):void;
   }

}
```

The `PublishObject` instance contains all of the information that we need, so it's the only parameter we'll pass to this method.

Now add stub `publish()` functions to both `SDKRequestor.as` and `HTTPRequestor.as`:

```
public function publish(a_publishObject:PublishObject):void
{

}
```

You will also need to import `PublishObject` in both of those classes:

```
import graph.apis.base.PublishObject;
```

We'll start, as usual, by writing the code for `HTTPRequestor`, so change the line in the `constructor` function of `CustomGraphContainerController.as` that instantiates the `_requestor` object so that it creates an `HTTPRequestor`:

```
_requestor = new HTTPRequestor();
```

Finally, change `CustomGraphContainerController.as` so that its `publish()` method calls the `publish()` method of the `Requestor`:

```
override public function publish(a_publishObject:PublishObject):void
{
    super.publish(a_publishObject);
    _requestor.publish(a_publishObject);
}
```

Everything's in place, but how do we post the message from the Visualizer to our actual Facebook Wall?

Request methods

Publishing a message to a user's Wall isn't any more complex than filtering information from it—we use the Graph URL, `https://graph.facebook.com/me/feed`, and pass it two parameters:

- ◆ The access token, and
- ◆ The message to post

The difference comes in how we pass those parameters. We cannot simply load the URL anymore. Try it yourself: browse to `https://graph.facebook.com/me/feed?access_token=«access_token»&message=Hello`. It will return your feed in JSON format, but won't post to it.

We still use a `URLLoader` and a `URLRequest`, but we use a different `request` method.

What's a request method?

An HTTP `request` method is a way of telling the web server what kind of action we want it to take when we ask it for a page or some other resource.

By default, an AS3 `URLRequest` uses an HTTP `request` method called `GET`; this is a "safe" method, so-called because it doesn't ask the server to change any information, merely to pass some back—which is all what we've needed up to this point in the book.

Publishing a wall post obviously causes a change, so we should use an "unsafe" method—in this case, POST. This is the same method used when submitting a web page form that changes or adds some data, like when ordering a book from Amazon.

 For security reasons, Flash Player 10 and above will allow only the POST method to be used if the user initiates the load. This means that your application cannot post to the Graph automatically (for instance, based on how long the user has been logged in); instead, you must always publish from, say, a button's MOUSE_CLICK event handler function.

Time for action – using the POST method

1. To specify that we want to use the POST method, we change the method property of URLRequest (after all, POST is a request method). Another class, flash.net.URLRequestMethod, contains consts with all the permitted values, so import it in HTTPRequestor.as:

```
import flash.net.URLRequestMethod;
```

2. We set up the URLLoader, URLRequest, and URLVariables instances in the same way as we do in the request() and search() methods:

```
public function publish(a_publishObject:PublishObject):void
{
  var loader:URLLoader = new URLLoader();
  var urlRequest:URLRequest = new URLRequest();
  var variables:URLVariables = new URLVariables();
}
```

3. Because we want to post to our own Wall, we use our profile's feed connection as the URL—there's no separate **Post to Wall** URL:

```
public function publish(a_publishObject:PublishObject):void
{
  var loader:URLLoader = new URLLoader();
  var urlRequest:URLRequest = new URLRequest();
  var variables:URLVariables = new URLVariables();

  urlRequest.url = "https://graph.facebook.com/me/feed";
}
```

4. Now we use the POST const from the URLRequestMethod class to set the request method:

```
public function publish(a_publishObject:PublishObject):void
{
```

```
    var loader:URLLoader = new URLLoader();
    var urlRequest:URLRequest = new URLRequest();
    var variables:URLVariables = new URLVariables();

    urlRequest.url = "https://graph.facebook.com/me/feed";
    urlRequest.method = URLRequestMethod.POST;
}
```

5. The URL parameters required are the `message` (which can be found in the `PublishObject` parameter) and the `accessToken`. Add them like so:

```
public function publish(a_publishObject:PublishObject):void
{
    var loader:URLLoader = new URLLoader();
    var urlRequest:URLRequest = new URLRequest();
    var variables:URLVariables = new URLVariables();

    urlRequest.url = "https://graph.facebook.com/me/feed";
    urlRequest.method = URLRequestMethod.POST;

    if (this.accessToken != "")
    {
        variables.access_token = this.accessToken;
    }
    variables.message = a_publishObject.message;
    urlRequest.data = variables;
}
```

6. Next, add the usual event listeners to the `URLLoader`, and tell it to start loading (which in this case means posting):

```
public function publish(a_publishObject:PublishObject):void
{
    var loader:URLLoader = new URLLoader();
    var urlRequest:URLRequest = new URLRequest();
    var variables:URLVariables = new URLVariables();

    urlRequest.url = "https://graph.facebook.com/me/feed";
    urlRequest.method = URLRequestMethod.POST;

    if (this.accessToken != "")
    {
        variables.access_token = this.accessToken;
    }
    variables.message = a_publishObject.message;
```

```
    urlRequest.data = variables;

    loader.addEventListener(Event.COMPLETE, onPublishComplete);
    loader.addEventListener(IOErrorEvent.IO_ERROR, onIOError);
    loader.load(urlRequest);
}
```

7. Create an event handler function for the `COMPLETE` event:

```
private function onPublishComplete(a_event:Event):void
{
    dispatchEvent(new DialogEvent(DialogEvent.DIALOG,
        "Publish complete!"));
}
```

> Remember, the `DialogEvent` can be used to display a dialog box within the Visualizer project, containing any message you please. You'll need to `import events.DialogEvent` to use it, though.

Compile, upload, and execute the SWF and you will find that... it doesn't work.

What just happened?

To find out why this didn't work, we can add a new type of event listener to the `URLLoader`—an `HTTPStatusEvent` listener.

This type of event is returned by the server and dispatches before the `IO_ERROR` or `COMPLETE` events. Its `status` property contains the "HTTP code" of the response, which is a simple shorthand to explain the response status. For example, `404` is an HTTP status code meaning "Not Found". There's a full list at `http://en.wikipedia.org/wiki/List_of_HTTP_status_codes`, but in general you will see:

- `200`: If there were no problems
- `400`: If the request you sent was badly formed (most likely due to a typo in the URL variables)
- `403`: If you are not allowed to access whichever resource you requested
- `404`: If the resource that you requested was not found on the server
- `500`: If there was another problem (like insufficient permissions)

(You may also see `0` if Flash Player is unable to detect the HTTP response code due to some condition in its environment.)

This can be useful additional information to have to help narrow down an `IO_ERROR` problem, or to detect a problem that doesn't dispatch an `IO_ERROR` event.

So, to find out what's causing the problem, let's add an event listener to our `URLLoader`.

Time for action – listening for errors

1. To listen for the `HTTPStatusEvent`, we must first import the class to `HTTPRequestor.as`:

```
import flash.events.HTTPStatusEvent;
```

2. Next, add the listener to the `URLLoader` within the `publish()` method:

```
public function publish(a_publishObject:PublishObject):void
{
  var loader:URLLoader = new URLLoader();
  var urlRequest:URLRequest = new URLRequest();
  var variables:URLVariables = new URLVariables();

  urlRequest.url = "https://graph.facebook.com/me/feed";
  urlRequest.method = URLRequestMethod.POST;

  if (this.accessToken != "")
  {
    variables.access_token = this.accessToken;
  }
  variables.message = a_publishObject.message;
  urlRequest.data = variables;

  loader.addEventListener(Event.COMPLETE, onPublishComplete);
  loader.addEventListener(IOErrorEvent.IO_ERROR, onIOError);
  loader.addEventListener(HTTPStatusEvent.HTTP_STATUS,
    onHTTPStatusReturned);
  loader.load(urlRequest);
}
```

...and add a handler function:

```
private function onHTTPStatusReturned(a_event:HTTPStatusEvent):void
{
  dispatchEvent(new DialogEvent(DialogEvent.DIALOG,
    "HTTP status: " + a_event.status));
}
```

3. For the full gamut of response collection, we might as well add a "security error" event listener; this type of event is dispatched to report some of the types of security errors that occur while trying to do some sort of asynchronous operation (like load data).

```
import SecurityErrorEvent:
import flash.events.SecurityErrorEvent;
```

...add an event listener to the URLLoader:

```
public function publish(a_publishObject:PublishObject):void
{
  var loader:URLLoader = new URLLoader();
  var urlRequest:URLRequest = new URLRequest();
  var variables:URLVariables = new URLVariables();

  urlRequest.url = "https://graph.facebook.com/me/feed";
  urlRequest.method = URLRequestMethod.POST;

  if (this.accessToken != "")
  {
    variables.access_token = this.accessToken;
  }
  variables.message = a_publishObject.message;
  urlRequest.data = variables;

  loader.addEventListener(Event.COMPLETE, onPublishComplete);
  loader.addEventListener(IOErrorEvent.IO_ERROR, onIOError);
  loader.addEventListener(HTTPStatusEvent.HTTP_STATUS,
      onHTTPStatusReturned);
  loader.addEventListener(SecurityErrorEvent.SECURITY_ERROR,
    onSecurityError);
  loader.load(urlRequest);
}
```

...and create a handler function:

```
private function onSecurityError(a_event:SecurityErrorEvent):void
{
  dispatchEvent(new DialogEvent(DialogEvent.DIALOG,
    "Security error: " + a_event.text));
}
```

4. Compile, upload, and execute the Visualizer, and try to post on your own Wall again.

It still won't work, but you'll see a dialog like this:

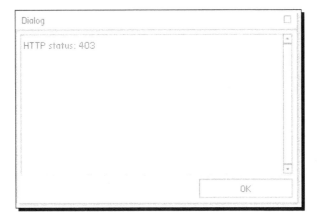

What just happened?

The dialog says **HTTP status: 403**. As mentioned earlier, this means that we are not allowed to access the resource that we were trying to access—that is, we're not allowed to post to the Wall. In other words, we don't have permission... or rather, we haven't been granted the extended permission required.

It's possible that you'll see an HTTP status code response of 500, instead. That's okay—it's a fairly generic error message which means "there was a problem," in this case. The cause is likely still the lack of the extended permission.

Of course, if you had granted your application the permission needed earlier in the book, you won't have seen any problems at all!

Time for action – granting the required permission

1. Before this can work, we must grant the application the publish_stream extended permission, so alter the onRequestorInitialize() function within CustomGraphContainerController.as, like so:

```
private function onRequestorInitialize(a_event:Event):void
{
  _requestor.attemptToAuthenticate(
    ExtendedPermissions.READ_STREAM,
    ExtendedPermissions.PUBLISH_STREAM);
}
```

2. Compile, upload, and try it again. You'll see the **Request for permission** pop up when you load the page:

3. Click on **Allow**, then open your `feed` List Renderer, and click on **Publish**. Enter some text in the box:

...and click on **Post**. Check your Wall on the Facebook website:

 Michael James Williams Hello World!
5 seconds ago via MichaelJW's Visualizer 🔒 · Like · Comment

Did it work?

If so, congratulations! If not, check that:

◆ Your access token is still valid,

◆ Your URLVariables parameters have the correct names, and

◆ You have definitely granted the application the correct permissions (check your **Application Settings** on the Facebook website)

What just happened?

You've successfully published data on Facebook without using the Facebook website itself.

On your Wall post, check out the "via" text—it's a link to your application's profile page. This helps prevent developers from impersonating users or applications; everyone can see which application made the post. It also helps your application to spread, as other Facebook users can see the posts that your application makes and click the link to find out how to install.

You may find it annoying to have a dialog pop up with the HTTP status code every single time, so I recommend changing the onHTTPStatusReturned() method inside HTTPRequestor.as so that it displays the dialog only if there's a problem—that is, if the HTTP code returned is anything other than 200 or 0:

```
private function onHTTPStatusReturned(a_event:HTTPStatusEvent):void
{
    if ((a_event.status != 0) && (a_event.status != 200))
    {
        dispatchEvent(new DialogEvent(DialogEvent.DIALOG, "HTTP status:
" + a_event.status));
    }
}
```

We've managed to create a post from scratch; now let's do it using the SDK.

Time for action – posting via the SDK

There are two ways to post data to Facebook using the SDK. The first involves the Facebook.api() method that we've been using all along, so let's start with that.

Normally, we pass three parameters to this method:

◆ A URL stub

◆ A callback function

◆ An AS3 object containing the arguments to pass to Facebook (in this case, just message)

When publishing, we need to pass a fourth variable:

- The HTTP `request` method to use

From our work with the HTTP Requestor, you already know that this needs to be `POST`. So, modify the `publish()` method of `SDKRequestor.as`, like so:

```
public function publish(a_publishObject:PublishObject):void
{
  var urlStub:String = "/me/feed";
  Facebook.api(urlStub, publishComplete,
    { message:a_publishObject.message },
    URLRequestMethod.POST
  );
}
```

Make sure that you import `flash.net.URLRequestMethod`.

Next, you'll need to create the `publishComplete()` function to be used as a callback:

```
private function publishComplete(result:Object, fail:Object):void
{

}
```

We don't need to add event listeners for HTTP statuses or security errors when using the SDK; just check whether the `result` is `null`; if so, more details should be in the `fail` object:

```
private function publishComplete(result:Object, fail:Object):void
{
  if (result != null)
  {
    dispatchEvent(new DialogEvent(DialogEvent.DIALOG,
      "Publish complete!"));
  }
  else
  {
    dispatchEvent(new DialogEvent(DialogEvent.DIALOG,
      "Publish failed. Details: " + String(fail)));
  }
}
```

Make sure that you import `events.DialogEvent` if you want to use it.

That's all that we need to do. Open `CustomGraphContainerController.as` and instantiate the `Requestor` as an SDK `Requestor` in the `constructor` function:

```
_requestor = new SDKRequestor();
```

We've already granted our application the `publish_stream` extended permission, so there's no need to do that again, but feel free to remove it and request it again. (See Chapter 3 for more information.)

Compile the Visualizer, upload it, and load it in your browser, making sure that you go to the right web page. The results should be the same as with the HTTP `Requestor`:

 Michael James Williams Hello World!
5 seconds ago via MichaelJW's Visualizer 🔒 · Like · Comment

If not, check the dialog box to see what information the `fail` object contains.

What just happened?

You're now able to post to your own Wall either through the custom code we built, or through the official SDK. In both cases, a `URLRequest` is used, though the SDK encapsulates it so that you don't have to deal with it.

As mentioned earlier, the SDK contains two methods for posting to the Graph—the second is to use the `Facebook.postData()` method. This takes three arguments:

- ◆ A URL stub
- ◆ A callback function
- ◆ An `AS3` object containing the arguments to pass to Facebook

...and posts them to Facebook. Under the surface (at least at the time of writing), all it does is call the `Facebook.api()` method that we're using, passing it the three arguments listed, plus `POST`. This means that there's no important difference between the two, so it doesn't matter which one you use.

Going further with Wall Posts

The simple message we just posted is properly called a **Status Message**, which is defined as a single piece of text, posted on the user's own Wall (see `http://developers.facebook.com/docs/reference/api/status`). If you look at the metadata of the `Graph` Object representing the Wall post that you just created in your feed, you'll see its `type` property is `status`.

But Wall posts can feature more than just plain text:

Michael James Williams

Michael found a lost Groovy Cow on their farm. Oh no!
Michael was tending their cows when a confused but charming Groovy Cow caught their eyes! This Groov...

See more

 3 seconds ago via FarmVille · Comment · Like · Adopt the Groovy Cow

Michael James Williams

Michael's chickens are mighty hungry!
Michael could use some help feeding their chickens! Happy, fed chickens give more Mystery Eggs!

18 seconds ago via FarmVille · Comment · Like · Feed their chickens

This type of Wall post is called a Post object by the Facebook documentation (`http://developers.facebook.com/docs/reference/api/post`). The distinction between a Post and a Status Message is arbitrary, though, as Post objects still have a `type` property of `status` and still use the same code interface. The practical difference is a Status Message will appear beside your name on the Facebook website, while a Post will not.

Let's see how to create a Post.

Time for action – publishing rich posts

To avoid confusion, I'll use the term **rich post** to refer to a Wall post that uses more than just plain text. Besides `message`, there are eight additional parameters we can pass to the `URLVariables` object:

- `picture`
- `link`
- `name`
- `caption`
- `description`
- `source`
- `actions`
- `privacy`

We'll concentrate on `message`, `picture`, `link`, `name`, `caption`, and `description` first, and find out what they do by publishing a rich post that uses them.

The Visualizer can be configured to display a window with input fields for all six of these parameters, instead of just `message`. To do so, find this line in `CustomGraphContainerController.as`:

```
this._publishingCapability = PublishingCapabilities.BASIC;
```

...and replace it with this:

```
this._publishingCapability = PublishingCapabilities.COMPLETE;
```

When you click on the **Publish** button on your `feed` List Renderer, you'll see the new window:

The **Post** button still passes an instance of `PublishObject` to the same function, `publish()`, in the class that `CustomGraphContainerController` extends. The difference from before is that the `PublishObject` has more properties set.

Specifically, it can have any of these properties:

◆ `message`

◆ `pictureURL`: Corresponds to `picture`

◆ `linkURL`: Corresponds to `link`

- linkName: **Corresponds to** name
- caption
- description

Our existing code already passes the instance of PublishObject to the publish() method of whichever Requestor is currently being used, so those are the only methods we need to alter.

Open HTTPRequestor.as and edit its publish() function like so:

```
public function publish(a_publishObject:PublishObject):void
{
  var loader:URLLoader = new URLLoader();
  var urlRequest:URLRequest = new URLRequest();
  var variables:URLVariables = new URLVariables();

  urlRequest.url = "https://graph.facebook.com/me/feed";
  urlRequest.method = URLRequestMethod.POST;

  if (this.accessToken != "")
  {
     variables.access_token = this.accessToken;
  }
  variables.message = a_publishObject.message;
  variables.picture = a_publishObject.pictureURL;
  variables.link = a_publishObject.linkURL;
  variables.name = a_publishObject.linkName;
  variables.caption = a_publishObject.caption;
  variables.description = a_publishObject.description;
  urlRequest.data = variables;

  loader.addEventListener(Event.COMPLETE, onPublishComplete);
  loader.addEventListener(IOErrorEvent.IO_ERROR, onIOError);
  loader.addEventListener(HTTPStatusEvent.HTTP_STATUS,
     onHTTPStatusReturned);
  loader.addEventListener(SecurityErrorEvent.SECURITY_ERROR,
     onSecurityError);
  loader.load(urlRequest);
}
```

Similarly, edit the `publish()` function in `SDKRequestor.as`:

```
public function publish(a_publishObject:PublishObject):void
{
  var urlStub:String = "/me/feed";
  Facebook.api(urlStub, publishComplete,
   {
      message:a_publishObject.message,
      picture:a_publishObject.pictureURL,
      link:a_publishObject.linkURL,
      name:a_publishObject.linkName,
      caption:a_publishObject.caption,
      description:a_publishObject.description
   },
    URLRequestMethod.POST
   );
}
```

Test the Visualizer on your host. Here's some test data from Wikipedia and Wikimedia Commons:

- `message`: Hello Britain!

- `picture`: http://upload.wikimedia.org/wikipedia/commons/thumb/a/ ae/Flag_of_the_United_Kingdom.svg/200px-Flag_of_the_United_ Kingdom.svg.png

- `link`: http://en.wikipedia.org/wiki/Union_Flag

- `name`: Union Flag

- `caption`: en.wikipedia.org

- `description`: The Union Flag, also known as the Union Jack, is the flag of the United Kingdom

This is the result:

What just happened?

It's easier to see what the different properties represent with a labeled screenshot:

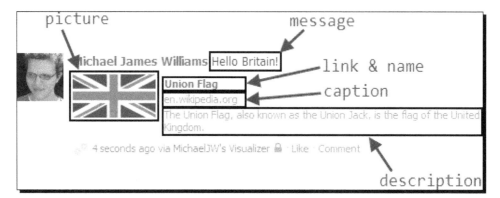

You don't have to use all of the properties possible in a rich post; look at these Farmville rich posts again:

These don't use a `message` or a `caption`.

It is common to allow only the user to set the message: if the user has just set a high score in your game and you want to allow them to post about it on their Wall, you might allow them to write a message while you set the image, link, description, and caption. This will help you maintain your game's branding while your users spread the word about it on their Walls.

A note on images: That small image in the post is still hosted on Wikimedia Commons, but is accessed via a proxy PHP hosted on Facebook's server—`http://platform.ak.fbcdn.net/` in this case. The `crossdomain.xml` on that server is as follows:

```
<cross-domain-policy>
    <site-control permitted-cross-domain-
policies="master-only"/>
    <allow-access-from domain="*"/>
</cross-domain-policy>
```

This means that your application can access the `BitmapData` of the image directly without any sandbox security issues, no matter where the original image was hosted.

The actual Graph Object created looks like this:

```
{
 "id": "«redacted»",
 "from": {
   "name": "Michael James Williams",
   "id": "«redacted»"
 },
 "message": "Hello Britain!",
 "picture": "http://platform.ak.fbcdn.net/www/app_full_proxy.php?a
pp=«redacted»&v=1&size=z&cksum=«redacted»&src=http%3A%2F%2Fupload.
wikimedia.org%2Fwikipedia%2Fcommons%2Fthumb%2Fa%2Fae%2FFlag_of_the_
United_Kingdom.svg%2F200px-Flag_of_the_United_Kingdom.svg.png",
 "link": "http://en.wikipedia.org/wiki/Union_Flag",
 "name": "Union Flag",
 "caption": "en.wikipedia.org",
 "description": "The Union Flag, also known as the Union Jack,
     is the flag of the United Kingdom.",
 "icon": "http://graph.facebook.com/images/icons/hidden.gif",
 "actions": [
   {
     "name": "Comment",
     "link": "http://www.facebook.com/«redacted»/posts/«redacted»"
   },
   {
     "name": "Like",
     "link": "http://www.facebook.com/«redacted»/posts/«redacted»"
   }
 ],
 "privacy": {
   "description": "Friends only",
```

```
    "value": "ALL_FRIENDS"
  },
  "type": "link",
  "created_time": "2010-11-19T00:28:10+0000",
  "updated_time": "2010-11-19T00:28:10+0000",
  "attribution": "MichaelJW's Visualizer"
}
```

Note the fields: `message`, `picture`, `link`, `name`, `caption`, `description`. For a non-rich post (a Status Message), these fields simply aren't included, rather than being empty strings.

The icon and attribution fields refer to the application's settings: the icon is `hidden.gif` because it hasn't been changed from the default. Note that there's no indication of the ID of the application (other than in the URL of the image via proxy), so unfortunately we can't figure out the link to the profile page of the application that posted this message using the Graph API.

Something else to note: the `type` field is set to `link` rather than `post`. This means that there are three separate types of Graph Object—Status Message, Post, and now Link (`http://developers.facebook.com/docs/reference/api/link`)—which are essentially the same, but with different amounts of data attached.

Have a go hero

You know those quizzes of the formula, "Which (Member of Currently Popular Band)/(Character in Classic Animated Movie)/(Type of Ice Cream) Are You?"

Make one of those in Flash. The actual UI should be pretty easy to create, and the questions should be fun to think up (I don't think those quizzes use particularly advanced expert systems to make their match). The key part here is posting the data to the quiz taker's wall. A rich post is perfect for this; you can include an image of the person/character/food that the user was matched up with and a link to the quiz for others to take.

Posting to another Wall

The authenticated user is not the only one with a Wall. Everyone on Facebook has a Wall, and so do all the Pages and Groups and Events. How can we post to those?

It's even simpler than adding new variables. We just change the URL that we want to post to—to post to the Wall of Bob Smith (`bob.smith`), instead of `https://graph.facebook.com/me/feed` we'd open a `URLRequest` to `https://graph.facebook.com/bob.smith/feed` (or, if using the SDK, use a Graph URL stub of `/bob.smith/feed`).

The same is true for any other Object with a Wall: POST the message to `https://graph.facebook.com/«ID»/feed`. You can publish rich posts to these too, and the JSON looks the same.

You don't even need a different extended permission for this; `publish_stream` will let you post to the user's Wall, the user's friends' Walls, and the Walls of Pages, Groups, Events, and anything else with a feed.

Time for action – posting to another Wall using the Visualizer

The `PublishObject` that gets passed to the `publish()` method of the `Requestor` contains a property, owner ID with the value of the ID of the Graph Object owning the connection list whose **Publish** button was pressed.

This makes it very simple to construct the Graph URL (or Graph URL stub) required. Open `HTTPRequestor.as` and modify the `publish()` method as follows:

```
public function publish(a_publishObject:PublishObject):void
{
  var loader:URLLoader = new URLLoader();
  var urlRequest:URLRequest = new URLRequest();
  var variables:URLVariables = new URLVariables();

  urlRequest.url = "https://graph.facebook.com/";
  urlRequest.url += a_publishObject.ownerID;
  urlRequest.url += "/feed";
  urlRequest.method = URLRequestMethod.POST;

  if (this.accessToken != "")
  {
     variables.access_token = this.accessToken;
  }
  variables.message = a_publishObject.message;
  variables.picture = a_publishObject.pictureURL;
  variables.link = a_publishObject.linkURL;
  variables.name = a_publishObject.linkName;
  variables.caption = a_publishObject.caption;
  variables.description = a_publishObject.description;
  urlRequest.data = variables;

  loader.addEventListener(Event.COMPLETE, onPublishComplete);
  loader.addEventListener(IOErrorEvent.IO_ERROR, onIOError);
  loader.addEventListener(HTTPStatusEvent.HTTP_STATUS,
     onHTTPStatusReturned);
  loader.addEventListener(SecurityErrorEvent.SECURITY_ERROR,
     onSecurityError);
  loader.load(urlRequest);
}
```

Make this similar change to the `publish()` method in `SDKRequestor.as`:

```
public function publish(a_publishObject:PublishObject):void
{
  var urlStub:String = "/" + a_publishObject.ownerID + "/feed";
  Facebook.api(urlStub, publishComplete,
    {
      message:a_publishObject.message,
      picture:a_publishObject.pictureURL,
      link:a_publishObject.linkURL,
      name:a_publishObject.linkName,
      caption:a_publishObject.caption,
      description:a_publishObject.description
    },
    URLRequestMethod.POST
  );
}
```

That's all you need to do; now you can post on any Wall you have access to.

Actions, privacy, and source

The `actions`, `privacy`, and `source` parameters are a little more complicated than the others, as they require a JSON to be passed, rather than just a `String`. Fortunately, it's just as easy to create a JSON from a native `AS3` object as it is to do the opposite.

Actions

Let's start by looking at the `actions` parameter. Take another look at the JSON representation of the Graph Object that we created earlier in the chapter. It contains a node called `actions`:

```
"actions": [
  {
    "name": "Comment",
    "link": "http://www.facebook.com/«redacted»/posts/«redacted»"
  },
  {
    "name": "Like",
    "link": "http://www.facebook.com/«redacted»/posts/«redacted»"
  }
]
```

Now look again at the Wall post:

The `actions` are the links underneath the post that other Facebook users can click.

We can add our own user-defined action, such as "Visit my website" or "Plant some crops", by passing it in a JSON to the `actions` parameter.

Time for action – literally

1. Open `HTTPRequestor.as` and find the `publish()` function. Create a native AS3 object within the function like so:

```
var actionObj:Object = [ {
    name:"Visit my Twitter Page",
    link:"http://twitter.com/MichaelJW"
} ];
```

Square brackets define an array, so we could type this as an `Array` rather than an `Object`, but it doesn't really matter.

2. Next, in the same function, use the JSON library that we've used before to decode this object into a JSON string:

```
var actionString:String = JSON.encode(actionObj);
```

3. Now, add this `String` as a property of the `URLVariables` object, called `actions`:

```
variables.message = a_publishObject.message;
variables.picture = a_publishObject.pictureURL;
variables.link = a_publishObject.linkURL;
variables.name = a_publishObject.linkName;
variables.caption = a_publishObject.caption;
variables.description = a_publishObject.description;
variables.actions = actionString;
urlRequest.data = variables;
```

4. Make similar changes in `SDKRequestor.as`:

```
public function publish(a_publishObject:PublishObject):void
{
  var urlStub:String = "/" + a_publishObject.ownerID + "/feed";
  var actionObj:Object = [ {
    name:"Visit my Twitter Page",
    link:"http://twitter.com/MichaelJW"
  } ];
  var actionString:String = JSON.encode(actionObj);
  Facebook.api(urlStub, publishComplete,
   {
      message:a_publishObject.message,
      picture:a_publishObject.pictureURL,
      link:a_publishObject.linkURL,
      name:a_publishObject.linkName,
      caption:a_publishObject.caption,
      description:a_publishObject.description,
      actions:actionString
   },
      URLRequestMethod.POST
   );
}
```

5. You will need to import `com.adobe.serialization.json.JSON`. Test this out:

What just happened?

You've added an **app-specific action** to posts coming from your project. You can add only one such action to each post, but of course, it doesn't have to be the same for every single post.

The `action` is a functional hyperlink; clicking on it would take you to my Twitter page. Facebook adds a URL parameter, `ref=nf`, to the end of all such links, though, so test them out first—for example, trying to load `http://google.com?ref=nf` gives you a `404` message.

Many applications and games use some user-specific data in the URL. For example, a game's link might point to `http://gamehomepage.com/user.php?ID=«user_id»`, where the User ID is filled in with code at the time of posting.

Privacy

Look again at the JSON Post from earlier—this time, at the `privacy` node:

```
"privacy": {
    "description": "Friends only",
    "value": "ALL_FRIENDS"
},
```

My default privacy setting is to have my Wall posts be visible to my friends only (as denoted by the little lock icon to the left of the action links). However, we can change this for specific posts.

Time for action – setting a Post's privacy settings

We set this option in much the same way as we set the app-specific action—using an AS3 object encoded into a JSON string.

1. In the `publish()` function of `HTTPRequestor.as`, create a new object:

```
var privacyObj:Object = {
    value:"EVERYONE"
}
```

2. As before, encode it into a JSON string:

```
var privacyString:String = JSON.encode(privacyObj);
```

...and pass it to the `URLVariables`:

```
variables.message = a_publishObject.message;
variables.picture = a_publishObject.pictureURL;
variables.link = a_publishObject.linkURL;
variables.name = a_publishObject.linkName;
variables.caption = a_publishObject.caption;
variables.description = a_publishObject.description;
variables.actions = actionString;
variables.privacy = privacyString;
urlRequest.data = variables;
```

3. Add similar code to `SDKRequestor.as`:

```
public function publish(a_publishObject:PublishObject):void
{
  var urlStub:String = "/" + a_publishObject.ownerID + "/feed";
  var actionObj:Object = [ {
    name:"Visit my Twitter Page",
    link:"http://twitter.com/MichaelJW"
  } ];
  var actionString:String = JSON.encode(actionObj);

  var privacyObj:Object = {
    value:"EVERYONE"
  }
  var privacyString:String = JSON.encode(privacyObj);

  Facebook.api(urlStub, publishComplete,
   {
     message:a_publishObject.message,
     picture:a_publishObject.pictureURL,
     link:a_publishObject.linkURL,
     name:a_publishObject.linkName,
     caption:a_publishObject.caption,
     description:a_publishObject.description,
     actions:actionString,
     privacy:privacyString
   },
     URLRequestMethod.POST
   );
}
```

4. By setting `value` to `EVERYONE`, we will make the post visible to anyone who can see your Wall, not just your friends.

What other options are there?

Well, `value` can be set to:

- ❏ `EVERYONE`
- ❏ `ALL_FRIENDS`
- ❏ `NETWORKS_FRIENDS`
- ❏ `FRIENDS_OF_FRIENDS`

The meanings of those are pretty obvious, apart from NETWORKS_FRIENDS (which allows your friends plus anyone in your networks to see the post).

There's one other possible setting for value: CUSTOM. Using this allows you to specify two other properties of privacyObj—networks and friends.

For the networks property, enter a comma-separated list of the IDs of the networks that should be allowed to see your post, like so:

```
var privacyObj:Object = {
  value:"EVERYONE",
  networks:"network1,network2,network3"
}
```

To allow all networks to see the post, just enter 1 as the value.

For the friends property, enter one of the following:

- EVERYONE
- NETWORKS_FRIENDS
- FRIENDS_OF_FRIENDS
- ALL_FRIENDS
- SELF
- NO_FRIENDS

Again, it's pretty clear what each of these do. NO_FRIENDS lets you allow only people in specified networks to see the post.

There is another possible setting for friends: SOME_FRIENDS. This gives you another pair of properties that you can set for privacyObj—allow and deny. Each of these properties takes a comma-separated list of user IDs (mixed with friend list IDs); allow defines who can see the post, while deny defines who cannot.

So, your privacyObj could look like this:

```
var privacyObj:Object = {
    value:"CUSTOM",
    networks:"network1,network2,network3",
    friends:"SOME_FRIENDS",
    allow:"bob.smith,joe.q.faikname",
    deny:"bill.the.jerk"
}
```

What just happened?

As you can see, you have fine-grained control over the level of privacy of posts on a user's Wall. The "correct" settings to use depend entirely on your application and its audience; just be aware of what's possible.

 You cannot control the privacy setting of posts that your users publish on the Walls of other users, Pages, Events, or Groups; these are always able to be seen by anybody who can see the other Wall.

Source

The `source` parameter supposedly allows you to embed small photo galleries, Flash objects (like video clips), and MP3 music into a Post, as well as custom key-value pairs that (although invisible on the Facebook website) can be read later on by your application or any other.

Unfortunately, at the time of this writing this feature is not working correctly with the Graph API. Take a look at what can be done with the `source` parameter here: `http://developers.facebook.com/docs/guides/attachments`. With luck, the feature will be fully implemented and documented by the time you read this paragraph.

Deleting Graph Objects

We've mastered adding posts, but what about removing them later?

Time for action – deleting a Post

Facebook's interface for deleting a post is a **Remove** button that appears on hover:

The Visualizer project also has a **Delete** button; let's see how to add it.

Time for action – deleting Posts using the Visualizer

1. We can enable the **Delete** button of the Visualizer by using yet another hidden option. In the `constructor` function of `CustomGraphContainerController.as`, set `this._showDeleteButtons` to `true`:

```
public function CustomGraphContainerController(a_
graphControlContainer: GraphControlContainer)
{
  super(a_graphControlContainer);
  this._showListCounts = true;
  this._showListFilters = true;
  this._canShowSearchUI = true;
  this._publishingCapability = PublishingCapabilities.COMPLETE;
  this._showDeleteButtons = true;

  _requestor = new SDKRequestor();
  addEventListenersToRequestor();
  //we must wait for the Requestor to initialise before we can do
  // anything else with it
  _requestor.addEventListener(Event.COMPLETE,
     onRequestorInitialize);

  _requestor.initialize();
}
```

2. The next time you load the SWF, you'll see this new button in the List Renderer:

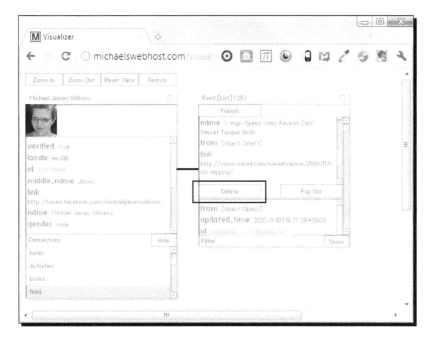

Like the **Publish** button, when **Delete** is clicked it calls a method, deleteGraphObject(), in the class that CustomGraphContainerController extends. Let's override this function so that we can use it. In CustomGraphContainerController.as, add this:

```
override protected function deleteGraphObject(a_objectID:String):void
{
  super.deleteGraphObject(a_objectID);


}
```

Note that the ID of the Graph Object whose **Delete** button was pressed is passed to the function. That's all we need!

1. We'll add similar deleteObject() methods to the Requestors. In IRequestor. as, add this line:

```
package graph.apis.base
{
  import flash.events.IEventDispatcher;
  import graph.GraphRequest;

  public interface IRequestor extends IEventDispatcher
  {
    function request(a_request:GraphRequest):void;
    function attemptToAuthenticate(...permissions):void;
    function initialize():void;
    function search(a_query:String = "", a_type:String = "",
      a_userID:String = ""):void;
    function publish(a_publishObject:PublishObject):void;
    function deleteObject(a_objectID:String):void;
  }

}
```

2. Now, add this stub function to both SDKRequestor.as and HTTPRequestor.as:

```
public function deleteObject(a_objectID:String):void
{

}
```

3. Make sure that you call this function in CustomGraphContainerController.as:

```
override protected function deleteGraphObject (a_objectID
:String):void
{
  super.deleteGraphObject(a_objectID);
  _requestor.deleteObject(a_objectID);
}
```

We'll start (as always) with the code for HTTPRequestor, so make sure that your project is set up to instantiate _requestor as an HTTPRequestor rather than an SDKRequestor. We can re-use much of the code from publish(); modify the deleteObject() function of HTTPRequestor.as like so:

```
public function deleteObject(a_objectID:String):void
{
  var loader:URLLoader = new URLLoader();
  var urlRequest:URLRequest = new URLRequest();
  var variables:URLVariables = new URLVariables();

  if (this.accessToken != "")
  {
    variables.access_token = this.accessToken;
  }
  urlRequest.data = variables;

  loader.addEventListener(Event.COMPLETE, onDeleteComplete);
  loader.addEventListener(IOErrorEvent.IO_ERROR, onIOError);
  loader.addEventListener(HTTPStatusEvent.HTTP_STATUS,
    onHTTPStatusReturned);
  loader.addEventListener(SecurityErrorEvent.SECURITY_ERROR,
    onSecurityError);
  loader.load(urlRequest);
}
```

4. Note that instead of using onPublishComplete() as the COMPLETE event handler function, we're using onDeleteComplete(), so create that function:

```
private function onDeleteComplete(a_event:Event):void
{
  dispatchEvent(new DialogEvent(DialogEvent.DIALOG, "Deleted!"));
}
```

Which URL do we need to use? It's simple: we use the Graph URL of the Graph Object that we want to delete. So:

```
public function deleteObject(a_objectID:String):void
{
  var loader:URLLoader = new URLLoader();
  var urlRequest:URLRequest = new URLRequest();
  var variables:URLVariables = new URLVariables();

  urlRequest.url = "https://graph.facebook.com/";
  urlRequest.url += a_objectID;

  if (this.accessToken != "")
```

```
    {
       variables.access_token = this.accessToken;
    }
    urlRequest.data = variables;

    loader.addEventListener(Event.COMPLETE, onDeleteComplete);
    loader.addEventListener(IOErrorEvent.IO_ERROR, onIOError);
    loader.addEventListener(HTTPStatusEvent.HTTP_STATUS,
       onHTTPStatusReturned);
    loader.addEventListener(SecurityErrorEvent.SECURITY_ERROR,
       onSecurityError);
    loader.load(urlRequest);
}
```

5. What about HTTP `request` methods? There's one called `DELETE`, which is definitely not a "safe" method, and does exactly what we want. Unfortunately, due to security concerns, we can only use it in AIR. Here's the code, in case you write an AIR application later:

```
public function deleteObject(a_objectID:String):void
{
  var loader:URLLoader = new URLLoader();
  var urlRequest:URLRequest = new URLRequest();
  var variables:URLVariables = new URLVariables();

  urlRequest.url = "https://graph.facebook.com/";
  urlRequest.url += a_objectID;
  urlRequest.method = URLRequestMethod.DELETE;

  if (this.accessToken != "")
  {
     variables.access_token = this.accessToken;
  }
  urlRequest.data = variables;

  loader.addEventListener(Event.COMPLETE, onDeleteComplete);
  loader.addEventListener(IOErrorEvent.IO_ERROR, onIOError);
  loader.addEventListener(HTTPStatusEvent.HTTP_STATUS,
      onHTTPStatusReturned);
  loader.addEventListener(SecurityErrorEvent.SECURITY_ERROR,
     onSecurityError);
  loader.load(urlRequest);
}
```

If you're making a regular Flash Player SWF, though, the `URLRequestMethod` class won't even have a `DELETE` const.

For regular SWF-based applications, it's not that much more complicated. We have only two choices of `request` method—`GET` and `POST`. Because `GET` is a safe method, we can't use it to delete an object from the server, so we must use `POST`:

```
public function deleteObject(a_objectID:String):void
{
  var loader:URLLoader = new URLLoader();
  var urlRequest:URLRequest = new URLRequest();
  var variables:URLVariables = new URLVariables();

  urlRequest.url = "https://graph.facebook.com/";
  urlRequest.url += a_objectID;
  urlRequest.method = URLRequestMethod.POST;

  if (this.accessToken != "")
  {
     variables.access_token = this.accessToken;
  }
  urlRequest.data = variables;

  loader.addEventListener(Event.COMPLETE, onDeleteComplete);
  loader.addEventListener(IOErrorEvent.IO_ERROR, onIOError);
  loader.addEventListener(HTTPStatusEvent.HTTP_STATUS,
    onHTTPStatusReturned);
  loader.addEventListener(SecurityErrorEvent.SECURITY_ERROR,
     onSecurityError);
  loader.load(urlRequest);
}
```

...but we can easily tell Facebook to treat it as a `DELETE` request by passing a new parameter—`method=delete`:

```
public function deleteObject(a_objectID:String):void
{
  var loader:URLLoader = new URLLoader();
  var urlRequest:URLRequest = new URLRequest();
  var variables:URLVariables = new URLVariables();

  urlRequest.url = "https://graph.facebook.com/";
  urlRequest.url += a_objectID;
  urlRequest.method = URLRequestMethod.POST;
```

```
if (this.accessToken != "")
{
  variables.access_token = this.accessToken;
}
variables.method = "delete";
urlRequest.data = variables;

loader.addEventListener(Event.COMPLETE, onDeleteComplete);
loader.addEventListener(IOErrorEvent.IO_ERROR, onIOError);
loader.addEventListener(HTTPStatusEvent.HTTP_STATUS,
    onHTTPStatusReturned);
loader.addEventListener(SecurityErrorEvent.SECURITY_ERROR,
    onSecurityError);
loader.load(urlRequest);
}
```

This works just as well as the AIR version, and only costs us one extra line of code.

To delete an object using the SDK, we could use `Facebook.api()`, but there's a shortcut method: `Facebook.deleteObject()`. This takes two parameters—the ID of the Graph Object to delete, and a callback function. This makes the required code very simple; add this to `SDKRequestor.as`:

```
public function deleteObject(a_objectID:String):void
{
  Facebook.deleteObject(a_objectID, deleteComplete);
}

private function deleteComplete(result:Object, fail:Object):void
{
  if (result != null)
  {
    dispatchEvent(new DialogEvent(DialogEvent.DIALOG, "Deleted!"));
  }
  else
  {
    dispatchEvent(new DialogEvent(DialogEvent.DIALOG,
      "Deletion failed. Details: " + String(fail)));
  }
}
```

Compile, upload, and test the new changes by deleting one of your posts from your Wall.

What just happened?

You should have seen a Wall post get deleted from Facebook.

 Stop Press: Shortly before this book was published, Facebook appeared to change the Graph API so that Wall posts could only be deleted by an application if that application was used to publish them in the first place. Previously, it was possible to delete any posts on the logged-in user's Wall, as well as any posts made by the user on other Walls. At time of this writing, the official Graph API documentation does not mention this restriction. So, if you're having problems deleting posts, try creating one through the Visualizer first, and then deleting that.

Once again this requires only the `publish_stream` extended permission; by now you should have a good idea of how powerful this permission is. You can use the same code to delete other kinds of Graph Object, not just posts. If your application has permission to modify or create an object, it has permission to delete it, too.

If you try to delete a post through the Facebook website, it will ask for confirmation:

This is a good idea, and worth using for the interface of your own projects. The Visualizer doesn't ask for confirmation, and doesn't even remove the Post from the List Renderer once deleted—though this does let you see what happens if you try to remove a Post that's already been deleted...

Publishing other kinds of Graph Object

All the types of Graph Object that can be created can be created with the same basic steps as a Wall Post:

◆ Use `POST HTTP` request method

◆ Set parameters with a `URLVariables` object

◆ Make sure that you have an access token and the required permissions

The Graph List Renderer's **Publish** button always creates a window with inputs that are appropriate to the Graph List being rendered, and this in turn always passes its values to the `publish()` function of `CustomGraphContainerController`, inside a `PublishObject` instance, so you can experiment with the different types.

The `PublishObject` also includes the type of connection to which the user is attempting to publish, in a property called `connectionType`. You can use this to decide which parameters to pass to the Graph, and also to construct the Graph URL to `POST` these parameters to.

An up-to-date list of the properties of each Graph Object that can be set when publishing them can be found through the documentation, available here: `http://developers.facebook.com/docs/reference/api/`.

Let's go through them in turn.

Comments

Comments are text messages that can be left on Wall Posts, and look like this:

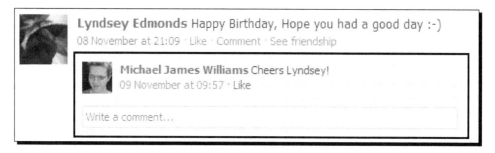

The URL to request is: `https://graph.facebook.com/«post_id»/comments`.

There's only one possible parameter: `message`, the text to be displayed.

They require the `publish_stream` permission.

Comments do not display the name of the application that created them.

Likes

When a user "likes" a Wall Post that fact shows under the post, visible to all:

The user will also receive e-mails and notifications whenever someone comments on that post. It's like a mini-subscription, as well as a sign of approval.

The URL to request is:

`https://graph.facebook.com/«post_id»/likes.`

There are no possible parameters.

Likes require the `publish_stream` permissions.

What about "liking" other Graph Objects?

In Chapter 2, we looked at how "like" connections joined people to TV shows, movies, music, interests, and activities; the "like" connection is responsible for many of the strands in the Graph's Web. Yet, the Graph API will not allow us to "like" anything other than posts (even trying to like a comment will result in an `HTTP Status Code 500`).

Facebook has said that they have no plans to allow developers to create "likes" for anything else. It seems their aim is to make sure no user ever clicks an unofficial "like" button (or at least, a "like" button in a context that Facebook hasn't approved; `Yelp.com` has its own design of "like" button, as they are a partner site to Facebook).

So, unfortunately, it's not possible to alter the user's television, movies, interests, or activities through the Graph API.

Deleting Likes

Likes don't have their own ID, so we can't delete a like by attempting to delete `https://graph.facebook.com/«like_id»`. Instead, we must use this URL: `https://graph.facebook.com/«graph_object_id»/likes`.

As you know, this is the Graph URL for a connection, which would return a Graph List if we tried to load it in a browser. However, when we try to delete the URL using the process described in the *Deleting Graph Objects* section, it will make the authorized user "unlike" the Graph Object.

Notes

Notes are like little blog posts:

The URL to request is: `https://graph.facebook.com/«id»/notes`.

The ID can only be that of the current user, or of a Page which the user administers.

Despite generally being longer than Wall Posts—and being able to support images, links, and formatted text—they take only two parameters:

- `message`: This is an HTML string (so that explains the ability to add images and formatting)
- `subject`: The title of the note

To post a note, your application will need the `publish_stream` permission.

Events

Events look like this:

Like a Page, an Event has a Wall, which can be posted to using the /«event_id»/feed URL stub. Events also have lists of members, but they are divided into four categories:

- ◆ Attending: /«event_id»/attending
- ◆ Maybe attending: /«event_id»/maybe
- ◆ Not attending: /«event_id»/declined
- ◆ Awaiting reply: /«event_id»/noreply

Guests can be invited and can RSVP with any of the first three categories; this makes scheduling somewhat easier.

Another connection, /«event_id»/invited, contains a list of everyone that has been invited to the event, regardless of their RSVP.

To create an Event, POST to this URL: https://graph.facebook.com/«id»/events.

(As with Notes, the ID can only be the current user's or that of a Page which the user administers.)

Three parameters are required:

+ name: The title of the event
+ start_time: The time and date the event will start
+ end_time: The time and date the event will finish

Both dates must be entered in **ISO 8601** format. Wikipedia has more information than you'll ever need to know on ISO 8601 (http://en.wikipedia.org/wiki/ISO_8601); a quick summary is that **1:25pm UTC, November 8, 2010** is represented as 2010-11-08T13:25Z. If you let the user enter the time manually, make sure that you alter it to match the UTC time zone!

To create an event, your application will need the create_event permission.

Event RSVPs

Rather than having a single URL to POST an RVSP to, and setting the type of RSVP in the parameters, Facebook uses three separate URLs:

+ https://graph.facebook.com/«event_id»/attending: attending
+ https://graph.facebook.com/«event_id»/maybe: maybe attending
+ https://graph.facebook.com/«event_id»/declined: not attending

When RSVPing through the website interface, Facebook will ask the user for an (optional) note to go along with it (such as, "Sorry I can't make it that day," or "Really looking forward to it!"). However, the preceding three URLs take no parameters; if you want to let the user post an RSVP note, simply publish it to the /feed connection as a Post.

RVSPs aren't written in stone; the user can change their mind later. Bear this in mind when designing an application for this! Don't stop them from setting their RSVP status just because they already have one.

To RSVP, your application will need the rsvp_event permission.

Albums

An **Album** is a collection of `Photo` objects.

To create an album, request this URL: `https://graph.facebook.com/«id»/albums`.

As with Events and Notes, the ID can be either the authenticated user's, or that of a page which the user administers.

Only two parameters are supported:

◆ `name`: The title of the album

◆ `description`: The album's description (optional)

Creating a new album requires the `publish_stream` permission. You may want to grant the `user_photos` permission as well to allow the user to view the actual album and photos!

Photos

To upload a photo to an album, we must post two parameters to `https://graph.facebook.com/«album_id»/photos`:

- `message`: The caption of the photo
- `source`: The actual photo file (JPG, PNG, and so on)

To get the photo file from the user's computer to the `source` parameter, we can use a `FileReference`. Full documentation for the `FileReference` class is available here: `http://help.adobe.com/en_US/FlashPlatform/reference/actionscript/3/flash/net/FileReference.html`.

To allow the user to select a local file, import the `flash.net.FileReference` class.

Create a new instance of this class:

```
var fileRef:FileReference = new FileReference();
```

Add an event listener to the class to call a function once the user has selected a file:

```
fileRef.addEventListener(Event.COMPLETE, onSelectFile);
```

Use the `browse()` method to create a OS-specific dialog that will allow the user to select a file from their hard drive:

```
fileRef.browse();
```

The **Publish** window of the Visualizer for a `photos` connection takes care of all this, passing the `FileReference` instance to the `publish()` method as a property of `PublishObject` called `source`.

To actually upload the file through our `HTTPRequestor`, we cannot use a `URLLoader`. Instead, we must load the file using the `FileReference` itself. So, instead of this:

```
variables.message = a_publishObject.message;
variables.picture = a_publishObject.pictureURL;
variables.link = a_publishObject.linkURL;
variables.name = a_publishObject.linkName;
variables.caption = a_publishObject.caption;
variables.description = a_publishObject.description;
variables.actions = actionString;
variables.privacy = privacyString;
urlRequest.data = variables;

loader.addEventListener(Event.COMPLETE, onPublishComplete);
loader.addEventListener(IOErrorEvent.IO_ERROR, onIOError);
```

```
loader.addEventListener(HTTPStatusEvent.HTTP_STATUS,
    onHTTPStatusReturned);
loader.addEventListener(SecurityErrorEvent.SECURITY_ERROR,
    onSecurityError);
loader.load(urlRequest);
```

...we must do this:

```
variables.message = a_publishObject.message;
variables.source = a_publishObject.source;
urlRequest.data = variables;
a_publishObject.source.addEventListener(
    DataEvent.UPLOAD_COMPLETE_DATA, onPublishComplete);
a_publishObject.source.addEventListener(IOErrorEvent.IO_ERROR,
    onIOError);
a_publishObject.source.addEventListener(HTTPStatusEvent.HTTP_STATUS,
    onHTTPStatusReturned);
a_publishObject.source.addEventListener(
    SecurityErrorEvent.SECURITY_ERROR, onSecurityError);
a_publishObject.source.upload(urlRequest);
```

No real changes are needed for the SDK Requestor; it uses a `FileReference` and encapsulates the upload process. This means that we can just call `Facebook.api()` as usual:

```
Facebook.api(urlStub, publishComplete,
  {
    message:a_publishObject.message,
    source:a_publishObject.source
  },
  URLRequestMethod.POST
);
```

In each case, remember to change the URL stub to /«album_id»/photos.

Uploading a photo to an Album requires the `publish_stream` permission. As with Albums, you may want to grant the `user_photos` permission as well.

Not surprisingly, in order to add a photo to an Album, the user must either own the Album, or administer the Page which owns the Album.

Checkins

Checkins are used by Facebook Places and allow the user to post their current location and a message about that place.

To create a checkin, POST to this URL: `https://graph.facebook.com/«user_id»/checkins`.

The only ID allowed is that of the authenticated user (so you could use `me` instead).

Three parameters are supported:

- `coordinates`
- `place`
- `message`

The `coordinates` parameter must be a JSON string containing two properties—`latitude` and `longitude`. Use the `JSON.encode()` method from earlier in this chapter to turn a native AS3 object into a JSON string.

The `place` parameter should be the ID of a Place corresponding to the place the user is currently visiting. In Chapter 5, we saw how to search for Places near a given location, and retrieve their IDs.

The `message` parameter is optional—it's a simple comment by the user about what they're doing. For example, "Just went on the Log Flume at Alton Towers."

Creating a checkin requires the `publish_checkins` permission. You may wish to grant the `user_checkins` permission as well to allow the user to view their other checkins.

What about...?

There are a lot of things you can do via Facebook's website interface, but not through the Graph API. We've already looked at the restrictions to the "like" feature; what else is missing?

Sending inbox messages

It's possible to read inbox messages (as we saw in Chapter 5) but not to create and send them. Facebook had planned to allow apps to create inbox messages but this plan appears to have been scrapped. It's possible that this functionality will be included as part of the new messages; see Chapter 8 for a little more information on this.

Creating Pages, Groups, Applications, and Videos

It's not possible to create any of these types of Graph Object via the Graph API.

This is a little surprising—a Group is not that different from an Event, and a Page, in turn, is not that different from a Group. The lack of video creation ability is even stranger, as it means it's not possible to create a mobile application that uploads video directly to Facebook.

Not being able to create applications through other applications makes some sense though!

Changing biographical information

Your application can't alter the user's relationship status, current location, favorite quotations, record of education, or anything of the sort. Because the Graph API doesn't allow "liking/unliking" anything other than Wall posts, it means the user's entire Info box is "look but don't touch."

Making Friends

It's not possible for an application to send a friend request to another user, or to remove someone from the current user's friend list. (Although you can send other users enough rude messages to encourage them to remove the current user from their friend list.)

Inviting Friends to Events

You can create Events, but you can't invite anyone to them. Go figure.

Pop Quiz

1. Why do we need to use a different HTTP request method all of a sudden?

    a. We should have been using POST all along

    b. The Graph API changed since you read the previous chapter

    c. HTTP requires that we use an "unsafe" method when changing data

2. Why bother listening for different types of HTTP Status Codes?

    a. We need to do this now that we are using a different HTTP request method

    b. These codes can give us extra information about why a publishing attempt failed

3. What can we publish without an access token?

    a. Nothing

    b. Just Status Messages

    c. Just Likes

    d. Anything

Summary

So, you've learned how to create lots of different types of Graph Object: Posts, Comments, Events, and so on. You've also learnt how to destroy them if need be.

Were you surprised at what you couldn't do with the Graph API?

In the next chapter, we'll go back to examining the Graph, but we'll use a powerful new tool—**Facebook Query Language**.

Key takeaways:

◆ To publish via HTTP, use a `URLRequest`/`URLLoader`/`URLVariables` setup as usual, and include parameters for the new Graph Object in the `URLVariables` instance, alongside the access token.

    ❑ The URL to use is `https://graph.facebook.com/«id»/«connection»`. Make sure to use `flash.net.URLRequestMethod.POST`.

◆ To publish via the SDK, call `Facebook.api("«id»/«connection»", «callback», {parameter1:"value1", parameter2:"value2"}, URLRequestMethod.POST)`.

◆ Uploading photos requires a `FileReference`. Use `FileReference.browse()` to let the user pick an image from their hard drive.

    ❑ To upload via HTTP: Use `FileReference.upload()` rather than `URLLoader.load()`.

    ❑ To upload via the SDK: just pass the `FileReference` as the value of the `source` parameter in the `URLVariables` instance, and call `Facebook.api()` as usual.

◆ You cannot "like" anything other than a Post through the Graph API. This means we can't alter the user's interests or favorite TV programs.

- ◆ At the time of writing, we can only delete Posts that were created using the same application.

    - ❑ To do so via HTTP, just pass `method=delete` to `https://graph.facebook.com/«id»`, using `URLRequestMethod.POST`.

    - ❑ If using AIR, you can simply load `https://graph.facebook.com/«id»` using `URLRequestMethod.DELETE`.

    - ❑ To delete via the SDK, call `Facebook.deleteObject("«id»", «callback»)`.

    - ❑ The exception is when deleting a "like"; in this case, the URL stub to delete is `«id»/likes`.

- ◆ A full list of parameters and permissions required for publishing is available at `http://developers.facebook.com/docs/reference/api`.

- ◆ For security reasons, Flash Player 10 and above will not let your application publish anything via the `HTTP POST` method unless the user initiated the action (for instance, by clicking a button).

7
FQL Matters

The Graph is a terrific model for accessing the data in Facebook; it manages to take the huge amount of information on the site and make it easy and simple to access it.

Sometimes, however, we want a little extra control and a little extra power. That's where FQL comes in. It's a programming language designed for searching the Facebook databases – and it doesn't use the Graph.

In this chapter we shall:

- ◆ Recap the different models of data representation and visualization
- ◆ Get comfortable with FQL by using it to grab some Facebook data
- ◆ Learn how to use FQL to do (almost) anything we could do with the Graph
- ◆ Discover what the Graph is better at than FQL
- ◆ Find out how to detect which extended permissions have been granted
- ◆ Look at some advanced FQL features

So let's get on with it...

What is FQL?

FQL (pronounced as the acronym, "eff-cue-ell") is Facebook's version of the database language SQL. Don't know what SQL is? Don't worry, you don't need to. In this chapter, I'll assume you don't know anything about FQL, SQL, or databases yet. So before getting into what FQL is, let's take a step back and look at databases.

But what if I do already know SQL?

Even if you know SQL, it's worth reading this chapter to brush up on some concepts and learn the differences between FQL and regular SQL. In particular, check out the **Restrictions** section.

If you're experienced with SQL, you may be surprised by how many features FQL is missing. Most notably, there are no `INSERT`, `DELETE`, or `UPDATE` clauses. Also, `JOIN`, `GROUP BY`, and `LIKE` are missing; you must specify a set of fields to be returned, rather than typing `SELECT *`, and you can only specify one table in the `FROM` clause.

Understanding the FQL interface

We've been looking at the Facebook data as though it were structured in the Graph format laid out in Chapter 2, but really, this is just a model for the data; the Graph API acts like a wrapper, making it appear as though the data is structured in that way. It's not.

Does it matter how the data is structured? Not for our purposes. What matters is the interface we are given to access it with. So far, that interface has been the Graph API; we've obtained all our data through Graph URLs and processed them with AS3.

But there is another way of looking at the data, which is like a traditional database structure. In this case, all the data is kept in **tables**, organized into **columns, rows**, and **fields**. It's easier to explain with an example:

user						
uid	first_name	middle_name	last_name	name	sex	username
123456	Michael	James	Williams	Michael James Williams	male	michael_james_williams
789012	Joe	Quincy	Faikname	Joe Q Faikname	male	joe_q_faikname

Some columns have been left out for brevity.

This is one **table** of data. Specifically, it's the `user` table, as you can see from the following heading:

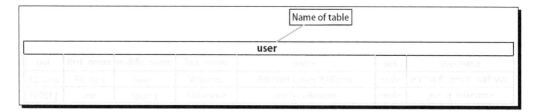

Each **column** represents an attribute of the data:

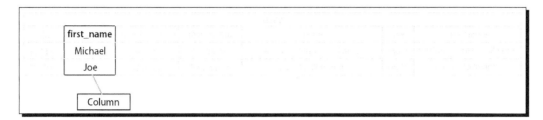

Each **row** corresponds to a single object, with all its attributes:

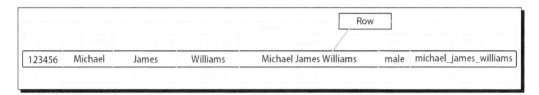

The intersection of a row and a column – that is, a single attribute of a single object – is called a **field**:

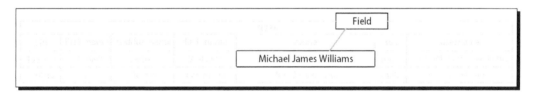

You could alternatively think of this like a spreadsheet; this is the simple, natural way of storing data in a grid. (Of course, if you're familiar with relational databases, you could just think of it as a relational database's table!)

Models of data

So now we've got three different models we can use when thinking about Facebook data:

1. The **AS3 object-oriented** model: We have classes containing certain properties, and instances of those classes containing information about a specific item. For example, we could have a class called User which contains certain properties, and define an instance of that class:

```
class User
{
  public var uid:int;
```

```
    public var first_name:String;
    public var middle_name:String;
    public var last_name:String;
}

var michael_james_williams:User = new User();
michael_james_williams.uid = 123456;
michael_james_williams.first_name = "Michael";
michael_james_williams.middle_name = "James";
michael_james_williams.last_name = "Williams";
```

2. The **Graph** model: items are all nodes in a graph, connected by edges. Each node contains information about its item, like name or ID.

3. The **relational database** model: all data is stored in tables, each having a column for each attribute and a row for each object, so as to form grids.

Representations of data

We also have multiple ways of *representing* data: we've used JSON throughout the book, but we could use XML, or a spreadsheet, or even just lists of properties in plain text.

The difference is, the three models are for visualizing the data, while JSON and so on are methods for storing, transmitting, and receiving data. The former is abstract and theoretical; the latter is concrete and practical.

Getting information

We know how to get information out of the database by means of the Graph model: we request an object (or list of objects), subject to certain criteria, and we retrieve a JSON representation of that object (those objects). The obvious next question is: how do we get this data if we're thinking in terms of a relational database model?

For this we use **Facebook Query Language** (**FQL** for short). It's a language quite different to object-oriented languages; it's designed specifically for getting information out of a relational database, unlike AS3 which is not designed to solve any specific problem. It differs heavily in syntax, too, as we'll see.

Let's take a look at an example, getting some information out of the `page` table:

page
page_id
name
website
type
location

Each of these – `page_id`, `name`, `website`, `type`, and `location` – are columns, just as `uid`, `first_name`, `middle_name`, `last_name`, `name`, `sex`, and `username` are for the `user` table.

Time for action – retrieving info from the Page table

So how do we use it? Well, we can't request objects, of course, because we're not using an Object model – but we don't even request rows, which are their close equivalents. We request specific fields. If all we're interested in is the URLs of Pages' associated websites, we can just request results from the "website" column:

```
SELECT website
```

Next, we have to specify the table we're interested in. In this case, that's "page":

```
SELECT website
FROM page
```

Now we specify a condition to narrow down the search:

```
SELECT website
FROM page
WHERE name = "Facebook"
```

(Note that when checking this condition, we use = rather than ==, unlike in AS3.)

These three elements make up a single "query". When we **run this query** – analogous to compiling an AS3 – we will receive `http://www.facebook.com/`, as this is the value of the field in the `website` column in the `page` table, in the row whose `name` is set to `Facebook`.

 It's common to see the FQL keywords typed in all capitals, like SELECT, FROM, and WHERE, but this isn't strictly necessary. It does help readability though.

So how do we run the query? Do we have to use a compiler? No, actually. All we have to do is pass it to Facebook using an API URL, which is very similar to a Graph URL except that it doesn't use the word "graph". No surprise there, as we're no longer viewing the data using the Graph model.

The API URL for an FQL query looks like this:

```
https://api.facebook.com/method/fql.query?query=FQL_QUERY
```

The API URL for an FQL query after entering all the details is as follows:

```
https://api.facebook.com/method/fql.query?query=SELECT website FROM
page WHERE name = "Facebook"
```

(Don't worry that we've removed the from the query; they don't matter.) Type this into your web browser and it'll encode it to:

```
https://api.facebook.com/method/fql.query?query=SELECT%20website%20
FROM%20page%20WHERE%20name%20=%20%22Facebook%22
```

When you load the page, what you'll see depends on the browser you're using. In Chrome, you'll just see this:

```
http://www.facebook.com/
```

Note: this is not JSON! No curly braces to be seen... still, that's what we expected, right?

View the source of the page (this is what you may see already if using a different browser):

```
<fql_query_responsexmlns="http://api.facebook.com/1.0/"
xmlns:xsi="http://www.w3.org/2001/XMLSchema-instance" list="true">
<page>
<website>http://www.facebook.com/</website>
</page>
<page>
<website/>
</page>
</fql_query_response>
```

This is XML-formatted data. I won't go into this now. It's good to know XML output is available, but we've used JSON so far, so why stop here? Let's ask Facebook to give us the results in JSON form; use the same URL but add a new parameter: "format=json".

Load this URL: `https://api.facebook.com/method/fql.` `query?format=json&query=SELECT%20website%20FROM%20page%20WHERE%20` `name%20=%20%22Facebook%22`

...to get this result:

```
[{"website":"http:\/\/www.facebook.com\/\n"},{"website":""}]
```

That's more like it. We've got two JSON objects, each with a single property called "website".

 If you prefer XML, you can use that instead. Just use the parameter "`format=xml`" instead of "`format=json`".

What just happened?

But wait – why do we have two fields, and why does the second have nothing in its `website` property?

We can find out by getting the IDs of each page, instead of the names, and using these IDs to view their related Graph Objects. First, construct a new FQL query:

```
SELECT page_id
FROM page
WHERE name = "Facebook"
```

Then, pass this to the relevant API URL:

`https://api.facebook.com/method/fql.query?format=json&query=SELECT%20` `page_id%20FROM%20page%20WHERE%20name%20=%20%22Facebook%22`

You'll get this output:

```
[{"page_id":20531316728},{"page_id":107885072567744}]
```

Load the Graph Objects for each ID, using the Graph URLs. First, the Page with ID of 20531316728:

`https://graph.facebook.com/20531316728`

```
{
    "id": "20531316728",
    "name": "Facebook",
    "picture": "http://profile.ak.fbcdn.net/hprofile-ak-snc4/
      hs624.snc3/27535_20531316728_5553_s.jpg",
    "link": "http://www.facebook.com/facebook",
    "category": "Technology",
```

```
    "username": "facebook",
    "founded": "February 4, 2004",
    "company_overview": "Millions of people use Facebook everyday to
       keep up with friends, upload an unlimited number of photos,
       share links and videos, and learn more about the people they
       meet.\n\n\"Like\" this page for ongoing updates on new products,
       announcements and stories. \n\nOther ways to connect with us:\
       nVisit the Facebook Blog at http://blog.facebook.com\nFollow us
       on Twitter: @facebook\nSubscribe to more video at
       http://www.youtube.com/facebook\n\n",
    "mission": "Facebook's mission is to give people the power to share
       and make the world more open and connected.",
    "fan_count": 17565186
}
```

Then, the Page with ID of 107885072567744:

```
https://graph.facebook.com/107885072567744

    {
        "id": "107885072567744",
        "name": "Facebook",
        "link": "http://www.facebook.com/pages/Facebook/107885072567744",
        "category": "Interest",
        "is_community_page": true,
        "description": "<p><b>Facebook</b> is a <a href=\"/pages/
           w/107511275938278\">social networking</a> website launched in
           February 2004 that is operated and privately owned by Facebook,
           Inc., with more than 500 million active users in July 2010.
           </p>",
        "fan_count": 299474
    }
```

Aha! The second one is a **community page** – a page about Facebook created and owned by Facebook users, rather than by Facebook itself. And if you load this Page on the Facebook website (using the URL in the link property) in your browser, you'll see there's nothing set for the Website field, which is why the second result we got from our first query was blank. Mystery solved.

Have a go hero – creating an FQL query builder

Create a Flash application that allows you to enter an FQL query, runs it, and displays the result. You'll need to make use of a, like we did back in Chapter 2. This will make it much easier to test the queries in the rest of the chapter!

What about connections?

So that's essentially the FQL equivalent of retrieving a single Graph Object. But what's the equivalent to getting a Graph Object's connections?

Understanding the way connections are formed in a database model is a much harder concept to grasp than with the Graph API model. (I wouldn't be surprised if this were one of the main motivations beyond the Graph API.) You have to work backwards, in a sense.

Let's use the idea of an album full of photos as an example. First, imagine we create an empty album called "Michael's Awesome Vacation Photos." It'll look like this, in the database model:

album		
aid	**owner**	**name**
«automatic»	«my user ID»	Michael's Awesome Vacation Photos

The `album` table has a `cover_pid` field, which is set to the ID of a picture that I want to set as the cover photo. So let's suppose I take a picture of the airport and upload it as my cover photo; it'll be auto-assigned an ID.

Now we can enter the airport photo's ID as the value for the album's `cover_pid` field:

album			
aid	**owner**	**name**	**cover_pid**
«automatic»	«my user ID»	Michael's Awesome Vacation Photos	«ID of airport photo»

We can illustrate this like so:

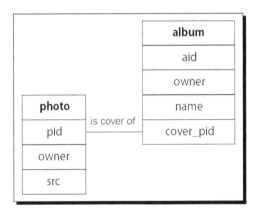

Read the line from left to right using the names of the tables (not the fields), and the verb written above the line: "The photo is the cover of the specified album."

Notice also that the photo table has a field called `aid`, which is set to the ID of the album that the photo belongs to. So the airport photo's table looks like this:

photo		
pid	**aid**	**owner**
«automatic»	«ID of album»	«my user ID»

Now we can draw another of these lines:

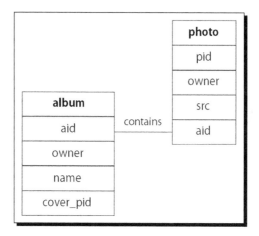

"The album contains the specified photo."

Of course, now we have the problem that we want to display both on the same diagram to make things neat, and that generally requires either tangling the lines, duplicating a table, or using awkward wording. We get off lightly in this example:

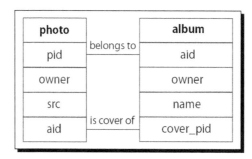

Okay, so that explains how one photo is connected to one album. We can find out which album has a certain photo as its cover with this FQL query:

```
SELECT aid
FROM album
WHERE cover_pid = «specific photo's ID»
```

Conversely, we can find which photo is the cover for an album with this query:

```
SELECT pid
FROM photo
WHERE pid = «album's cover_pid»
```

...actually, we can find out which photos are *in* an album with a very similar query:

```
SELECT pid
FROM photo
WHERE aid = «album's ID»
```

This can be considered "backwards" compared to the Graph model, because with the Graph you take the album object and ask for all its related photos: "`album/photos`"; with the database model you take the photo table and ask for all rows belonging to an album: "`FROM photo WHERE aid = «album id»`".

Photos, Albums, and their Owners

Did you notice that both the `photo` and `album` tables have a field called "`owner`", containing the owner's user ID? Now, surely we can connect these. A first attempt at doing so might look like this:

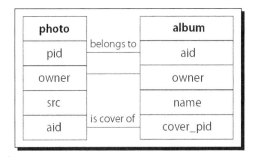

What word would go above that line? A smart guess would be "is", since the owners are the same – watch out, because this is a trap.

These "entity relationship" lines don't connect *fields* in the database tables; they connect entire tables, *using* the fields as a "key". Remember the rule of reading the verbs from left to right. If we used "is" as the verb, it would say, "The photo is the specified album" which is clearly wrong.

We can't connect the two tables directly because their relationship is through another entity. Let me show you what I mean:

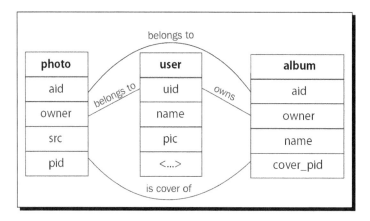

We've now got three tables (photo, album, user) and four relationships:

- The photo belongs to the specified album
- The photo is a cover of the specified album
- The photo belongs to the specified user
- The user owns the specified album

So we can get the URLs of all of a specific user's photos using this query:

```
SELECT src
FROM photo
WHERE owner = «user's ID»
```

Have a go hero – getting a user's albums

See if you can write an equivalent query for getting the URLs of all of a specific user's albums. The names of the tables and columns that you'll need to use are in the diagram above, but you can find more information at `http://developers.facebook.com/docs/reference/fql/`.

Remember, you can always check your query using an API URL call.

Primary keys

Have you noticed how one side of a relationship line always points to the main ID of a table?

- `photo.pid`
- `user.uid`
- `album.aid`

Each of these fields is called the **primary key** of its table. This means any given row can be identified using that field (and only that field); every row has a value in its primary key's field, and no two rows have the same primary key value.

We can make it easier to understand the relationships between tables by writing the names of the primary keys in bold type.

We also have a name for fields that link to primary keys of other tables, like:

- `photo.owner` (links to `user.uid`)
- `photo.aid` (links to `album.aid`)
- `album.cover_pid` (links to `photo.pid`)

We call these **foreign keys** and tend to write these in italics in any diagram.

Our earlier diagram of the **photo**, **user**, and **album** tables can thus be redrawn as shown in the next screenshot:

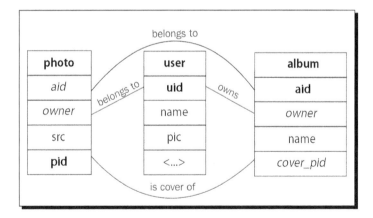

Crow's feet

So we have two lines connecting the album table and the photo table.

For a given album, what's so different about the results of these two queries?

```
SELECT pid
FROM photo
WHERE aid = «album ID»
```

and

```
SELECT pid
FROM photo
WHERE pid = «album's cover_pid»
```

The answer is, the first may return several photos' IDs, while the second will only ever return one. We can clarify this in the wording of our relationship sentences like so:

"The album contains **zero or more** photos"

"The album's cover is **one and exactly one** photo"

Note I've had to reverse the sentences to start with "the album" rather than "the photo" for these to make sense.

We can also represent this in the diagram; we use what's called **crow's foot notation**:

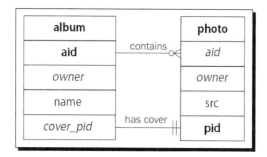

The three prongs ("**crow's foot**") on the right of the top line means "many" and the circle means "zero," so this reads as "zero to many" or "zero or more". The pair of dashes across the right of the bottom line means "one and exactly one".

This doesn't tell the whole story, though. Not all photos are the cover photo for an album. We need to reverse the sentences to explain that in words:

"The photo belongs to **one and exactly one** album"

"The photo is the cover of **zero or one** albums"

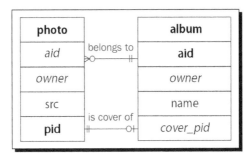

Here, the pair of dashes on the top line again means "one and exactly one," while the circle and dash means "zero or one." I've left the other markings on the lines, but since the tables are the other way around now, they're on the left rather than the right.

It's tricky to read these diagrams at first; the best thing to do is break them down into pairs of sentences like we've done here. You'll get the hang of it eventually.

Have a go hero – drawing your own crows' feet

Another way to learn how to use crow's foot notation is to draw your own diagrams. Redraw the diagrams connecting the photo, user, and album tables and add the appropriate markers to each side of the lines. Remember to start with the pairs of relationship sentences to figure out what you need to say!

You can do this with pencil and paper, but if you want to go further and draw diagrams for all the tables, consider using a piece of software like DbSchema: `http://www.dbschema.com/`. Remember, the list of tables and their columns is available at `http://developers.facebook.com/docs/reference/fql/`.

Link tables

How can we create the same links between friends? Well, this has to be a relationship between the user table and itself, so a good first guess would be:

"A user is friends with **zero or more** users"

...with the reverse sentence being exactly the same. So far, so good. It gets trickier when we try to draw it, though. Do either of these work?

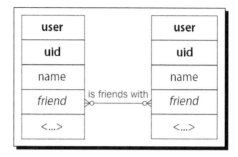

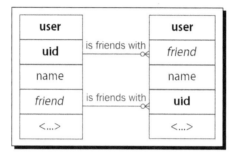

No. And this is a basic rule of the database model: you can't have "many-to-many" relationships between tables. Here we tried it where both tables were the same, but this rule applies even if that's not the case.

I guess we'd better give up then. Not really, of course. Instead, we use what's called a "link table":

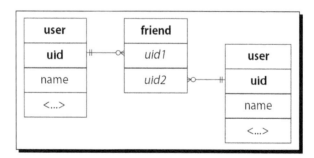

Labels for these relationships are tricky; since the link table is not a tangible thing, the proper label has to be something like, "is assigned to," which is not helpful. Really, the link table itself expresses the relationship, so you can often omit the labels altogether. Alternatively, label them as if they were connecting through the link table, like "is friends with".

This makes searching for a user's friends a little harder than searching for their photos. However, we can get a list of friends' IDs like so:

```
SELECT uid2
FROM friend
WHERE uid1 = «user's ID»
```

What just happened?

That query will get a list of IDs of all users that are friends with the specified other user. Don't worry, every row is duplicated with the order of IDs switched; if there's a row with "uid1 = 123" and "uid2 = 456" then there's another row with "uid1 = 456" and "uid2 = 123". This means you won't miss anyone if you only ask for values of uid2.

Getting a list of a user's friends' names is harder. Let's think about how we'd do it with the help of AS3.

Time for action – getting a user's friends' names with AS3

We can start by getting a list of the IDs of a user's friends using the query above:

```
SELECT uid2
FROM friend
WHERE uid1 = «user's ID»
```

From earlier in the chapter, you know that we can call this API URL to get that list:

```
https://api.facebook.com/method/fql.query?access_token=«access_
token»&format=json&query=SELECT%20page_id%20FROM%20page%20WHERE%20
name%20=%20%22Facebook%22
```

Except, actually, that won't work. Just like when using the Graph API to access private information, you'll need to use an access token. (See Chapter 3 for a reminder of how to generate one of these.)

The correct API URL, then, is:

```
https://api.facebook.com/method/fql.query?access_token=ACCESS_
TOKEN&format=json&query=SELECT%20page_id%20FROM%20page%20WHERE%20
name%20=%20%22Facebook%22
```

Given a user's ID, we can get their name using this query:

```
SELECT name
FROM user
WHERE uid = «user's ID»
```

So, we can loop through the JSON object returned to make a query like that for each user:

```
for each (var uid:String in jsonListOfFriendIDs)
{
  var query:String = "SELECT name FROM user WHERE uid = " + uid;
  callFQL(query);    //function that calls the API url with this query
}
```

What just happened?

We got a list of names of all the specified user's friends. Easy! But unfortunately this requires making an API call for each friend of the user. Facebook says the average number of friends per user is 160, so that's 161 API calls, just for a list of names... isn't there an easier way?

Time for action – an easier way

FQL's WHERE clause doesn't have to use an equals sign. We can use less than, more than, greater than or equal to, and so on — but more interestingly we can use an operator called **IN**.

1. Its working is shown in the following code:

```
SELECT name
FROM user
WHERE uid IN ('123', '456', '789')
```

2. That query will get the names of the three users with IDs of 123, 456, and 789. Since a query is just a string, we can construct one from a list of User IDs as shown in the following lines of code:

```
var query:String = "SELECT name FROM user WHERE uid IN ("
for each (varuid:String in jsonListOfFriendIDs);
{
  query += "'" + uid + "',";
}
query = query.substring(0, query.length - 1) + ")";  //replace
last comma with a closing parenthesis
callFQL(query);    //function that calls the API url with this
query
```

What just happened?

This code gets us the same information as before, but only requires two API calls, which is a pretty big improvement. If only we could get it down to one...

Time for action – getting it down to one API call

1. There's another way to use the IN operator:

```
SELECT name
FROM user
WHERE uid IN (
  SELECT uid2
  FROM friend
  WHERE uid1 = «user's ID»
)
```

2. Again, the whitespace doesn't matter, and is only to help readability; you can call it in a single line like so:

```
SELECT name FROM user WHERE uid IN (SELECT uid2 FROM friend WHERE
uid1='123')
```

3. Try it out using an API URL.

What just happened?

The query inside the parentheses is called a "**sub-query.**" Essentially we are making FQL do the same thing we just did with AS3: retrieve a list with one query and use it in another query.

Have a go hero – Mutual friends

I want to issue you the challenge of writing a query that gets all the mutual friends of two users: the logged-in user, and one other person. Unfortunately, just as you can't access a user's friend list through the Graph unless they've given your app permission to do so, you can't retrieve the same list through FQL (even as a sub-query) unless they've added the app.

Still, it's a good exercise. Get a friend to add your app, and try to write code that gets a list of the mutual friends of you and that person. Can you do it in a single FQL query?

Also, if you did write an FQL query builder in as part of the *Have A Go Hero* section earlier in the chapter, try adding the ability to authenticate with Facebook.

The Graph as a layer

For a given user — let's say the user with ID 123456789 — we can get info about all their friends using this Graph call:

```
123456789/friends
```

This will give us their friends' names and IDs. We can get exactly the same information from an FQL query as shown in the following code:

```
SELECT name, uid
FROM user
WHERE uid IN (
  SELECT uid2
  FROM friend
  WHERE uid1 = '123456789'
)
```

In fact, for *any* Graph API call, we can construct an equivalent FQL query. This means we can look at the Graph model as a layer on top of the database model; it gives us a simple way of accessing a limited number of FQL queries, almost like a collection of pre-programmed macros.

The converse is not true, however. Any Graph API call can be constructed in FQL, but there are a lot of FQL queries that have no equivalent Graph call. Master FQL, and you have a lot of control over the data returned. Here's a really simple example that demonstrates my point:

```
SELECT name, uid, pic
FROM user
WHERE uid IN (
  SELECT uid2
  FROM friend
  WHERE uid1 = '123456789'
)
```

This query gives us the same information as that `123456789/friends` Graph query, but it also gives us the URL to each user's profile picture (via the `pic` field), with just that one call.

Have a go hero – recreating existing Graph API calls in FQL

Look back at your most commonly used Graph API calls. How could you recreate them in FQL? More importantly, how could you enhance them with FQL? What extra data could you obtain?

Permissions

Just because you're not accessing data through the Graph doesn't mean you can grab whatever information you want. You're still subject to the same authentication requirements as before. For instance, you need an access token to run this query:

```
SELECT uid
FROM user
WHERE name="Michael James Williams"
```

Extended permissions are still relevant when using FQL. If you try to query the `mailbox_folder` table without any permissions, you'll receive an `error 612`, telling you that **mailbox requires the read_mailbox extended permission.**

At time of writing, there is no guide in the documentation that explains which extended permissions are required to access given tables (or fields). The closest is this page, which gives descriptions in terms of the Graph: `http://developers.facebook.com/docs/authentication/permissions`.

Checking existing permissions

One great feature that the database model offers but the Graph does not is a means to get a list of extended permissions granted to the current user.

This is by way of the `permissions` table, which has many columns:

 ◆ `uid` (integer) – A User ID (must be of the current user) or Page ID
 ◆ `publish_stream` (Boolean) – returns 1 if the user or page has the `publish_stream` permission, 0 otherwise
 ◆ `create_event` (Boolean) – returns 1 if the user or page has the `create_event` permission, 0 otherwise
 ◆ `rsvp_event` (Boolean) – returns 1 if the user or page has the `rsvp_event` permission, 0 otherwise

and so on. The table has one column for each of the possible permissions; in each case, the value will be 1 or 0.

So if the current user's ID is 123456, we can find out whether they have granted our app the `publish_stream` permission using the following FQL query:

```
SELECT publish_stream
FROM permissions
WHERE uid=123456
```

The JSON result looks like the following code:

```
[{"publish_stream":1}]
```

You can check multiple permissions at once:

```
SELECT publish_stream, create_event, rsvp_event
FROM permissions
WHERE uid=123456
```

giving you something like the following code:

```
[{"publish_stream":1,"create_event":0,"rsvp_event":0}]
```

Remember, a list of all extended permissions is available in the following URL: http://developers.facebook.com/docs/authentication/permissions.

Be careful when using this; it's not entirely reliable. Thanks to caching, the data in the table may be up to 15 minutes old, so you can't guarantee that it's true. You should still prepare your code for situations where it expects the user to have a certain extended permission but they don't.

Getting more information

Another table, `permissions_info`, holds information about the permissions themselves. It contains three columns:

- permission_name (string) – the name of the permission, like "publish_stream"
- header (string) –the name of the permission in plain English, like "Publish to my Wall"
- summary (string) – a short description of what the permission allows, like "publish content to my Wall"

Restrictions

The biggest restriction of FQL is that it cannot be used to do anything other than search. We can't use FQL to add, edit, or delete any data – it's strictly look, but don't touch.

This means you can't use an FQL query to delete all the wall posts you made in the middle of the night, to edit the captions of all the photos in an album, or to send a message to all your friends who live in the same neighborhood. Instead, you'll need to use a query to find the wall posts, photos, or friends in question, and then use AS3 and the Graph API to perform the actual actions.

Searches must use an indexable field

To speed up the performance of FQL searches, Facebook creates **indexes** of each table: copies of the tables that only contain a few of the columns of the originals. Much like the index in the back of a technical book, this makes it much faster to find something – as long as it's in the index.

For example, the `user` table is indexed by the `name` field (which contains the full name of the user), the `username` field, and also by its primary key, `uid`. Imagine that there are three separate lists created, each containing just the IDs, usernames, and full names of all the users; one list is ordered by ID, in numerical order, one by username, and the other is by full name in alphabetical order. If you now call this query:

```
SELECT uid
FROM user
WHERE name = "Michael James Williams"
```

then the database can take the list that is ordered by name, skip to the "M" section, and look for "Michael James Williams" within that section, finding matches much faster than if the results were in, say, the order in which the users signed up. That's roughly how indexing works.

Many databases will allow you to search for anything, but provide significantly faster results if your `WHERE` clause queries fields are **indexable**. With FQL, however, you can only call a query if your `WHERE` clause contains at least one indexable field.

So, what happens if we query the `user` table with a `WHERE` clause that only refers to the `first_name` field (which is not indexable, even though `name` is)?

```
SELECT uid
FROM user
WHERE first_name="Michael"
```

Try it out with an API URL:

```
https://api.facebook.com/method/fql.query?format=json&query=SELECT
uid FROM user WHERE first_name="Michael"
```

```
{"error_code":604,"error_msg":"Your statement is not indexable. The WHERE
clause must contain an indexable column. Such columns are marked with *
in the tables linked from http:\/\/wiki.developers.facebook.com\/index.
php\/FQL_Tables ","request_args":[{"key":"method","value":"fql.query"},
{"key":"format","value":"json"},{"key":"query","value":"SELECT uid FROM
user WHERE first_name=\"Michael\""}]}
```

At least we get a useful error message, rather than a blank JSON. (Well, quite useful; the URL needs to be changed to `http://developers.facebook.com/docs/reference/fql/`.)

Note that this restriction only requires *at least one* of the fields queried to be indexable. The fields specified in the SELECT clause can be any fields in the table specified in the FROM clause. And later in the chapter, you'll see how to query multiple fields at once inside a single WHERE clause, only one of which needs to be indexable.

Does this matter in practice?

In general, the fields that you actually need to use in a search query are indexable; it's rare that you'll want to search for a user based on the URL of their profile picture. There are exceptions to watch out for, though. For instance, in the event table, only the eid field (the primary key) is indexable, meaning that you cannot search across all events in the database to find one taking place in a specified location, or containing a specified term in its name.

Advanced FQL

What we've covered so far is enough to cover most of what you can do with Graph calls, and some more besides. Let's take a look at the more advanced features of FQL.

Operators

Just like if statements in AS3, FQL's WHERE clause can take both logical and comparison operators.

Comparison

We can use the mathematical comparison operators =, <, >, <=, >=, and !=. (An alternative to != is <>, which you may see in examples online.)

These all work the same as in AS3, with the exception of =, which is like AS3's ==; it's used for checking equality rather than assigning a value.

The most useful scenario for using these is when you want to filter out objects past a certain age.

Logical

AND, OR, and NOT will be familiar to you, although in AS3 we would write them as &&, ||, and !, respectively.

We already covered IN earlier in the chapter; this allows us to check whether a given item exists in a given list.

Have a go hero – getting a list of your events based on location

Earlier in the chapter we learned that we couldn't run this query:

```
SELECT eid
FROM event
WHERE location = 'london'
```

This is because the only indexable field in event is eid.

Here's one sneaky way around it:

```
SELECT eid
FROM event
WHERE eid != -1 AND location = 'london'
```

Unfortunately, it doesn't work. Facebook will tell you that "your statement is not indexable." Ah well.

So come up with a query that searches for events taking place in London that the current user is already aware of – you'll need to create a sub-query using the event_member table and the IN operator for this.

(The event_member table is a link table with two indexable fields: uid, which corresponds to a user, and eid, which corresponds to an event.)

Have a go hero – finding gatecrashers

Want a bigger challenge?

Pick an event where lots of photos were taken. Using FQL and AS3, write code that will take the ID of an event and a list of IDs of photo albums of that event, and output a list of names of people who were tagged in the albums but not invited to the event.

Ordering

The ORDER BY clause allows us to sort results on a specific field. For example, you can get a list of your own friends as shown in the following lines of code:

```
# SELECT name
# FROM user
# WHERE uid IN (

    * SELECT uid2
    * FROM friend
    * WHERE uid1 = « your User ID »
```

You can display them in alphabetical order by adding the following new clause:

```
SELECT name
FROM user
WHERE uid IN (
  SELECT uid2
  FROM friend
  WHERE uid1 = «your User ID»
)
ORDER BY name
```

Write `ORDER BY name DESC` to sort in descending order, or `ORDER BY name ASC` to sort in ascending order. The default is `ASC`.

This is great when retrieving data that needs to be displayed in a certain order inside Flash; all the work can be done at the server end, rather than having to take all the data and sort it with AS3. It cannot be done with a Graph call.

Paging

As with the Graph, there are two main methods of paging: by date, or by number.

Paging by date uses comparison operators:

```
SELECT aid
FROM album
WHERE owner = «your User ID» AND created < «latest date» AND created >
«earliest date»
```

You can also use arithmetic operators (+, -, /, *) to make date comparisons easier to read:

```
SELECT aid
FROM album
WHERE owner = «your User ID» AND created < «certain date» AND created
> «certain date» - 10
```

Paging by number uses `LIMIT` and `OFFSET`, just like with a Graph call:

```
SELECT aid
FROM album
WHERE owner = «your User ID»
LIMIT 15
OFFSET 30
```

See *Chapter 4* for more information on paging.

Extra functions

FQL supports a few extra functions; some make constructing queries easier, others add more power:

- `now()` – returns the current time
- `me()` – returns the ID of the current user
- `rand()` – returns a random number
- `strip_tags(field)` – removes HTML markup and encoding from the specified field
- `strlen(string)` – returns the length of the specified string
- `substr(string, startpos, length)` – returns a substring of the specified string
- `strpos(string, term)` – returns the position of the specified term within the specific string
- `lower(string)` – returns the specified string, converted to lower case
- `upper(string)` – returns the specified string, converted to upper case

You can use `now()` and `me()` to simplify the examples from Paging:

```
SELECT aid
FROM album
WHERE owner = me() AND created < now() AND created > now() - 10
```

Have a go hero – combining what you've learned

Can we use the `substr()` function to create an FQL call that gets a list of all the people whose name starts with M? If so, write the query; if not, explain why.

What about a list of people who are friends with the authenticated user and whose name starts with M?

Calling multiple queries at once

If you know you need to call more than one query, and the order in which these queries are called is not important, you can increase performance by calling them all with one API URL. All the results will be returned at once.

The syntax is:

```
https://api.facebook.com/method/fql.multiquery?queries=["SELECT x
FROM a WHERE c", "SELECT y FROM b WHERE d"]&access_token=«access_
token»
```

Although in this example I've only used very simple queries, you are not restricted to these.

Pop Quiz

1. When does it make sense to use FQL instead of the Graph API?

    a. When publishing information to Facebook

    b. When trying to retrieve a specific list of fields

    c. When attempting to find out the user's extended permissions

2. When does it make sense to use the Graph API instead of FQL?

    a. When publishing information to Facebook

    b. When trying to retrieve a specific list of fields

    c. When attempting to find out the user's extended permissions

3. How do columns and rows within database tables correspond to objects and properties within the AS3 model?

    a. Columns are like properties, rows are like objects

    b. Columns are like objects, rows are like properties

Summary

In this chapter, you went from knowing absolutely nothing about FQL to being able to do more advanced search queries with it than you could with the Graph API. You also learned about some techniques that the Graph API does not support, like how to get a list of extended permissions that the current user has been granted.

The key points are as follows:

◆ Databases arrange data into tables, columns, rows, and fields

◆ FQL stands for Facebook Query Language

◆ The API URL for submitting an FQL query is `https://api.facebook.com/method/fql.query?access_token=ACCESS_TOKEN&format=FORMAT&query=FQL_QUERY` – FORMAT can be either `json` or `xml`

◆ FQL queries must query an indexable field

◆ Read entity-relationship lines by combining the names of the two tables (not columns!) with the verb before the line

◆ The `permissions` table can be queried to find out which extended permissions an authenticated user has been granted

◆ A list of tables and their columns (with a guide to which fields are indexable) can be found at `http://developers.facebook.com/docs/reference/fql/`

In the next chapter, we'll wrap up everything we've learned throughout the book and wrap up your application as a whole.

8
Finishing Off

You know what the Graph is. You understand how it represents all of Facebook's data. You know how to read it, how to search it, how to add to it. You even understand how to treat the data as a traditional database, for cases when the Graph representation just won't do.

In short, you're a Graph guru. Congratulations!

So what's left? Well, you may have the technical knowledge required to use the Graph in your AS3 applications and games, but we've barely touched on the more practical issues, like deploying and publicizing your creations.

Therefore, in this chapter we'll look at:

- ◆ The different ways of putting your applications on Facebook
- ◆ How to host your application outside of Facebook
- ◆ Helping people get to know about your application
- ◆ Useful resources to build on what you've learned

So let's get on with it...

Putting it online

Let's assume you've used everything you've learned so far to build an awesome, social application or game. What are your choices for making it available to other people?

On Facebook

At time of writing, there are three ways to allow users to access your application from within the Facebook website: in an **IFrame**, through **FBML**, and in a **Page Tab**. We'll go through what each of these is, and how to use all of them, in turn.

IFrame

Remember frames? They're back...

Back in the nineties, every other website used the HTML `<frame>` tag to lay out their pages. This fashion was eventually dropped in favor of cleaner, bookmark-friendly methods, and has not been missed.

But now frames are back in common usage – or rather, their sister tag the **<iframe>** is.

An **IFrame**, or "inline frame," allows you to embed one complete web page entirely inside another, even if the two pages are on different servers and domains. If you view the source for, say, the FarmVille application page (`http://apps.facebook.com/onthefarm/`) you'll see that this is the case as shown in the next screenshot:

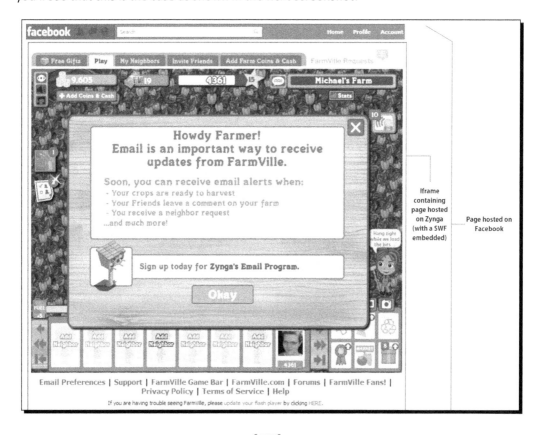

The page on the Facebook site is called the **Canvas** (not to be confused with HTML5's canvas).

Now, we've already got a page hosted on an external host (with an SWF embedded): `http://host.com/visualizer/index.html`. We don't need to make any changes to this page to load it inside an IFrame on Facebook; the settings are all in the Facebook Developer application.

Time for action – setting up an IFrame application

Browse to `http://www.facebook.com/developers/apps.php` and find your application in the list. Select it, then click **Edit settings**. Choose **Facebook Integration** from the menu on the left.

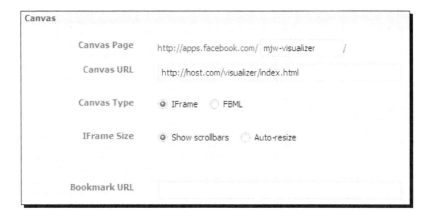

The settings can be seen in the previous screenshot. Here's what they mean, and what to set them to:

◆ **Canvas Page**: This is the URL, within Facebook, that users will browse to in order to load your application. As we saw above, FarmVille uses `http://apps.facebook.com/onthefarm`. Type something short and descriptive; it doesn't have to be too clever as users are more likely to reach the page through a Facebook Bookmark, rather than by typing in the URL. You can change this URL later.

◆ **Canvas URL**: This is the URL of the page that gets loaded into the IFrame that sits inside the Canvas page. Your application can contain multiple HTML pages that the user can navigate between; the Canvas URL is the first page that will be loaded. Set this to your application's URL, that is `http://host.com/visualizer/index.html`.

◆ **Canvas Type**: IFrame or FBML. We're using IFrame at the moment; we'll look at FBML later in the chapter.

- ◆ **IFrame Size**: If you use Facebook's official JavaScript SDK, and your IFrame's contents are likely to change size, you can call a JavaScript function to automatically resize the IFrame to fit. We don't need this for what we've covered in the book, so stick with the default **Show scrollbars** option.

- ◆ **Bookmark URL**: As mentioned above, your application can contain multiple HTML pages. This URL is the one that the IFrame will point to if the user accesses the application via a Facebook Bookmark. This is useful if you want new users to see a beginner's guide, while allowing returning users to skip straight to the application. In this example it's been left blank, since the Visualizer only has one page; this means that the Canvas URL will be used.

Make your edits and click on **Save changes**.

What just happened?

If you included the full path to the web page where the SWF is embedded (including the `.html` extension), you will have received this error:

Canvas Callback URL must point to a directory (i.e., end with a "/") or a dynamic page (i.e., have a "?" somewhere).

Facebook wants a URL of the form `http://host.com/«folder»/`, with no "`«page»`. `html`" at the end. If you don't specify a page, your server has a list of default filenames which it tries to serve, one by one, until it finds one that exists. For example, this might be "`index.html, index.htm, default.html`". Delete or rename any other pages in the application's directory that look like they might appear on that list (besides `index.html`). Try loading `http://host.com/visualizer/` in your browser to make sure it loads the right page – if it doesn't, check your webhost's support to find out what you need to do.

If your web page is not called `index.html`, then the simplest thing to do is rename it so that it is. Otherwise, you'll need to find out how to change your server's list of default filenames so that it includes your web page's name.

As a hacky alternative, you could trick Facebook into thinking that the static HTML page is actually dynamic, by adding a fake parameter to the end of the URL: `http://host.com/visualizer/page.html?pretendtobedynamic=true`.

Go back to the Facebook Integrations settings and re-enter a Canvas Page URL. Enter the new **Canvas URL**. Click on **Save Changes** again – this time, there should be no error.

Now go to your application page: `http://apps.facebook.com/mjw-visualizer` (replace "`mjw-visualizer`" with the string you entered as the Canvas Page).

You may discover that, when you load the application's page within Facebook, the authentication pop-up window does not appear.

Why is this? Check the source — nope, the JavaScript is intact. You can check to see whether it's being run (it will be). Perhaps it's because you're using an IFrame, and Facebook is blocking the ExternalInterface code?

Actually, it's much simpler than that; it's probably the browser's pop-up blocker. The code we've used so far works fine from an IFrame, so allow pop ups for your site and you'll be fine. Now you have a fully integrated Flash Facebook application, running from within the Facebook website. Nice work.

FBML

Take another look at the next screenshot:

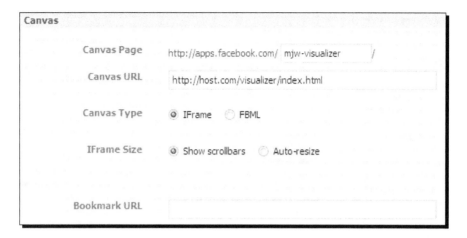

You can see that we have a choice between creating an IFrame application and an FBML application. FBML is a markup language, like HTML; essentially, it gives you Facebook-specific tags you can use in your application web page (not the SWF) to insert a Friends list or a "like" button.

However, by the time this book is published (or very soon after), Facebook will drop the option to create FBML applications – the **Canvas Type** option might already have been removed from your Facebook Integration settings.

So don't bother creating an FBML canvas application. Stick with IFrames.

Page tab

At the top of each Page's profile is a set of tabs:

You can allow Pages to add your application to their profile as a tab. The options for this are again in the **Facebook Integration** settings.

Time for action – adding an application to a Page tab

To add your application as a tab on a Page that you administer, you must first mark it as being able to be embedded in a tab. Open the application's settings, and navigate to the Facebook Integration section. In the **Page Tabs** sub-section, enter the following:

- **Tab Name**: The name to be displayed on the tab (keep it short)
- **Tab URL**: The filename of the application's web page, relative to the **Canvas URL**
- **Edit URL**: Leave this blank

Next, browse to the application's Application Profile Page from the **Developers** dashboard, and click on **Add To My Page** from the menu on the left:

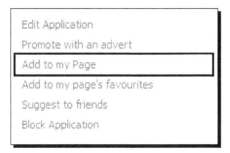

 Add to my page's favorites adds a link to the application's profile to your Page, rather than the application itself.

You'll be given a list of Pages that you control; if you don't have any Pages, you can follow the instructions at `http://www.facebook.com/FacebookPages` to learn how to create one.

Select the desired Page:

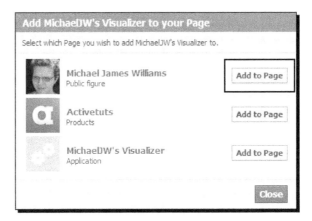

Note that you can even add the application as a tab in its own profile page!

Check out your Page:

Success! Well... not quite. Click on the tab, and you may see this error message appear:

Application temporarily unavailable

Parse errors:

FBML Error (line 31): illegal tag "body" under "fb:tab-position"

Runtime errors:

Cannot allow external script

What just happened?

The problem here is, the HTML in the Tab URL's web page is trying to run some JavaScript to deal with authentication, and Facebook does not allow this within tabs.

Or at least... it doesn't at time of writing. Currently, tabs require FBML, rather than IFrames. But by the time you read this – and as already mentioned above – tabs will not accept FBML and will require IFrames. The documentation explaining how to incorporate IFrames into tabs does not exist yet, and it can't be tested, so unfortunately this book cannot explain how to do it. Sorry!

But let's look at what you'll need to know about tabs for when you can create them.

From a technical point of view, the most important point is that tabs have a width of only 520 pixels, so bear this in mind when laying out your application and its tab page. You may even wish to create a separate web page to house the SWF – or even a separate SWF – for use inside a tab.

If you've made an advergame for a company, with Facebook integration to use the player's own name inside the game and let them post their score on their **Wall**, you could put the game in a tab on that company's Facebook page, rather than just using a standalone application page for it.

Adobe took such an approach with their Flex quiz game, **Cube Builder**:

The previous screenshot shows the game's leaderboard, rendered inside an SWF, in a tab on the Adobe Flash Facebook Page (`http://www.facebook.com/flashplatform/`). Clicking on **Play The Game** takes you to the Cube Builder game itself, as an Application on Facebook (`http://apps.facebook.com/cubebuilder/`).

This is also a good example of how to deal with the 520 pixel limit on the IFrame's width; the Cube Builder game SWF is considerably wider than this, so the tab shows a much narrower SWF with completely different content, rather than attempting to cram the game into the smaller space.

Off Facebook

As we discussed, Facebook is not restricted to the `Facebook.com` website. Blogs let you log in with your Facebook account to post a comment, IMDB lets you "like" movies through their website (and automatically updates your Facebook profile info accordingly), and Xbox 360 games can post your awesome gaming achievements to your Wall. In the same spirit, your Facebook-integrated applications and games don't have to be stuck inside the Facebook site.

Your own website

You've been hosting the Visualizer application on your own website all through this book — no need to explain this.

Although we've embedded the SWF in such a way that it stretches to the edge of the browser window, there's no requirement to do this. Treat it like a regular SWF in a regular page. You do need to include that JavaScript (either to create the pop-up window, if using the HTTP Requestor, or to embed the Facebook JS scripts, if using the SDK) to handle the authentication, but nothing else needs special treatment. Even then, you only need to include the authentication code if your application needs to use an access token.

You could use the same page for your application's canvas IFrame, its profile tab, and its own web page, but it seems unlikely that the same design would look great in all three situations. A more flexible solution is to have three different web pages, but embed the same SWF in each one.

Flash game portals

If you're a Flash game developer, you know that many games get the majority of their traffic through Flash game portals like `Kongregate.com` and `Newgrounds.com`, rather than through the game's home page. It would be great to add Facebook integration to games played through these sites, but there are a few obstacles that make it difficult.

Portals might prevent SWFs from loading data from external sites, which would mean that accessing even public Graph data would be tricky or impossible. This is not particularly likely – if external resources are completely blocked, how could in-game advertising work? – but it's worth looking out for.

The true problem lies in authentication. This is for two reasons:

- In order to obtain an access token, we call a JavaScript function within the page where the SWF is embedded. But Flash game portals don't give us access to the source of the web page, so we can't insert this JavaScript function to be run. On top of that, portals are likely to prevent SWFs from using `ExternalInterface` to call JavaScript functions, because they pose a potential security risk.

- In Chapter 3, we learned that we had to set the Site URL to match the base domain name of our application's host. If these didn't match – say, if your application was at `http://portal.com/games/awesomegame.html` but the Site URL was set to `http://host.com/`– Facebook would not let the user authenticate. This means we can't allow games hosted on different portals to authenticate through the same Facebook application.

So, sadly, Facebook did not design their applications model for SWFs that can be run from different sites. A possible workaround is to import a separate SWF, hosted on your own server, into the main game SWF, and let that separate SWF handle authentication... but implementing that is beyond the scope of this book.

However, you don't have to do all that work yourself! If you don't need access to the entire Graph API, and only want to be able to post messages on the user's Wall, retrieve their profile information, and obtain a list of their Facebook friends, then you can use the Mochi Social Platform.

This is a freeActionScript API, provided by Mochi Media, which ties in to the Facebook, Twitter, and MySpace APIs, allowing you to post to and access data from all three social networks. It also allows you to store arbitrary data about the player and link it to their social networking profile. This means you can store their top scores, other stats, or even entire custom levels that they've built.

For more information, visit `http://www.mochimedia.com/developers/social.html`.

As a desktop AIR application

Although much of the `HTTPRequestor` code we've written will work in a desktop AIR application without any changes, there's one sticking point: authentication. Since, when using AIR, we don't have an SWF embedded in an HTML page, how can we display the Facebook authorization page, obtain the access token, and pass it to an AS3 function?

Time for action – authorizing through AIR with HTTP

Rather than placing our application inside an HTML page, we must place an HTML page inside our application. To do this, we can use an HTMLLoader.

The `flash.html.HTMLLoader` class, only accessible in AIR, is a type of `DisplayObject` that acts as a container for HTML content. We use it to load the Facebook login page for our application, much like we did with a pop-up window in Chapter 3. Back in that chapter, once the user had logged in, the pop-up window redirected to another page, passing the access token as part of the hash, and JavaScript in this page's source extracted the hash and passed it to the SWF. In AIR, our application will use an event listener to detect this redirection, and extract the hash directly.

Here's how that breaks down. These are general instructions, rather than being tied to the Visualizer, so implement them however best fits your project:

1. First, import HTMLLoader.

```
import flash.html.HTMLLoader;
```

2. Next, create an instance of this class, and add an event listener for when its contents are redirected.

```
var htmlLoader:HTMLLoader = new HTMLLoader();
htmlLoader.addEventListener(Event.LOCATION_CHANGE, onRedirect);
```

(Don't forget to `import flash.events.Event`.)

3. The HTMLLoader will have a width and height of zero, by default, which is not useful since we need the user to click a button inside it! So, resize it.

```
var htmlLoader:HTMLLoader = new HTMLLoader();
htmlLoader.addEventListener(Event.LOCATION_CHANGE, onRedirect);
htmlLoader.width = 640;
htmlLoader.height = 480;
```

4. Add it to the display list so that it can be seen.

```
var htmlLoader:HTMLLoader = new HTMLLoader();
htmlLoader.addEventListener(Event.LOCATION_CHANGE, onRedirect);
htmlLoader.width = 640;
htmlLoader.height = 480;
addChild(htmlLoader);
```

5. The HTMLLoader needs to load the Facebook Authorize URL, `https://graph.facebook.com/oauth/authorize?client_id=«application_id»&type=user_agent&redirect_uri=«redirect_url»`. The contents of the web page hosted at the redirect URL don't actually matter; you could use an empty web page, the Google home page again, or even a URL that points to a site that doesn't exist. Load the URL.

```
var htmlLoader:HTMLLoader = new HTMLLoader();
htmlLoader.addEventListener(Event.LOCATION_CHANGE, onRedirect);
htmlLoader.width = 640;
htmlLoader.height = 480;
addChild(htmlLoader);
var authURL:String = "https://graph.facebook.com/oauth/
authorize?client_id=«application_id»&type=user_agent&redirect_
uri=«redirect_url»";
htmlLoader.load(new URLRequest(authURL));
```

(Make sure you `import flash.net.URLRequest`.)

6. The `onRedirect()` function will be triggered when the user successfully authenticates, but may be triggered at other times (like when the initial page is loaded), so check that there is a hash in the URL (which will, remember, be something like `http://«redirect_url»#access_token=«access_token»`.

7. Unfortunately, and unlike in JavaScript, there's no `location.hash` property in AS3, so we have to do this manually.

```
private function onRedirect(a_event:Event):void
{
  var htmlLoader:HTMLLoader = a_event.target as HTMLLoader;
  if (htmlLoader.location.indexOf("#") != -1)
  {
    //hash is in URL
  }
}
```

8. Extract the hash:

```
private function onRedirect(a_event:Event):void
{
  var htmlLoader:HTMLLoader = a_event.target as HTMLLoader;
  if (htmlLoader.location.indexOf("#") != -1)
  {
    var hash:String = htmlLoader.location.substr
      (htmlLoader.location.indexOf("#") + 1);
  }
}
```

Great! The code from `HTTPRequestor.setAccessToken()` can be re-used here to extract the actual access token.

What just happened?

You just obtained the access token for your application and the current user, entirely in AS3, using AIR.

It would be a good idea to hide the `HTMLLoader` now that it's no longer needed:

```
private function onRedirect(a_event:Event):void
{
  var htmlLoader:HTMLLoader = a_event.target as HTMLLoader;
  if (htmlLoader.location.indexOf("#") != -1)
  {
    var hash:String = htmlLoader.location.substr
      (htmlLoader.location.indexOf("#") + 1);
    setAccessToken(hash);
    removeChild(htmlLoader);
  }
}
```

This access token can now be used in exactly the same way that we used it throughout the book; there's no need to open any more web pages, so there's no need to change any other code.

Of course, you'll want to add more error checks and handlers – like, what happens if the user does not click on **Accept**, or is not connected to the Internet – but that's par for the course.

You might consider using the static `HTMLLoader.createRootWindow()` method, instead of `HTMLLoader.load()`, as this creates a new window to contain the loaded web page, rather than loading it into a `DisplayObject`. It has the same functionality, but it may make for a cleaner interface in your application. Check out the AIR LiveDocs on `HTMLLoader` for more information.

Time for action – authorizing through AIR with the SDK

The Adobe ActionScript 3 SDK for Facebook Platform can also be used with AIR, if a few changes are made to your code. The biggest change required is the class used: we've used the `com.facebook.graph.Facebook` class throughout this book, but for AIR we must use `com.facebook.graph.FacebookDesktop`.

This has a few differences. Let's go through them. Again, these are general instructions, so implement them as best fits your project.

1. It's easiest to start with the code we've already been using for SWF-based authentication, and modify it to work with AIR; there aren't too many differences. First, import the `FacebookDesktop` class.

```
import com.facebook.graph.FacebookDesktop;
```

2. Now, replace every reference to the `Facebook` class with a reference to `FacebookDesktop`.

3. The `FacebookDesktop.login()` method takes a slightly different pair of arguments to `Facebook.login()`. Instead of the second parameter being an object with this format:

```
{perms: "permission1,permission2,permission3"}
```

...it's an array with the following format:

```
["permission1", "permission2", "permission3"]
```

4. In other words, your `FacebookDesktop.login()` call needs to look like this:

```
FacebookDesktop.login(loginComplete, ["permission1",
"permission2", "permission3"]);
```

5. Another notable change is that, upon successfully authenticating, the `FacebookDesktop` class will automatically request the `me` object, and return it as a property, `user`, of the first parameter passed to the callback function. This means that you can get details like the user's name without having to request anything:

```
private function loginComplete(success:Object, fail:Object):void
{
  if (success is FacebookSession)
  {
    trace(success.user.name);  //logged-in user's name
  }
}
```

What just happened?

You're now able to authenticate your users with Facebook regardless of whether your project is an SWF or an AIR application, using either HTTP or the official SDK.

There are a few other small differences between `Facebook` and `FacebookDesktop`, but none involving the methods we've used throughout the book. To be safe, check the SDK's documentation for the class you want to use.

Consider using AIR even when developing Facebook-related projects that you intend to deploy as SWFs; it gives you the huge benefit of being able to test locally – that means no copying files across to an FTP server, or deleting objects from your cache – and with very few changes to the code. It may save you a lot of time in testing.

As an AIR for Android Application

The methods for obtaining Graph API data through instances of the URLLoader class work fine in AIR for **Android** applications; once again, the issue is with authenticating the user.

The SDK does not officially support AIR for Android for authentication, unfortunately. However, we can get an access code manually, as we did when authorizing through AIR via HTTP.

AIR for Android does not have the HTMLLoader class, but it does have something similar: the StageWebView class. Let's look at using this.

Time for action – authorizing on Android

1. First, import the StageWebView class.

```
import flash.media.StageWebView;
```

2. Then, create an instance of it, set the size, and add an event listener.

```
var stageWebView:StageWebView = new StageWebView();
stageWebView.stage = this.stage;
stageWebView.viewPort = new Rectangle(0, 0, stage.stageWidth,
stage.stageHeight);
stageWebView.addEventListener(LocationChangeEvent.LOCATION_CHANGE,
onRedirect);
```

3. This is very similar to what we did with desktop AIR, except that:

 ❑ Instead of using addChild() to add the StageWebView to the display list, we set its stage property to the stage, because StageWebView is not a DisplayObject

 ❑ Instead of setting the width and height separately, we use a Rectangle object to define an area onscreen to display the web page contents

 ❑ Instead of listening for an Event, we listen for a LocationChangeEvent

4. To deal with these changes, import the required classes:

```
importflash.media.StageWebView;
import flash.geom.Rectangle;
import flash.events.LocationChangeEvent;
```

5. Load the Facebook Authorize URL:

```
varstageWebView:StageWebView = new StageWebView();
stageWebView.stage = this.stage;
stageWebView.viewPort = new Rectangle(0, 0, stage.stageWidth,
stage.stageHeight);
stageWebView.addEventListener(LocationChangeEvent.LOCATION_CHANGE,
onRedirect);
var authURL:String = "https://graph.facebook.com/oauth/
authorize?client_id=«application_id»&type=user_agent&redirect_
uri=«redirect_url»";
stageWebView.loadURL(authURL);
```

6. Note that the `StageWebView.loadURL()` method does not require a `URLRequest`, but a `String`.

7. Extract the access token from the hash in the same way as before:

```
private function onRedirect(a_event:LocationChangeEvent):void
{
  varstageWebView:StageWebView = a_event.target as StageWebView;
  if (stageWebView.location.indexOf("#") != -1)
  {
    var hash:String = stageWebView.location.substr
      (stageWebView.location.indexOf("#") + 1);
    setAccessToken(hash);
  }
}
```

8. You can't use `removeChild()` to remove the `StageWebView`, so use this method:

```
private function onRedirect(a_event:LocationChangeEvent):void
{
  varstageWebView:StageWebView = a_event.target as StageWebView;
  if (stageWebView.location.indexOf("#") != -1)
  {
    var hash:String = stageWebView.location.substr
      (stageWebView.location.indexOf("#") + 1);
    setAccessToken(hash);
    stageWebView.stage.nativeWindow.close();
  }
}
```

That will work! There's just one small tweak we have to make. On Android, the StageWebView uses the Android OS system web control (in desktop AIR, the internal AIR WebKit engine is used). Since we don't have full control over this, we need to make sure it doesn't do anything unexpected, like open the browser application.

9. To do this, prevent the `StageWebView` instance's default action as soon as it dispatches the `LOCATION_CHANGING` event (this is dispatched just before the location changes):

```
var stageWebView:StageWebView = new StageWebView();
stageWebView.stage = this.stage;
stageWebView.viewPort = new Rectangle(0, 0, stage.stageWidth,
stage.stageHeight);
stageWebView.addEventListener(LocationChangeEvent.LOCATION_CHANGE,
onRedirect);
stageWebView.addEventListener(LocationChangeEvent.LOCATION_
CHANGING, onRedirecting);
var authURL:String = "https://graph.facebook.com/oauth/
authorize?client_id=«application_id»&type=user_agent&redirect_
uri=«redirect_url»";
stageWebView.loadURL(authURL);

private function onRedirecting(a_event:LocationChangeEvent):void
{
  varstageWebView:StageWebView = a_event.target;
  a_event.preventDefault();  //stop any unexpected default
behavior
  stageWebView.loadURL(a_event.location);  //...but continue
loading the URL
}
```

What just happened?

Using a `StageWebView`, you authenticated a user with Facebook through an AIR for Android application. Since `URLLoader` instances can be used in the same way in AIR for Android as they can in a regular SWF, this means that you can now make Android applications that are totally integrated with Facebook, using Flash.

Have a go hero – modifying the SDK for Android

At time of writing, the SDK uses an `HTMLLoader` for AIR authentication, and JavaScript for SWF authentication, so cannot be used to authenticate an Android application. If you really want to use the SDK for your Android projects, you'll have to make some changes of your own.

Add `StageWebView`-based login functionality to the SDK. Rather than modifying existing SDK class files, create new class files that extend existing ones – that way, they won't be lost if you update the SDK in future.

It's a tricky challenge because you'll be modifying someone else's code, but worth it if you want to use the SDK.

Choosing your application's Facebook settings

There's more to an application's settings than Canvas URLs. Here are some of the more interesting options:

♦ **Advanced | Deauthorize Callback**: Here you can specify a URL that will get called whenever a user removes your application; the ID of the user will be passed to this URL. In order to do something with this ID, you'll need to use a server-side scripting language – see "*What Next?*" later in this chapter. More information on decoding the info is available here: `http://developers.facebook.com/docs/ authentication/`.

♦ **About | Developers**: Allows you to set other users as a developer of your application, giving them access to the application settings.

♦ **Advanced | Sandbox Mode**: Very useful for testing, this will only allow a user to sign in to your application if they are listed as a developer of that application.

♦ **Facebook Integration | Bookmark URL**: On the left side of the Facebook home page, you can see a list of applications and games that you've used:

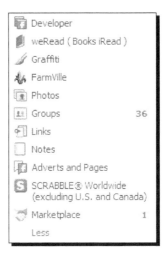

♦ These are called **Bookmarks**; setting the Bookmark URL lets you choose where these links point to.

The number to the right of a Bookmark is called a **Counter**, and lets the user know about notifications and changes within the application. Read more about Counters here: `http://developers.facebook.com/docs/guides/ canvas/#bookmarks`.

♦ **About | Icon** and **About | Logo:** The icon appears next to Bookmarks and below wall posts created via your app, while the logo appears in the authorization page and in search results.

Getting your application out there

All the development work you've done is pointless if nobody ever uses your application.

If you've created a Flash project that only uses Facebook as an extra feature – a **Post To Facebook** button, for example – then this section will not be too relevant. But if your project is built around Facebook, with the Graph API at its core, or perhaps even embedded in Facebook, then you will benefit from making it visible on the Facebook website.

Editing the application's profile page

First impressions count. If you want people to use and install your application, you need to impress them with your application's profile page.

Here's an example of a lame profile page:

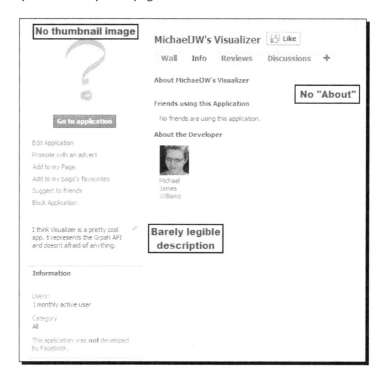

The page gives you absolutely no indication of what the application is about, or why you should bother using it. It doesn't exactly look like the developer has put much effort into the page, so why should the user believe that the application is any better?

Compare it to the profile page for Graffiti (http://facebook.com/graffitiwall), a Flash application that allows you to draw images on Facebook for your friends:

The thumbnail image was drawn using Graffiti, giving a quick example of what it can do. The **About** paragraph sums up the purpose of the application concisely, and the description adds a little social proof: "lots of other people like this, so you probably will too!"

Actually, a lot of the page is about social proof (perhaps not surprising for a social application on a social network):

- Display of your friends who use the application
- Average user rating (4.3 out of 5)
- Large number of reviews

◆ Millions of monthly active users

◆ Huge number of people who have clicked that **Like** button

Obviously you don't have any direct control over these! But they do play a large part in how people perceive your application or game, so bear that in mind.

Have a go hero – creating your application's profile page

Browse to your list of applications inside the Developers application, select your application from the list, and click on **Application Profile Page**.

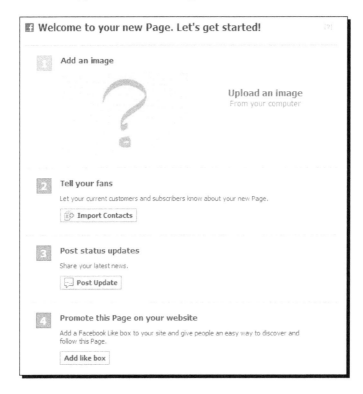

The **Get started** tab will guide you through setting everything up with a profile picture, status updates, and basic information. Remember your main aim is to get people to click the **Go to application** button!

Custom tabs

The Graffiti application does not just have the four default tabs, **Wall**, **Info**, **Reviews**, and **Discussions**. It has two custom tabs:

- ◆ **Tutorial**, which contains embedded videos explaining how to use the drawing interface.
- ◆ **Graffiti**, which contains the latest images drawn by other users.

Like the **About** paragraph and the description, these help potential users understand what the application is for, and how to use it, in a way that's targeted specifically to the Graffiti application. The **Graffiti** tab, rather than the **Info** tab, is set to be opened by default when clicking through to the application's profile, because it gives a much stronger first impression.

Likewise, when clicking through to FarmVille's profile (`http://www.facebook.com/FarmVille`), this **Play Now!** tab is displayed, which contains nothing more than a button that takes the user to the game:

Clearly, the FarmVille developers' first priority is to get users playing the game rather than reading about it.

You can create a custom tab for your application by following the instructions in Page Tab, earlier in this chapter. To set it as the default landing tab, click the Wall tab, and then the **Settings** button. Select your custom tab from the **Default landing tab for everyone else** drop-down list.

The Facebook Application Directory

Once you've built your application, tested it, and set up a profile page, you're ready to go live. Check out the **Facebook Application Directory** here: `http://www.facebook.com/apps/directory.php`.

Applications in this directory are visible throughout Facebook: as well as being able to search for them via the directory itself, they'll also turn up in the general Search box.

There is a catch – your application needs to have:

◆ Ten people who have used it within the last month, or

◆ Five people who have added it to their Bookmarks

So you'll need to get some people to join in by sending them the canvas page URL. Also, you can't submit applications that are still under construction.

Once that's sorted, browse to your list of applications, and select the one you want to submit. Click the link reading **submit it to the Application Directory**.

You'll then be prompted to set up a logo, a name, a contact e-mail, and a description:

After that, it'll be in the Directory! Look for it using the main Search box.

Watch out for these policies!

You must have read the scare stories about how Facebook is taking over the world because they have so much information on us, and how terrible it is that so many people trust it with so much of their personal data. We should be cautious of what we put on there, to be sure.

The same fears apply to you now, since you now know how to access all of that information.

Facebook has a list of policies that you, as a developer, must follow when creating your applications. Since this is continually updated, I won't go into much detail; the full list can be found here: `http://developers.facebook.com/policy/`. In general:

1. You mustn't spam.
2. You must respect users' privacy.
3. You mustn't mislead users.

There are some specific policies that you might easily overlook, though (like, "your web site must include a Log Out option"), so make sure you read it through carefully before publicizing your application.

Make sure you're aware of any privacy policies that apply in your country, or in the country where your web host is based. For example, UK developers are subject to the Data Protection Act of 1998, which defines the laws regarding data collected on living people.

What next?

We've covered the important technical concepts of Facebook and the Graph API, but there's plenty more to learn if you're eager.

The Official AS3 Facebook SDK

There are parts of the SDK that we never needed to use for the Visualizer, but that you may want to look in to. We only ever used it as a basic interface for the Graph API.

For example, it includes a `DisplayObject` called `Distractor`, which is a Flash version of the throbber animation used on Facebook when objects are loading:

Find out more online:

1. The official home page for the SDK is: `http://www.adobe.com/devnet/facebook.html`.

2. The URL for the associated Google Code project (where support issues can be brought up and the latest version can be downloaded) is `http://code.google.com/p/facebook-actionscript-api/`.

3. You can discuss the project in its Google Group: `http://groups.google.com/group/facebook-actionscript-api`.

4. The official documentation can be found at `http://facebook-actionscript-api.googlecode.com/svn/release/current/docs/index.html`.

Other Facebook APIs

We've focused on the Graph API in this book, and spent some time diving in to FQL – all accessed through AS3 with HTTP or the SDK. These aren't the only Facebook APIs, though.

JavaScript SDK

Facebook officially supports one, a JavaScript SDK, which is available here: `http://developers.facebook.com/docs/reference/javascript/`

It's a good idea to learn this if you want to add Facebook integration to the web pages around your SWFs, rather than just the SWFs themselves. Since you already understand the core concepts behind the Graph (like the concept of Graph Objects and connections, and OAuth 2.0), you shouldn't find this difficult to pick up. Plus, the AS3 SDK is based on this, so a lot of it will be familiar to you already.

The JS SDK also allows you to use FBML and the "like" button in your web pages.

Insights API

Facebook has a tool called Insights that can collect and analyze metrics about the usage of your applications or pages. Check it out at `http://www.facebook.com/insights/`. These metrics can be viewed on the website, but can also be accessed via the Graph API, so if you really wanted to, you could make a Flash application that analyzed its own usage.

To get started learning how to access this data, check out the Insights section of the Graph API documentation: `http://developers.facebook.com/docs/api`.

Facebook Chat API

The Facebook website's built-in chat client uses Jabber/XMPP, and really has nothing to do with the Graph API. Still, if you want to implement a Facebook chat client of your own, the information is here: `http://developers.facebook.com/docs/chat`.

Internationalization API

Facebook is available in over 70 languages (including, er, Pirate English), so why should your application be restricted to one? With the Internationalization API, you can encode all the text in your application so that it can be rendered in any supported language. You can even allow your users to submit translations, in case you're not septuaginalingual.

Adobe Social service

Adobe and Gigya provide a service called Social that allows developers to connect with Facebook, Twitter, MySpace, LinkedIn, Windows Live, OpenID, and many more social networks, all through a single shared API.

With Social, you can allow your users to log in to any of these social networks, and then obtain their name, avatar, list of friends, and other information given by that network. You can also use it to share information. It's totally encapsulated – for example, you can use the service to post to a user's wall, if logged in to Facebook, or publish a Tweet to the user's stream, if logged in to Twitter, with the same command.

Find out more about Social at `http://www.adobe.com/flashplatform/services/social/`.

Related Technologies

PHP

PHP is a **server-side scripting** language. That means it can generate HTML pages on the fly; to a web browser (or a `URLRequest`), a PHP page looks like a regular web page, but when it's loaded it can do all sorts of things behind the scenes.

For example, it can save and load information to and from a database on your own web server, allowing you to store information on users beyond what Facebook can carry: high scores, personal preferences, and so on.

As with JavaScript, there is an officially supported Facebook PHP SDK, available here: `http://github.com/facebook/php-sdk/`.

Another popular server-side scripting language you could learn is Microsoft's ASP.NET. This would be an ideal choice if you're already a .NET developer, as it's based on the same platform and languages.

Open Graph Protocol

The Open Graph protocol lets you represent any web page as a Graph Object. By implementing it on your site, every page can have the same functionality as a Facebook Page. Among other things, this means that if a Facebook user "likes" your web page, it will show up in their Interests. IMDB uses this to let users "like" movies.

There's a general overview of the Open Graph protocol here: `http://opengraphprotocol.org/`.

Information on using it specifically for Facebook can be found here: `http://developers.facebook.com/docs/opengraph`.

Real-Time Updates

With the Open Graph protocol, users can "like" a movie on the IMDB website, and it will appear in their Facebook profile's Interests. Real-time updates allow the reverse: when a user types a movie's name into their Interests box, IMDB will be notified, and can update the user's IMDB profile with that preference.

You'll need to understand a server-side scripting language (like PHP) in order to use real-time updates. More information can be found here: `http://developers.facebook.com/docs/api/realtime`.

Brand new and coming soon

Some Facebook features were announced too late to be included in this book. Let's take a look...

Facebook Credits

Facebook Credits are a form of micro transaction that has been available to certain developers (like Zynga, the company behind FarmVille) for a long time. Users spend real-world cash to buy these Credits, and can then spend these inside applications and games – for instance, to buy a special type of crop in FarmVille, or more storage space on a photo sharing application. The developers then receive a cut of the cash payment.

At time of writing, Facebook have not given a date for when all developers (not just those that have been invited) will be able to use Credits to sell virtual goods.

Test users

The Facebook policies prevent anyone from creating multiple user accounts. However, it's now possible to create up to 50 user accounts specifically for the purpose of testing an application, using the Graph API.

For more information, see `http://developers.facebook.com/docs/test_users`.

The New Messages

In November 2010, Facebook announced their highly-anticipated "Gmail killer," the new Messages. This allows users to combine messages, texts, chats, and emails into a single conversation thread, for cross-platform communication.

The Graph API and FQL will be able to be used to access these messages, through a new connection called `/thread/`.

For more information, see the documentation at `http://developers.facebook.com/docs/reference/api/thread`.

Facebook developer resources

Here are some excellent websites for your browser bookmarks and RSS readers.

Official Facebook resources

- The central source of information for all Facebook developers is `http://developers.facebook.com/`. From here you can access the massive set of documentation, which covers every part of the APIs, as well as the (very active) developer forums, where you can discuss application development with others.

- You can also check the current status of the Facebook Platform through the Platform live status page: `http://developers.facebook.com/live_status`. If something is going wrong with your application and you can't see any cause on your side, check this page to see whether the problem lies with Facebook.

- You should also be aware of the Facebook Platform Bug Tracker: `http://bugs.developers.facebook.net/`. Since changes are made to the platform very frequently, a few bugs pop up here and there. This bug tracker helps you to bring bugs to the attention of the Facebook administrators; it can also be used to figure out if an issue you're having is a common bug.

Other great websites

The entire InsideNetwork (`http://www.insidenetwork.com/`) is invaluable reading for Facebook developers. It consists of:

- ◆ Inside Facebook: `http://www.insidefacebook.com/` – news about Facebook and the Facebook Platform
- ◆ AppData: `http://www.appdata.com/` – analysis of metrics and traffic trends for Facebook applications
- ◆ PageData: `http://pagedata.insidefacebook.com/` – like AppData, but for Facebook Pages rather than applications
- ◆ Inside Virtual Goods: `http://www.insidevirtualgoods.com/` – research, data, and analysis regarding virtual goods (will be particularly relevant once Facebook Credits go public)
- ◆ Inside Social Games: `http://www.insidesocialgames.com/` – news and analysis of the growing social games market (including Facebook games)

Another great blog about Facebook game development is Facebook Indie Games: `http://fbindie.posterous.com/`.

As you read more and more of these sites, you'll come across all sorts of terms and acronyms that you may not recognize, like DAU, MAU, and K Factor. `Wavedash.net` has provided a useful reference for what many of these terms mean: `http://www.wavedash.net/2010/04/the-secret-glossary-of-social-games-analytics/`.

The blog "Cognition.ca" does not contain many posts on Facebook development, but it does have two that I found very useful:

- ◆ `http://www.cognition.ca/2007/11/using-ssh-tunnels-to-develop-facebook-applications.html`
- ◆ `http://www.cognition.ca/2008/02/facebook-application-development-how-to-11-tips-you-dont-want-to-miss.html`

Check out the comments on the latter post as well. Although some of the information is out-of-date, there's some really great advice about setting up a test version of your application so that you don't push untested changes to your live version.

In Chapter 6 I mentioned that Facebook won't allow you to "like" Graph objects (apart from posts) through anything other than the official Facebook Like Button. Well, that's not entirely true – the team at Hook seem to have cracked it. See this blog post for more details (but remember that Facebook don't want you to do this, so there's no guarantee this will work forever): `http://labs.byhook.com/2010/08/03/facebook-like-button-in-flash/`.

Me, me, me

My website is `http://michaeljameswilliams.com/`. Through there, you can find my blog of Flash game development tutorials, and get in contact if you want to ask any questions or hire me. I post on Twitter as @MichaelJW.

I'm also editor of `http://active.tutsplus.com/`, which publishes Flash tutorials on subjects including Facebook application development.

Yes, I'm on Facebook, but no, I probably won't add you – sorry! I like to keep my friends list pared down to people I know in real life. (Is that ironic?) However, you can connect to me through my public Page: `http://www.facebook.com/pages/Michael-James-Williams/169573433058884`– drop me a note and let me know what you thought of the book!

Keeping up with the Zuckerbergs

Facebook are always making changes and improvements to the service. Things change; as a developer you must deal with this.

More importantly, you must accept this. Every time Facebook announces a new feature, the removal of an old feature, or a change to an existing feature, developers rise up and complain that this is going to cripple their application, push them way back on schedule, and make them lose huge amounts of revenue and users.

It's fine to be vocal, but at some point it becomes denial. If you've been using the Facebook website for any length of time, you'll know that they will happily make big, sweeping changes – like the introduction of the News Feed, and the removal of Tabs and Boxes on user profiles – and stick with them despite complaints from users. And usually, their instincts in what will make the site better are right.

No surprise, then, that the same is true with the APIs. Maybe this isn't fair to developers, but it's not likely to change. So remember, as you build your project, that if it relies too much on one single feature of the Graph API (or the Facebook interface, or the data available), then you're in danger of having the rug swept out from under your feet. Remember to work out a pricing structure with your clients so that when changes need to be made to their project's Facebook integration code a few months later, you aren't contracted to do it for free.

Fortunately for you, your knowledge of the Graph API is based on core concepts, not on specific implementations. You understand the Graph itself, rather than just how to copy and paste snippets of Facebook-related AS3 code. This means you'll be able to cope with anything new.

Dealing with change

Keep an eye on these two pages:

* Facebook Developer Blog: `http://developers.facebook.com/blog/`

* Facebook Developer Roadmap: `http://developers.facebook.com/roadmap`

The blog announces changes relevant to developers, and the roadmap gives a brief summary of these upcoming changes.

In general, new changes are announced weeks or even months before they are implemented. Often, you'll be able to enable the changes in your application some time before the migration is forced upon you, which is useful for testing alterations you need to make to your code.

Now go and read the blog's archives dating from November 2010 onwards (the date when this book was completed), and then subscribe to it to receive regular updates. This way, you'll stay up-to-date.

Summary

In this chapter, we looked at how to move beyond the technical issues onto the practical ones, and where to go from here. All that's left is for you to go and make some fantastic Facebook applications!

I wish you the best of luck with your development. From me, and everyone else involved in this book, thanks for reading! I hope you've found it useful. And please let me know about any Facebook applications or games you develop – I'd love to see them.

Pop Quiz Answers

Chapter 2

1	a	It makes the metadata visible
2	d	Unlimited
3	a	True
4	b	False

Chapter 3

1	b	Stands in as the authenticated user's ID when used in a Graph URL.
2	c	We wanted to present the user with a genuine Facebook login page, for trust reasons
3	a	It's likely to scare users away

Chapter 4

1	b	It's a compromise between speed of access and amount of information provided
2	b	Restrict user access to a Graph Object for a certain time period
3	c	Date-based paging means Graph Objects won't be missed out if created or removed while paging

Chapter 5

1	d	Potentially any of the above
2	b	The first doesn't act as a filter for the second, unlike all the other Graph Search URLs
3	a, d	Results are personalised so that more relevant results rank higher
		More types of search (like user) can be used

Chapter 6

1	c	HTTP requires that we use an "unsafe" method when changing data
2	b	These codes can give us extra information about why a publishing attempt failed
3	a	Nothing

Chapter 7

1	b, c	When trying to retrieve a specific list of fields
		When attempting to find out the user's extended permissions
2	a	When publishing information to Facebook
3	a	Columns are like properties, rows are like objects

Index

C

checkins 230
comments 222
community page 24
COMPLETE event 109
compound object
  creating from list, results based 144
connections
  about 243
  exploring 40
  finding, in browser 36-40
  graph objects connections, rendering 46-48
  HTTP requestor, creating 48-54
  rendering 45
  requestor 48
connections object 38
constructor function 189, 199
controllers.CustomGraphContainerController
      class 28
controllers.GCController class 28
coordinates parameter 230
create_event (Boolean) 255
crows' feet
  about 248, 249
  drawing 249
CustomGraphContainerController 52, 137
CustomGraphContainerController.as 89, 137
CustomGraphContainerController class 28
CustomGraphContainerController.
      renderGraphObject() method 34
CustomGraphContainerController requests 41
CustomGraphContainerController.search()
      function 166
custom tabs 287

D

data
  based on data, requesting 131-133
  obtaining, in pages 126, 127
data-based filtering 130
data-based paging 139, 140
data models, FQL
  AS3 object-oriented model 237, 238
  graph model 238
  relational database model 238
data property 28

data representations 238
Date object 82
debugging 18
decodedJSON object 111
deleteGraphObject() method 216
deleteObject() function 217
deleteObject() method 216
De MonsterDebugger tool 19
DialogEvent 18
DialogEvent class 18
domain names 13
Don't allow dialog box 100

E

escape()method 132
event_member table 259
event RSVPs 226
events 225, 226
expires_in parameter 81, 96
extended permissions
  about 101
  dealing with 106
  obtaining 101, 102
  permanent access token, using 105
  requesting 102-105
ExtendedPermissions class 144
ExternalInterface 92
ExternalInterface call 92
ExternalInterface class 92

F

Facebook
  about 7, 23
  application, registering with 72, 73
  benefits 8-10
  biographical information, changing 231
  data posting, via SDK 197-199
  friends, making 231
  friends profile, checking out 65-68
  numbers 9
  policies 289
  privacy settings, viewing 68, 69
  settings, for application 283
  signing up 11
  statistics page 9
Facebook.api() method 110, 134, 167, 197, 199

lists
    number of objects, displaying 118, 120
    of posts, rendering 40-45
    rendering 40
load() method 28
loginComplete parameter 109
lower(string) function 261

M

me() function 261
message parameter 230
metadata=1 flag 46
metadata=1 parameter 38
metadata parameter 40
method=delete parameter 219
MinimalComps
    URL 18
MouseEvent.CLICK listener 48
multiple IDs
    requesting, at once 141

N

name property 32
networks
    about 66
    URL 66
networks property 213
news feeds
    searching for 171, 172
Notepad++
    URL 13
notes 224
now() function 261

O

OAuth 2.0 protocol 81
objects
    exploring 26, 27
    requesting 122-124
offset
    adding, to GraphRequest 128, 129
offset parameters 127
onAuthenticationComplete() function 89
onGraphDataLoadComplete() function 165
onGraphSearchComplete() function 165

onHTTPStatusReturned() method 197
onRequestorInitialize() function 195
Open Graph Protocol 292
operators
    comparision operator 258
    logical operator 258
ORDER BY clause 259
ordering 259

P

Page
    about 24
    creating 231
    loading 24
PageData
    URL 294
page tab
    about 270
    application, adding to 271-274
page table
    information, retrieving from 239-242
paging 125, 126, 260
paging node 140
paging object 43
permission_name (string) 256
permissions 67
permissions, FQL
    about 255
    existing permissions, checking 255
    permissions_info 256
personal profile 24
photo album 243-245
photos
    loading, from album 56-61
    uploading 228, 229
PHP 291
picture field 36
place parameter 230
Pop Out button 61
post
    deleting 214
    deleting, via visualizer 215-221
POST HTTP request method 221
POST method
    using 190-192
Powered by... 17, 18

since parameter 158
SOS max 19
source code 15
source parameter 208, 214
status message 199
status property 192
strip_tags(field) function 261
strlen(string) function 261
strpos(string, term) function 261
substr() function 261
substr(string, startpos, length) function 261
success parameter 111
summary (string) 256

T

tables
  linking 249, 250
TextMate
  URL 13
this.accessToken 96
time property 82
type parameter 153, 181

U

uid (integer) 255
until parameter 133, 158
upper(string) function 261
URLLoader request 48
URL parameter 191
URLRequestMethod class 190
URLRequest object 28, 114
URLVariables object 90, 200
URLVariables parameter 197

User Agent Flow 81
user/application authorization 70, 71
user_checkins permission 230
user feed
  posting to 185-189
user_interests extended permission 102

V

videos
  creating 231
visualizer
  about 15
  feeds, searching through 175-181
  search window, implementing in 163-166
Vizzy Flash Tracer 19

W

wall
  posting to, visualizer used 207, 208
wall posts
  searching for 171
web hosts
  about 11
  need for 12
  selecting, ways 12
  software, requisites 13
website property 241
window.open() 93

Z

Zoom In button 35

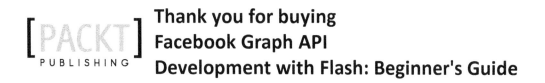

About Packt Publishing

Packt, pronounced 'packed', published its first book "Mastering phpMyAdmin for Effective MySQL Management" in April 2004 and subsequently continued to specialize in publishing highly focused books on specific technologies and solutions.

Our books and publications share the experiences of your fellow IT professionals in adapting and customizing today's systems, applications, and frameworks. Our solution-based books give you the knowledge and power to customize the software and technologies you're using to get the job done. Packt books are more specific and less general than the IT books you have seen in the past. Our unique business model allows us to bring you more focused information, giving you more of what you need to know, and less of what you don't.

Packt is a modern, yet unique publishing company, which focuses on producing quality, cutting-edge books for communities of developers, administrators, and newbies alike. For more information, please visit our website: www.PacktPub.com.

Writing for Packt

We welcome all inquiries from people who are interested in authoring. Book proposals should be sent to author@packtpub.com. If your book idea is still at an early stage and you would like to discuss it first before writing a formal book proposal, contact us; one of our commissioning editors will get in touch with you.

We're not just looking for published authors; if you have strong technical skills but no writing experience, our experienced editors can help you develop a writing career, or simply get some additional reward for your expertise.

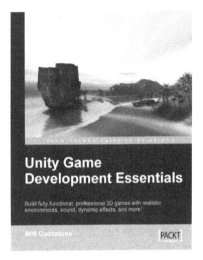

Unity Game Development Essentials

ISBN: 978-1-847198-18-1   Paperback:316 pages

Build fully functional, professional 3D games with realistic environments, sound, dynamic effects, and more!

1. Kick start game development, and build ready-to-play 3D games with ease

2. Understand key concepts in game design including scripting, physics, instantiation, particle effects, and more

3. Test & optimize your game to perfection with essential tips-and-tricks

4. Written in clear, plain English, this book is packed with working examples and innovative ideas

5. This book is based on Unity version 2.5 and uses JavaScript for scripting

Agile Web Application Development with Yii1.1 and PHP5

ISBN: 978-1-847199-58-4   Paperback: 368 pages

Fast-track your Web application development by harnessing the power of the Yii PHP framework

1. A step-by-step guide to creating a modern, sophisticated web application using an incremental and iterative approach to software development

2. Build a real-world, user-based, database-driven project task management application using the Yii development framework

3. Take a test-driven design (TDD) approach to software development utilizing the Yii testing framework

Please check **www.PacktPub.com** for information on our titles

Google App Engine Java and GWT Application Development

ISBN: 978-1-849690-44-7 Paperback:480 pages

Build powerful, scalable, and interactive web applications in the cloud

1. Comprehensive coverage of building scalable, modular, and maintainable applications with GWT and GAE using Java

2. Leverage the Google App Engine services and enhance your app functionality and performance

3. Integrate your application with Google Accounts, Facebook, and Twitter

4. Safely deploy, monitor, and maintain your GAE applications

XNA 4.0 Game Development by Example: Beginner's Guide

ISBN: 978-1-849690-66-9 Paperback: 428 pages

Create your own exciting games with Microsoft XNA 4.0

1. Dive headfirst into game creation with XNA

2. Four different styles of games comprising a puzzler, a space shooter, a multi-axis shoot 'em up, and a jump-and-run platformer

3. Games that gradually increase in complexity to cover a wide variety of game development techniques

4. Focuses entirely on developing games with the free version of XNA

Please check **www.PacktPub.com** for information on our titles

www.ingramcontent.com/pod-product-compliance
Lightning Source LLC
LaVergne TN
LVHW062306060326
832902LV00013B/2075